A Grammar of Spoken
Brazilian Portuguese

A GRAMMAR OF SPOKEN BRAZILIAN PORTUGUESE

by Earl W. Thomas

NASHVILLE
VANDERBILT UNIVERSITY PRESS
1974

Copyright © 1974 Vanderbilt University Press

Library of Congress Cataloguing-in-Publication data:

Thomas, Earl W.   1915–1993
    A grammar of spoken Brazilian Portuguese.

    1. Portuguese language—Dialects—Brazil.
2. Portuguese language—Spoken Portuguese. 3. Portuguese. 3. Portuguese language—Grammar—1950–

I. Title.
PC544.T43   469'.798   74-16228
ISBN 0-8265-1197-X

Printed in the United States of America
11th Printing 1995

Acknowledgments

I wish to thank Professor Alex Severino, my colleague, and Mrs. Severino, and Professor Alfred Hower of the University of Florida, who read the preliminary draft of this book and made numerous important suggestions and corrections.

My students in the Intensive Portuguese Course of 1972-73 used the preliminary draft and helped me greatly by catching inconsistencies, by making suggestions for explanations and arrangement of contents, and by testing the exercises. I therefore take this occasion to express my gratitude to Roger Andreae, Carolyn Brooks, Faith Brooks, Susan Carey, Allyson Hunter, Brian Solomon, Marilyn Thomas, Kristen Thweatt, Nancy Tuerff, John Walker, and Rebecca Webb, as well as to my unofficial student, Mrs. Julius Lachs. All of them helped enthusiastically to catch errors and to improve the text. I believe that all suggestions they made have been incorporated into the final text.

Finally, thanks are due the Department of Spanish and Portuguese at Vanderbilt University for encouragement and aid in this undertaking, especially to Charles Vance, chairman of the department, and to Sandra Reid, its secretary.

Contents

Introduction

Portuguese is the language of Portugal, including a large part of the people of its African and Asiatic territories, and of Brazil. There are also nuclei of Portuguese speakers in the former Portuguese territories in India and Indonesia and the United States. It is the language of more than 110,000,000 people and is thus one of the principal languages of the world.

There are several dialects and regional variants of Portuguese, as of most other languages. The most notable differences are found within Portugal and some of its older overseas territories. But the most important differences to the student of the language are those between the Portuguese of Portugal and its overseas provinces on the one hand and that of Brazil on the other. The pronunciation of Brazil is in some respects more archaic than that of modern Portugal, in others more innovative. The forms of verbs, nouns, and adjectives are generally the same in the two countries. But there are considerable differences in vocabulary and in syntax, especially in the spoken forms of the language. Within Brazil there are also regional differences, especially in pronunciation. However, Brazilians from any part of the country have no difficulty in understanding people from any other region.

The speech of east central Brazil, of which Rio de Janeiro is the principal center, is used as the basis of the present text, for several reasons. It is the speech with which most North Americans are likely to have contact. It is also the type of speech which has most influence within Brazil. The student is not likely to have difficulty with the speech of any region if he has become accustomed to that of Rio.

Any language which possesses a highly developed literature will show a number of differences between the language of books and the speech of the average educated person. In the Portuguese of Brazil the differences are rather large. Contrary to popular belief, the spoken language is usually more complex and more difficult for foreigners. However, a rather large proportion of American students of Portuguese will want to make use of it in oral communication. Besides, thorough learning of any present-day language is best acquired through oral learning of the normal spoken language. For these reasons, this text is based on the language as it is spoken by Brazilians of moderate education (and largely by the most highly educated as well), even in some cases in which those forms or constructions are not accepted by authorities on normative grammar. When the usages of literary writing differ from the forms given here, it is felt that they can best be learned later, in courses on composition. Thus, this text makes frequent references to the usages of BF (*brasileiro falado*, spoken Brazilian Portuguese).

For the same reasons, the vocabulary, both in Portuguese and in English, attempts to give the words and idiomatic constructions most used in speech. Thus in English, the verb "arrive" is given as the equivalent of *chegar*, but also other translations which are more frequent in spoken English, e.g., "come," "get here," etc. Similarly, the distinction between "Let's go" and "Let us go" is maintained, although literary English blurs it.

An important innovation of the present text is the order of presentation. In spite of all the attempts of writers of texts for the study of modern languages to introduce radical new

1

methods in recent years, practically all of them present the tenses of the verbs more or less in the "logical" order developed by the Roman grammarians. This is a reasonable order for the study of one's own language, but it is not the order of need in any foreign language—an order which varies somewhat from one language to another. The present writer has had considerable opportunity to observe the order in which the Brazilian child learns the forms of his verbs, an order which is undoubtedly dictated by the necessities of everyday speech. For example, after the infinitive and the present indicative (both simple and progressive), the Brazilian child learns the preterit rapidly, then the future subjunctive. He uses this last tense with great ease and correctness at an age when he knows only a few forms of the imperfect indicative and is confused by the present subjunctive. On the other hand, he has very little use for the forms of the future indicative and the conditional, except in a few short verbs. This text therefore introduces the future subjunctive early, but the future indicative and the conditional are presented much later.

The case of the personal infinitive is somewhat different. It is a very popular form in speech. It is somewhat difficult for the foreign student to grasp, however, since its use cannot be very well covered by rules. It is also always possible to express any sentence correctly by using other forms. But the usual place of the personal infinitive—near the end of the text—is too late for effective learning through practice. Therefore, a compromise solution places this form somewhat farther from the end.

This book does not assume that the instructor will use Portuguese exclusively from the beginning of the course. The practice gained from using and hearing the language from the beginning does not make up for the time which is necessarily lost in advancing through the course. There is a considerable amount of oral practice found in the exercises from the beginning, if the instructor will require these exercises to be done orally, rather than in writing. The reduced amount of practice in the early lessons will be more than made up in the following ones, as soon as the student has acquired the basic forms and enough vocabulary to say something. The exercises are numerous and varied; the instructor may choose which he wishes to use if he does not have time for all.

The text is planned for use in a three-hour course lasting two semesters. It is assumed that a reading text will be introduced sometime before the end of the first semester, largely as a basis of conversational practice. If reading is begun early, the assignments will necessarily be short, so that the student can study them intensively and use the new words and expressions in oral practice.

By midyear or thereabouts it should be possible to switch completely to Portuguese for everything but grammatical explanations, with good comprehension on the part of the students, as well as with reasonable ability to make brief answers in Portuguese. The three-hour, two-semester course in which this text is used serves to prepare students to take courses in language and literature given wholly in Portuguese.

Rules for Writing Brazilian Portuguese

Syllabification

Words are divided into syllables according to the following rules:

1. A single consonant always goes with the following syllable. In pronunciation, this applies to a final consonant followed by a word beginning with a vowel: *o animal é* o a-ni-ma-lé. The final *l* of *animal* has, therefore, the sound of an initial *l*, rather than that of final *l*.

2. When a consonant is followed by *r, l,* or consonantal *u*, both letters go with the following syllable: *a-bro, du-plo, i-gual.*

3. Any other group of two consonants is divided, one forming part of the preceding syllable, the other going with the following: *al-to, ar-de, es-te.*

4. Groups of three consonants are always made up of *s* or *x* (pronounced like *s,*) a stop, and *l, r,* or consonantal *u.* In this case the first consonant is a part of the preceding syllable, the other two of the second: *las-tro, ex-tra, res-guar-do.*

5. The consonants *p, g, b, d,* and *t* before a stop consonant, initial *p* before *s, b* anywhere before *s,* and *c* before stops in some words, require a vowel *i* to be pronounced after them, and form a separate syallable in pronunciation. This vowel is not written, but is universally pronounced *p(i)neu, ap(i)to, ob(i)ter, ad(i)mirável, arit(i)mética, dig(i)no, p(i)sicologia, ob(i)servar, ac(i)ne.*

6. *dj, tl, ch, lh,* and *nh* represent single consonant sounds, and go with the following syllable in pronunciation. But *dj* is separated in writing.

Stress

1. Words which end in a single vowel *a, e,* or *o,* or in one of these letters followed by *m, s,* or *ns,* are normally stressed on the next-to-last syllable: *fala, falam, come, homem, homens, coco, cocos, rio, Maria.*

2. Words which end in a single vowel *u* or *i,* or in one of these followed by *m, s,* or *ns,* are normally stressed on the last syllable: *peru, perus, comum, comuns, quati, quatis, assim, sagüins.*

3. Words whose final syllable contains a diphthong, oral or nasal, or a diphthong followed by *s,* are normally stressed on the last syllable: *comeu, falei, mingau, papai, papéis, irmão, capitães, lições.*

4. Words which end in any consonant except *m* or *s* are normally stressed on the last syllable: *papel, falar.*

Written Accents

1. The accents used in writing Portuguese are the circumflex, the acute accent, the grave accent, and the tilde.

2. The tilde is written over certain vowels and diphthongs to indicate nasality. They also indicate the stress, unless another accent is written on the word: *irmã, irmão, lições, pães, órgãos, bênçãos.*

3. The circumflex accent is written over the close pronunciations of the vowels *a, e, o,* when circumstances require a written accent.

4. The acute accent is written over the open sounds of these letters, and over *u* and *i,* when circumstances require the use of a written accent.

5. The grave accent does not indicate stress. It is used over the letter *a* in certain cases to show that the word is a contraction.

The accents are written in the following circumstances:

1. Over the vowel of a monosyllable which is stressed in the sentence: *vê, lê, pôs, nós, só, pé, pá,* etc.

2. Over final *a, e,* or *o,* followed or not by *m, s, ns,* when the final vowel is stressed: *avô, avó, cajá, Pelé, inglês, também, vinténs.*

3. Over the stressed vowel of a word ending in *u, i,* or a diphthong, or in a consonant other than *m* or *s,* but not stressed on the last syllable: *júri, Vênus, fáceis, órgão, fácil, ímpar, látex.*

4. Over a stressed vowel when it occurs in the third syllable from the end: *constância, independência, câmara, xícara, Mário, século, árvore.*

5. The acute accent is always written over the stressed vowel of the diphthongs *éi, éu, ói,* to distinguish them from the diphthongs in which the stressed vowel is closed: *réis, céu, dói.*

6. The circumflex accent is written over close *o* when it is followed immediately by final *o: vôo, vôos, perdôo.*

7. The circumflex accent is written over certain third-person plural verb forms whose corresponding singular form has the vowel *ê: têm* (s. *tem*), *contêm* (s. *contém*), *vêm* (s. *vem*), *lêem* (s. *lê*), *vêem* (s. *vê*).

8. The acute accent is written over *u* or *i* when it does not form a diphthong with the preceding vowel, but forms a separate stressed syllable. However, the accent is omitted before *nh,* and before *l, m, n, r,* and *z* when they are in the same syllable as the vowel: *saúde, juízo, viúva, baía,* but *tainha, Raul, juiz, ainda, ruim, construir.*

9. The following words have a written accent to distinguish them from other words otherwise spelled the same:

pôde,	pret. of *poder*	Cf. *pode,*	present
pôr,	verb	Cf. *por,*	preposition
pára,	verb	*para,*	preposition
pêlo,	noun	*pelo,*	contraction
pélo,	verb form	*pelo,*	contraction
pólo,	noun	*polo,*	archaic contraction

10. The grave accent is used to distinguish contractions of the preposition *a* with the feminine forms of the definite article, or with all forms of the demonstrative *aquele,* from these words when not contracted. This accent never indicates stress. *À, às, àquele, àquela,* etc., include the preposition *a.*

11. The dieresis is used over the letter *u* preceded by *g* or *q* and followed by *e* or *i,* when *u* is pronounced: *freqüente, liqüido, agüentar.*

Pronunciation of Brazilian Portuguese

The student can acquire a good pronunciation of Portuguese from the instructor, from tapes, or from native speakers. The following statements will help him to remember which sound is used in each case, after he has learned to distinguish and reproduce them. The descriptions given here are necessarily only approximate.

The vowels

There are seven oral and five nasal vowel sounds used in Portuguese, with variants of some of them used in certain positions in the word. A vowel is nasal in the following circumstances:

1. If it is written with a tilde, e.g., *irmã, lições.*

2. When followed by *m* or *n* in the same syllable, e.g., *campo, canto, entender.* The nasal consonant is usually not pronounced.

4

3. When stressed and followed by *m* or *n*, even though these consonants begin a new syllable and are pronounced as consonants, e.g., *mano, teme*.

4. Always before *nh*, e.g., *tenho, manhã, senhor*.

5. Optionally, if unstressed and both preceded and followed by *m* or *n*, e.g., *menino, mamãe*.

Sounds represented by the vocalic letters

a 1. An open vowel like Spanish or Italian *a*, used in the stressed syllable or preceding, when it is not nasal. Similar to English *ah*. Examples: *pá, má, cavalo, papagaio*.

2. A sound intermediate between the preceding and the sound of *a* in English *sofa*. It is found in syllables following the stress. Examples: *leva, xícara*.

3. Nasal *ã,* the sound of the preceding, nasalized. Similar to the vowel of English *hunh?* Examples: *irmã, canta, tomamos*.

e 1. Close *e*, similar to English *e* of *they,* but without the sound of *y*. It is more closed than any pronunciation of this letter in Spanish, and must be clearly distinguished from open *e* (2, below). It occurs in stressed syllables of some words and is the most usual sound of this letter when it precedes the stressed syllable. Examples: *lê, medo, verde, invejar, quererá*.

2. Open *e* is midway between the vowels of English *bed* and *bad*. It occurs frequently in the stressed syllable (one must learn whether a stressed *e* is open or close). It occurs in unstressed syllables in the following circumstances:

    a. In augmentatives and diminutives formed from words having open *e* in the stressed syllable. Examples: *velhinho*, from *velho, pezão*, from *pé*.

    b. In adverbs in *-mente* formed from adjectives having this vowel in the stressed syllable. Example: *completamente*.

    c. In the syllable or syllables preceding open *e* in the stressed syllable. Example: *perereca* (all three *e*'s)

    d. In the suffix *-vel*. Example: *impossível*.

3. Nasal *ẽ*. This is the sound of close *e* nasalized. But note that final *-em* is a diphthong. Examples: *entendo*.

4. Like Portuguese *i*, in the following circumstances:

    a. When unstressed before a vowel. Examples: *compreendo, teatro*.

    b. In the syllable preceding stressed *i. Menino, devia, feliz*.

    c. In initial position, especially before *s* or *x* and a consonant, and in the prefix *ex-* before a vowel. *Enorme, espaço, extensão, exame*.

    d. In unstressed monosyllables. *Me, lhe, se, de*.

    e. In many other words in which there is no clear reason. *Pequeno, Dezembro, dezesseis* (first *e* in each case).

    f. In unstressed final position. *Face, doce, leite*.

i 1. The usual pronunciation is similar to English *ee* of *meet*. It is somewhat more tense than in English and pronounced farther forward in the mouth. Cf. Spanish or French *i. Vi, si, fizesse*.

2. Unstressed before a vowel, *i* usually represents the sound of English *y. Iate, ia-iá, iara*.

5

3. Unstressed between vowels, *i* is often doubled, one part forming a diphthong with the preceding vowel, the other pronounced like English *y*. *Saia, bóia, caio.*

4. Nasal *ĩ*, the first sound above, nasalized. *Fim, língua, findar.*

o   1. Close *o*, similar to English *o* in *obey*. It is found in stressed syllables in many words, and is the most usual value in unstressed syllables, except the final one. *Pôr, vovô, ovelha.*

2. Open *o*, similar to the vowel of English *ought*. It occurs in the stressed syllable of many words (one must learn whether the *o* of a stressed syllable is open or close). In syllables preceding the stress, it is found in the following circumstances:

    a. In augmentatives and diminutives formed from words having this vowel. *Copinho* (from *copo*), *olhinhos* (from *olhos*).

    b. In adverbs in *-mente* based on adjectives having this vowel. *Somente* (from *só*).

    c. In syllables preceding stressed open *o*. *cotó, forrobodó.*

    ' This vowel is also used in the word *dona*, even though it is stressed before a nasal consonant. This is a unique case.

3. Like Portuguese *u* in the following cases:

    a. Usually when it occurs in the syllable before stressed *i*. *Dormimos, engoli.*

    b. In many words in which the reasons are not clear. This pronunciation varies greatly among the different regions of Brazil. *Jogar, fogão, poder, colégio.*

    c. In final unstressed position. *Pato, lado, falo.*

    d. In unstressed monosyllables. *No, nos, do.*

4. Nasal *õ*. The close *o* nasalized. *Bom, conto, bomba.*

u   1. Usually like the *oo* in English *root*, but with the lips more rounded. *Tu, puro, rural.*

2. Unstressed before a vowel, and especially following *g* or *q*, and followed by *a* or *o*, like English *w*. *Ué, Uaupés, guarda, quatro.*

3. Nasal *ũ*, the first sound given above, nasalized. *Um, conjunto, fumo.*

The diphthongs

    There are numerous diphthongs in Portuguese, both oral and nasal. They are formed by a combination of two vowels pronounced in one syllable. In each case, the second vowel is *u* or *i* and unstressed. The first, or stressed vowel should be pronounced clearly, with the quality described in the presentation of the vowels.

The oral diphthongs are:

au   pau, mau, Austrália

ai   pai, aipim

eu   eu, meu, seu (with close *e*).

ei   sei, leite (with close *e*). Note: The glide vowel *i* is usually lost in the suffix *-eiro, -eira*, and in unstressed syllables.

éu   céu, chapéu (with open *e*, always written with the accent).

éi   hotéis, réis (with open *e*, always written with the accent).

6

iu	sentiu, viu.

iu sentiu, viu.

ou vou, sou. Note The pronunciation is as in English *know* in stressed syllables. It is usually like Portuguese close *o* (without the *u*) in unstressed syllables. It is usually pronounced *u* when unstressed in the preterits and derived forms of *saber, caber,* and *trazer.*

oi The vowel *o* is close. *Boi, coisa, moita.*

ói The vowel *o* is open, as in English *boy.* It is always written with the acute accent. *Mói, dói, lençóis.*

ui Note that stress is on the first vowel. *Uivar, continui.*

The nasal diphthongs are: (Both vowels are nasal in these.)

ão This diphthong is written *-am* when it is unstressed in the final syllable of a verb form. *Pão, cão, capitão, falam.*

ãe This diphthong is also written *ãi* in the interior of a few words. *Mãe, pães, capitães, cãibra.*

-em (pronounced *ẽi*). Written *en* before final *s.* It is found only in the last syllable of a word, and may be stressed or not. *Têm, tém, bens, comem.*

õe (*oi* nasalized) *Lições, pões, cações.*

ui This diphthong occurs only in *muito*, an archaic short form of it, *mui*, and in variant pronunciation of a few other words.

The consonants

b Similar to its sound in English. Do not pronounce intervocalic *b* as in Spanish. *Nabo, roubo, bobo.*

Brazilians never end a syllable in *b*, although many words are so written. They add a vowel *i*, forming another syllable. *Abstrato, substituir, sob, abnegado.*

c 1. Like English *s* when followed by *e* or *i. Certo, cinco.*

2. Like English *k* before any other letter. When it comes at the end of a syllable, it is often followed by the vowel *i*, especially at the end of the stressed syllable or of the word. *Clava, crer, carro; acne, chic.*

ç This is used only before *a, o,* or *u* and has the sound of *s. Aço, açude, Açores.*

ch Like *sh* in English. *Chá, acho, chamar.*

d 1. Similar to the English *d,* but with the tip of the tongue touching the upper teeth. Do not pronounce intervocalic *d* as in Spanish. *Dado, dedo.*

2. Before the sound *i* (however it is written, or even if it is not written) like English *j.* This sound is not used in many parts of Brazil, nor in Portugal. *Digo, bode, admiração.*

This is also the sound of the combination *dj. Djacir, adjetivo.*

This consonant may not end a syllable in Brazilian pronunciation. When it is so written, a vowel *i* follows it, forming an extra syllable. *Admirar, advir.*

f Similar to English. *Chefe, fé.*

g 1. Like the second *g* of *garage,* when followed by *e* or *i. Geral, gente, girar.*

2. Before any other letter, like *g* in English *go*. Do not pronounce intervocalic *g* as in Spanish. *Grande, glória, garra*. *G* does not end a syllable in pronunciation. Where it is so written, a vowel *i* is added, but without affecting the pronunciation of *g*. *Digno, significar, dogma*.

gu   1. Before *e* and *i*, like *g* in *go*. In a few words, a trema above the letter *u* indicates it is to be pronounced. *Guerra, guincho, agüentar*.

        2. Before *a* or *o*, as *gw*. *Guarda*.

h   Silent in all cases, except as a part of the digraphs *ch, lh, nh*.

j   Like the second *g* of *garage*, in all cases. *Jeito, haja*.

k   Not used in Portuguese except in foreign names

l   1. At the beginning of the syllable, as in Spanish or French. *Lê, lá*.

      2. At the end of a syllable, as in English in the same position. *Sol, al*.

lh   1. Like Spanish *ll* in Old Castile. Similar to *lli* of English *million*. Do not use the pronunciations of Spanish *ll* heard in most American countries. *Lhama, filha*.

      2. Like initial *l*, in the words *lhe, lhes* and whenever *nh, lh* or consonantal *i* follows in the next syllable. *Filhinho, folhelho, alheio*.

m   1. At the beginning of a syllable, as in English. *Mão, fome*.

      2. At the end of a syllable, *m* is not pronounced as a consonant, but merely nasalizes the preceding vowel, *Bom, bamba, falam*.

n   1. At the beginning of a syllable, as in English. *Não, dona*.

      2. At the end of a syllable, but not at the end of a word, it is not pronounced as a consonant, but merely nasalizes the preceding vowel. *Canta, onze*. However, it is usually pronounced in the verbal ending *-ndo. Falando*.

      3. In final position in the word it may be pronounced as a consonant or it may merely nasalize the preceding vowel. *Ípsilon, hífen, côlon*.

nh   1. At the beginning of a word, like Spanish *ñ*, similar to *ny* in *canyon*. *Nhame, nhoque*. Some regions of Brazil do not use this sound initially, replacing it with consonantal *i*. *Iame, ioque*.

      2. Between vowels, like nasalized *y*. *Manhã, cunha*. The vowel which precedes it is also nasalized.

p   Similar to English *p*, but using less breath. *Pai, roupa*.

qu   1. Before *e* or *i*, like English *k*. But if a dieresis is written over *u*, the prouanciation is like *kw*. Many words vary from one region to another. *Quero, quis, freqüente, qüestão* or *questão*.

      2. Before *a* or *o*, like *kw*. *Quatro, quota*.

8

r 1. In initial position, when written double between vowels, or after *n, l,* or *s,* most of Brazil uses a pronunciation which may approximate any of the varieties of Spanish *j*. The four southern-most states of Brazil and most of Portugal use instead a strong trill of the tip of the tongue, like Spanish initial or double *r*. *Rio, carro, guelra, Henrique, Israel.*

2. When written singly between vowels, it is pronounced with a single stroke of the tip of the tongue against the upper gums. It is very similar to English *d*, except that the tip of the tongue is curved to produce the typical *r* quality. *Pára, caro.* This is the sound of Spanish *r* in this position.

3. At the end of a syllable, i.e., before a consonant, either the first pronunciation given in (1) above, or that given in (2) may be used. *Porta, carne.*

4. At the end of a word, either of these pronunciations may be used. However, most Brazilians do not pronounce a final *r* at all. *Falar, vir, conhecer.*

s 1. At the beginning of a word, following a consonant (with a few exceptions), or written double between vowels, *s* has the sound of English *s* in *sink. Senso, passo, observar.*

2. Written single between vowels, like English *z. Caso, coisa.*

3. In final position, not followed by another word, like *s* in sink (in Rio and some other areas, like a weak English *sh*). *Homens, nós.*

4. Before a consonant within a word or final before a consonant in a following word, it varies according to the type of consonant which follows. Before a voiceless consonant (c, f, p, q, s, t, ch, x), like *s* in *list* (in Rio and some other areas, like a weak *sh*). *Risco, caspa, esquilo, as camas, três corações.*

Before a voiced consonant (b, d, g, j, l, m, n, v, z), like English *z* (in Rio and some other areas, like a weak *s* in *measure*). *Desde, cosmos, as belas damas, as vacas.*

5. In final position before a word beginning with a vowel, like *z* (in all Portuguese-speaking areas). *Vamos andar, os outros.*

6. In the prefix *trans* before a vowel, and in the word *obséquio* and its derivatives, like *z*. *Transação, obsequiar.*

sc Like *s* (before e or i). *Nascer, descer.*

t 1. Similar to English *t* at the beginning of a syllable, except that the tip of the tongue touches the upper teeth, and less breath is used. *Pato, tomo.*
2. Before the sound *i* (no matter how it is written, or even if it is not written), like the *ch* of cheese. *Pote, tive, aritmética.* In many areas of Brazil this sound is not used, the letter being pronounced approximately the same in all situations.

tl This is a single consonant. The tongue assumes the position to pronounce *t*, but releases the air behind it by separating the *sides* of the tongue from contact with the upper part of the mouth. *Atlas, Atlântico.*

v Similar to English *v*, but more energetic. *Vou, vivo.*

w Used only in proper names of foreign origin. It is pronounced like English *w* in some of them, e.g., Wilson, but like *v* in others, e.g., *Waldemar.*

9

x   1. At the beginning of a syllable, like English *sh* in *sheep. Xícara, enxada.*

2. In the prefix *ex-* when followed by a vowel, like English *z. Exame, exausto.*

3. Preceding a consonant, like *s* (in Rio and some other areas, like a weak *sh*). *Extra.*

4. Between vowels *in a few words only,* like *ss. Trouxe, máximo, próximo,* and words derived from them.

5. Between vowels *in a few words only,* like *ks. Fixo, nexo, fluxo, flexo, sexo,* and derived words.

6. In the prefix *ex-* meaning former, as *is* (or *iz* before a voiced sound). *ex-professor, ex-maestro.*

7. In final position, usually *ks. látex.*

y   Used only in foreign words and names, pronounced as in the language from which it is taken.

z   1. At the beginning of a syllable, like English *z. Zero, zunir.*

2. At the end of a syllable or word, exactly as a Portuguese *s* would be pronounced in that position. Like *s* in *faz, luz, faz tudo;* like *z* in *fez um, traz barro.*

Conventional signs used in this text

In many cases it is necessary to indicate certain pronunciations which the spelling does not clarify. These are indicated in the vocabularies of each lesson and in the general vocabulary between slant lines, thus /i/, /ó/, etc., to represent the stressed vowel.

The open sounds of the vowels *e* and *o* are indicated by the acute accent: /é/, /ó/. The closed sounds are represented by the circumflex accent: /ê/, /ô/.

Words placed in parentheses in the exercises are explanations, sometimes translations, of the words given: He got there (arrived) at two o'clock.

Words placed in brackets are not to be translated: He went [over] to his friend's house.

A tilde placed over a vowel between slant lines indicates that it is a nasal vowel: *imenso* /ĩmẽsu/.

Lesson I

1. The noun. The Portuguese noun has gender and number. It is either masculine or feminine, and may be singular or plural. It has no case forms to express the usage as subject, object, etc.

2. Gender of nouns. The genders are simply classifications of the nouns which require agreement of adjectives and pronouns. The gender is obvious in most cases, from either the meaning or the form. Nouns which refer to male beings are usually masculine, and those which refer to female beings are usually feminine, without regard to the form of the noun.

homem	masculine	man
mulher	feminine	woman

The gender of other nouns is often easy to recognize from the form. Most nouns which end in *-a, -dade, -gem,* or *-ção* are feminine: *casa, universidade, viagem, acão.* Those which end in *-o, -me,* or stressed *-á* are usually masculine: *livro, nome, xará.*

3. Plurals of nouns. Nouns have plural forms with which all articles and other adjectives must agree. The usual sign of the plural is *-s.* However, the plural form sometimes embodies other modifications in addition to the final *s.*

a. Nouns which end in a single vowel, oral or nasal, or in an oral diphthong (not a nasal diphthong), simply add *s.*

livro	book	livros	books
casa	house	casas	houses
irmã	sister	irmãs	sisters
céu	sky, heaven	céus	skies, heavens

b. Nouns ending in *m* change this letter to *n* before adding *s*; this change is purely orthographical and has no effect on the pronunciation.

homem	man	homens	men
jardim	garden	jardins	gardens

4. The definite article. The Portuguese equivalent of *the* has four forms to express the two genders, each in the singular and plural. The form must agree with its noun in gender and number.

o homem	the man	os homens	the men
a casa	the house	as casas	the houses

a. Pronunciation of the definite article. The masculine forms are pronounced /u/, /us/. The *-s* of the plural forms is pronounced like the double *s* of *kiss* before a voiceless consonant (*c, f, p, q, x, s, t,* and *r*) at the beginning of the next word. Before a voiced consonant (*b, d, g, j, l, m, n, v, z*), or before a vowel, it is pronounced like English *z.*

os homens /z/
as casas /s/
as mesas /z/

Before *j* (or *g* when pronounced like *j*), *x, ch, s,* or *z.* the final *-s* of the article is usually absorbed and not heard as a separate sound. *As janelas, as xícaras, as chaves, os sacos, os zeros.*

5. Contractions of *de* and *em* with the definite article. These two prepositions form contractions with the various forms of the definite article. Those formed with *de* are obligatory; those formed with *em* are optional, but are usual in speech.

de + o = do /du/	em + o = no /nu/
de + a = da /da/	em + a = na /na/
de + os = dos /dus/	em + os = nos /nus/
de + as = das /das/	em + as = nas /nas/

Examples: do homem   of the man
da casa   of the house

6. Use of *em*. Some of the principal uses of *em* are the following:

a. As the equivalent of English *in,* referring to place or time.

Na casa	In the house	No verão	In summer
No livro	In the book		

b. Movement to the inside, English *into*.

Ele entra na casa.   He enters (goes into) the house.

c. English *on,* meaning either *on top of* or *on the surface of.*

Está na mesa.   It is on the table.
Está na parede.   It is on the wall

d. The equivalent of *at* when used of place.

João está na escola.   John is at school.
Eles estão em casa.   They are at home.

7. The possessive of nouns. Since the Portuguese noun has no case forms, possession is expressed by the preposition *de* placed before the noun denoting the possessor. The phrase follows the thing possessed.

A mesa do professor   The teacher's desk

Vocabulary

Prepositions

de /di/	of, from	atrás de	behind
em	in, on, at	perto /é/ de	near

Nouns		*Verbs*	
a aula /aula/	class, classroom	está	(he, she, it) is
o professor /ô/	teacher, professor	estão	(they) are
a porta /ó/	door, doorway	*Phrases*	
a cadeira /êra/	chair	em casa	at home
o estudante	student	na casa	in the house
a estudante	student	na cidade	in town, in the city, downtown

o livro	book
o homem	man
o jardim	garden, lawn, front yard
a janela /é/	window
a casa	house, home
o menino /mi/	boy
a menina /mi/	girl
a cidade	city
a mesa /ê/	table, desk
o português	Portuguese

Exercise A. Practice saying these expressions at a normal speed; be able to give them in either language on hearing them in the other:

1.	Os livros dos estudantes.	The students' books.
2.	O livro do professor.	The teacher's book.
3.	A mesa do professor.	The teacher's desk.
4.	A porta da aula /daula/.	The door of the classroom.
5.	A cadeira do estudante.	The student's chair.
6.	A cadeira está na aula. /sta naula/	The chair is in the classroom.
7.	A cadeira está atrás da porta.	The chair is behind the door.
8.	O estudante está na cadeira.	The student is on (in) the chair.
9.	O professor está na aula.	The teacher is in the room.
10.	O homem está na porta.	The man is in the doorway.
11.	Os estudantes estão na janela.	The students are at the window.
12.	Os homens da cidade.	The men of (from) the city.
13.	Os homens estão na cidade.	The men are in the city (downtown).
14.	A casa do estudante.	The student's house.
15.	O estudante está em casa.	The student is at home.
16.	O livro está na cadeira.	The book is on the chair.
17.	As mesas estão em casa.	The tables are at (my) home.
18.	As janelas da aula.	The windows of the classroom.
19.	O livro está na mesa.	The book is on the table.
20.	O estudante está atrás da porta.	The student is behind the door.
21.	O homem está perto da janela.	The man is near the window.
22.	Os meninos estão no jardim.	The children are on the lawn.
23.	A menina está atrás do professor.	The girl is behind the teacher.
24.	As casas da cidade.	The houses of the city.
25.	A menina na janela.	The girl at the window.

Exercise B. Give the plural forms of the following expressions, pronouncing the *s* of the article as indicated:

1. A aula /z/	5. O homem /z/	9. A cadeira /s/
2. O menino /z/	6. A mesa /z/	10. O livro /z/
3. A porta /s/	7. A cidade /-/	11. O professor /s/
4. A janela /-/	8. O jardim /-/	12. O estudante /z/

Exercise C. Put in the plural all possible words:

1. O livro do menino.	4. A janela da casa.
2. A porta da aula.	5. A cadeira da estudante.
3. O homem atrás da mesa.	6. A porta do jardim.

13

Exercise D. Pronounce the following pairs of words, distinguishing the quality of the stressed vowel:

/é/	/ê/	/ó/	/ô/
seca	seca	porto	porto
peco	peco	olho	olho
governo	governo	gosto	gosto
começo	começo	posso	poço
desprezo	desprezo	fosse	fosse
vedo	vedo	toco	toco
teso	teso	boto	boto
sede	sede	bordo	bordo
rego	rego	dose	doze
peso	peso	fora	fora
		vovó	vovô

Lesson II

8. Regular verbs of the first conjugation. The infinitive (e.g., *to speak*) of the first conjugation has the ending *-ar.* There are six personal endings, corresponding to the three persons in the singular and plural. However, the second person plural is completely archaic, never used in conversation. The second person singular has only limited use, and it is not necessary for the use of the foreign student. The complete conjugation, in all six forms, is given in the Appendix, but only the four forms usual in conversation in Brazil are given here. The third-person forms are used for the second person, usually along with the new subject pronouns.

To form the simple present indicative, remove the infinitive ending *-ar* and add to the stem the following endings:

Falar	to speak	fal o	I speak
		fal a	you speak, he speaks
		fal amos	we speak
		fal am	they speak

Important note: These forms are *not* used in BF to mean *I am speaking,* etc.

9. The personal pronoun subjects. The forms of the personal pronouns used as subjects of the verb are:

eu	I	nós	we
você	you (sing.)	vocês	you (pl.)
ele	he	eles	they (masc.)
ela	she	elas	they (fem.)

Você and *vocês* are the familiar or intimate second-person subjects. The more formal will be given later.

The subject *it* is not usually expressed. If it refers to a noun, it may be expressed by *ele* or *ela,* according to the gender of the noun.

The subject pronouns may be omitted whenever the subject is clear from the context. However, they are used more often than in Spanish and may be used at any time, but are not generally repeated immediately with a second verb.

14

10. Conjugation of the verb *estudar* in the simple present indicative, with subject pronouns.

Estudar to study	eu estudo	I study
	você estuda	you study
	ele estuda	he studies
	nós estudamos	we study
	vocês estudam	you study
	eles estudam	they study

11. The irregular verb *estar*, to be.

eu estou	I am	nós estamos	we are
você está	you are	vocês estão	you are
ele está	he is	eles estão	they are

12. Plurals of nouns. Nouns which end in *-r*, in *-z*, or in *-s* preceded by a stressed vowel, add *-es* to form the plural.

o professor	os professores
a flor	as flores
o português	os portugueses
a voz	as vozes

Vocabulary

Nouns

o inglês pl. ingleses	Englishman, English
o dia	day
a noite	night
a manhã	morning
o rapaz	(older) boy, fellow
a moça /ô/	girl, young woman, "lady"
a escola /ó/	school
a água	water
o leite	milk
o café	coffee; café
o café da manhã	breakfast

José /juzé/	Joseph, Joe
Maria	Mary
o Rio (de Janeiro)	Rio (de Janeiro)
a flor /ô/	flower, blossom
a voz /ó/	voice
o trem	train

Preposition

com	with

Conjunctions

mas /mais/	but
e /i/	and

Verbs

falar	speak, talk
trabalhar	work
estudar	study
passar	pass; spend (time)
brincar	play; "kid"
ficar	stay, remain; be (permanently located)

Adverbs

atrás	back, behind
lá	there, over there
para lá /pra lá/	there (to that place)
lá atrás	back there
perto /é/	near, nearby
depressa /é/	quick, fast
onde	where

15

Expressions

Bom dia	Good morning
Boa noite	Good evening; good night
Tomar o café da manhã	Have breakfast, eat breakfast

Exercise A. Read, putting all possible words in the plural form:

1. Ele fala inglês.
2. Eu trabalho na cidade.
3. Você estuda português.
4. O menino brinca no jardim.
5. O rapaz fica em casa.
6. O estudante está na escola.

7. Onde você toma café?
8. Onde está o trem?
9. A flor está na mesa.
10. Onde você passa a noite?
11. O inglês fica no trem.
12. A moça estuda na escola.

Exercise B. Read for practice at a normal speed; be able to give the equivalent of either language in the other, orally:

1. O homem está na cadeira. — The man is on the chair.
2. A menina brinca na escola. — The girl plays at school.
3. O professor passa o dia em casa. — The teacher spends the day at home.
4. José e Maria estão na aula. — Joe and Mary are in class.
5. O rapaz fica no trem. — The boy stays on the train.
6. O estudante toma água. — The student drinks water.
7. As moças passam para lá. — The girls go over there.
8. Os professores ficam na aula. — The teachers stay in the (class) room.
9. Você estuda inglês? — Do you study English?
10. A escola fica na cidade. — The school is downtown.
11. O professor fica atrás da mesa. — The teacher stays behind the desk.
12. Ele toma café com leite. — He takes milk in his coffee.
13. A menina fala na aula. — The girl speaks (up) in class.
14. O rapaz está no Rio de Janeiro. — The boy is in Rio de Janeiro.
15. Eu não fico atrás. — I don't stay (lag) behind.
16. Onde ele toma o café da manhã? — Where does he have breakfast?
17. José trabalha com o professor. — Joe works with the teacher.
18. José e Maria estudam português. — Joe and Mary study Portuguese.
19. Maria está no jardim. — Mary is in the yard.
20. Ela está na cadeira atrás de José. — She is in the chair behind Joe.

Exercise C. Say in Portuguese:

1. He is at school.
2. They speak English.
3. He drinks water.
4. You study English.
5. He works downtown.
6. He passes the city.
7. I stay at home.
8. Joe drinks coffee with milk.
9. Joe and Mary are in the classroom.
10. Good morning, Mary.

11. The girls play in the yard.
12. I study Portuguese from the book.
13. The student's book is on the table.
14. Mary passes the window.
15. The boy is near the window.
16. Joe's desk is back there.
17. Good night, Joe.
18. The flowers are on the table.
19. I spend the night at Joe's.
20. The coffee is back there.

16

Exercise D. Pronunciation of *j* and soft *g*. Read aloud:

1. José está no jardim.
2. O jornal de José está na janela.
3. Eu janto já.
4. Jamais janto na janela do jardim.
5. Jorge é gerente geral.
6. Geraldo ajuda a gente a girar.

Lesson III

13. The progressive form of the verb. As in English, the simple and progressive forms of the verb are carefully distinguished in BF, although not always in the literary language. There are occasional differences between usages in the two languages, but they usually correspond closely. The simple form cannot be used in place of the progressive form in the spoken language without constant misunderstanding, as in English.

The progressive is formed with the auxiliary *estar* (also with some others in certain situations), followed by the present participle (known as *gerúndio* in Portuguese) of the main verb. The present participle is regular in all verbs, and simply replaces the *-r* of the infinitive with *-ndo*. Contrary to usage in other situations, the letter *n* is pronounced as a consonant here. The preceding vowel is nasal. The present participle is invariable in form, and cannot be used as an adjective.

falar	to speak	falando	speaking
estar	to be	estando	being
estou falando		I am speaking	

14. Questions. In most cases in Portuguese, a question which does not begin with an interrogative word is placed in the same order as a statement. Only the tone of the voice (or the question mark which is placed after the sentence in writing) indicates that the sentence is a question. No auxiliary, such as the English *do,* is needed in the simple present tense.

Você fala inglês?	Do you speak English?
Você está trabalhando?	Are you working?

15. The indefinite article. The equivalent of English *a, an* is *um* /ū/ (masculine) and *uma* /ūma/ (feminine). The *m* of the feminine form is sometimes lost in pronunciation, especially before a word which begins with this sound.

um homem	a man
uma menina (often /ūa minina/)	a girl

16. Contractions with the indefinite article. The prepositions *de* and *em* may form contractions with the indefinite article, but they are not obligatory. Those with *de* are not usual in the speech of Rio; those with *em* are generally used.

de + um = dum	em + um = num
de + uma = duma	em + uma = numa
A casa de um (dum) professor.	The house of a teacher.
Ela está numa (em uma) aula.	She is in a class.

17

17.   Negation. The verb is made negative by placing the word *não* immediately before it. No auxiliary such as the English *do* is used.

Não falo.	I don't speak.
Nós não estamos trabalhando.	We are not working.

18.   The Portuguese equivalents of *yes* and *no*. In order to express affirmation in Portuguese, the verb of the question is repeated. The same tense is used as in the question, but the person of the verb varies to fit the logic of the circumstances. No pronouns, either subjects or objects, are used.

Você trabalha na cidade?	Trabalho.	Do you work downtown? Yes.
Vocês falam português?	Falamos.	Do you speak Portuguese? Yes.
Eles também falam?	Falam.	Do they speak it too? Yes.

If the verb of the question consists of more than one word, only the auxiliary is used in the answer.

Os meninos estão brincando? Estão.	Are the children playing? Yes.

In answer to a question that does not contain a verb, the expression is usually *é* (That's it).

Quente hoje, hein?	É.	Hot today, eh? Yes.

To answer in the negative, one may repeat the verb preceded by *não* or, more often, use *não* alone.

Você fala inglês?	Não *or* não falo.	Do you speak English? No.

19.   Emphatic affirmative and negative answers. To make an answer more emphatic, one may say *sim* or *não* after the verb form which expresses the answer, i.e., *yes* or *no*.

Você fala inglês?	Falo, sim.	Do you speak English? Yes, I do.
Ele não trabalha?	Trabalha, sim.	Doesn't he work? Yes, he does.
Você fala espanhol?	Não falo, não.	Do you speak Spanish? No, I don't.

Vocabulary

Nouns

o tempo	weather; time
o carro	car, automobile
a rua	street
a xícara	cup
o amigo	friend
a amiga	friend
o copo /ó/	glass
o chapéu	hat
o sapato	shoe

Adjectives

ruim	bad
frio	cold
quente	hot, warm

Conjunctions

ou	or
que	that

Interrogative pronouns

que? o que?	what?
quem? (s. & pl.)	who?

Verbs

entrar (em)	enter, come in, go in, get in (to)
achar	find; think, believe
acabar	finish, end
tirar	take off, take out
lembrar	remember
lembrar a (João)	remind (John)
pensar (em)	think (about), think (of)

18

Adverbs

bem	well	aqui	here
mal	badly, poorly	hoje /ô/	today
muito	very; much	devagar	slow(ly)
não	no; not	hein?/éĩ/	Eh? Hunh?
sim	See §19	daqui	from here

Expressions

Eu acho *or* Eu acho que sim.	I think so.
Eu não acho *or* Eu acho que não.	I think not.
Eu acho que ele trabalha.	I think he works.
Eu falo com o menino.	I talk to (chat with) the boy.
Está bem.	O.K.
Ele está bem.	He is well *or* He is O.K.

Exercise A. Pronunciation of initial *r*. Practice reading the following:

> Raivoso o rato roeu
> o rabo do rodovalho,
> e a Rita Rosa Ramalho
> do rato roer se ria.

Exercise B. Practice and be able to give either language when you hear the other:

1. O professor está falando com o amigo.   The teacher is talking to his friend.
2. Eu trabalho com um português.   I work with a Portuguese.
3. Ele passa perto de um carro.   He passes near a car.
4. José está com uma menina.   Joe is with a girl.
5. Um menino está brincando com um livro.   A boy is playing with a book.
6. Ele está na porta de uma casa.   He is in the doorway of a house.
7. As flores estão na mesa.   The flowers are on the table.

Exercise C. Say in Portuguese:

1. Of a classroom.
2. In a city.
3. Behind a table.
4. Near a teacher.
5. Of the friends
6. On the chair.
7. In the shoes.
8. With the book.
9. At (the) school.
10. At home.
11. From the city.
12. Of the boy.

Exercise D. Make the following expressions negative:

1. Eu acho.
2. Ele entra na aula.
3. Acabamos a lição hoje.
4. Estou tomando café.
5. Você está estudando?
6. O livro está perto do homem.
7. Vocês acham a porta.
8. Nós brincamos hoje.
9. Você fala espanhol.
10. Eu tiro o chapéu.

Exercise E. Answer the following questions with the equivalents of *yes* or *no*:

1. Você fica na aula?
2. Hoje está quente?
3. Maria estuda muito?
4. José está trabalhando?
5. Nós entramos na casa?
6. Maria está em casa?
7. Vocês acham que ele trabalha?
8. Vocês brincam hoje?
9. Você está falando português?
10. Você lembra o rapaz?

Exercise F. Answer the questions, using one of the suggested alternatives:

1. José trabalha bem ou mal?
2. Hoje está quente ou frio?
3. Você toma água de copo ou de xícara?
4. Você toma leite ou água?
5. Vocês ficam aqui ou lá?
6. Eu falo depressa ou devagar?
7. O professor é inglês ou português?
8. Você acha que acaba o trabalho ou não?
9. Você entra na casa ou fica na rua?
10. Maria é amiga ou irmã de João?

Exercise G. Give the corresponding progressive forms:

1. Eu falo.
2. Você brinca.
3. José passa.
4. O menino fica.
5. Ele toma leite.
6. O homem trabalha.
7. Você estuda.
8. O trem passa.
9. Nós brincamos
10. Ele pensa.
11. Ele tira o chapéu.
12. Eu acabo o livro.

Exercise H. Change these statements to questions by reading them with question intonation; no change in sentence order is needed:

1. Ele fala inglês.
2. Nós ficamos em casa.
3. Vocês estão trabalhando.
4. Eles tomam café.
5. Nós estamos estudando.
6. Os meninos estão brincando.
7. O trem passa lá.
8. Ela está falando português.
9. Ele está na cadeira.
10. Você brinca no jardim.

Lesson IV

20. Plurals of nouns and adjectives. Adjectives form their plurals in the same ways as nouns; thus, adjectives follow the rules given in the preceding lessons.

frio	cold	pl. frios
audaz	bold	audazes
bom	good	bons
falador	talkative	faladores
português	Portuguese	portugueses

a. Nouns and adjectives which end in -ão generally form the plural by changing this ending to -ões.

a lição	lesson	as lições
a ação	action	as ações
mandão	bossy	mandões

A few nouns and adjectives change -ão to -ães to form the plural.

o pão	bread	os pães
o cão	dog	os cães
alemão	German	alemães

A few others simply add -s to the ending -ão. These include, but are not entirely limited to, nouns not stressed on the last syllable.

o irmão	brother	os irmãos
a mão	hand	as mãos
o órfão	orphan	os órfãos
a bênção	blessing	as bênçãos

b. Nouns and adjectives ending in -s after an unstressed vowel do not change for the plural.

o ônibus	bus	os ônibus
o lápis	pencil	os lápis
simples	simple	simples

c. Nouns and adjectives ending in -l which is not preceded by i drop the final -l and add -is.

o animal	animal	os animais
o motel	motel	os motéis
o anzol	fishhook	os anzóis
o paul	swamp	os pauis
lateral	lateral	laterais
fiel	faithful	fiéis
espanhol	Spanish	espanhóis
azul	blue	azuis

Note: The accents on certain plural forms—those whose stressed *e* or *o* is open—obey the rule that the diphthongs *éi* and *ói* always bear a written accent.

d. Nouns and adjectives in -il change the ending to -is if the last syllable is stressed, but to -eis if it is not stressed.

o barril	barrel	os barris
imbecil	imbecile	imbecis
fácil	easy	fáceis
útil	useful	úteis

21. The feminine forms of adjectives. Adjectives in final -o change this vowel to -a to form the feminine. Most other adjectives have the same form in both genders.

aberto	open	fem. aberta
doente	sick	doente
comum	common	comum
azul	blue	azul
fácil	easy	fácil

Adjectives of nationality ending in a consonant add -a to form the feminine.

português	Portuguese	portuguesa
espanhol	Spanish	espanhola

Adjectives in -ão, -eu and some others have irregular feminine forms.

bom	good	fem. boa
mau	bad	má

The feminine form of the adjective is used to form adverbs by the addition of the suffix *-mente,* which corresponds fairly closely with the formation of adverbs in English by the addition of *-ly.*

aberto	adv.	abertamente
frio	.	friamente
fácil		facilmente
comum		comumente

22. Forms of the present tense of the verb *ser,* to be.

eu sou	nós somos
você é	vocês são
ele é	eles são

23. Uses of *ser* and *estar.* These two verbs are both translated *to be,* but they are not interchangeable and must be carefully distinguished.

a. Only *estar* may be used to form the progressive tenses.

Ele está falando.	He is talking.

b. *Ser* is used to form the passive voice.

A porta é aberta.	The door is opened.

c. *Ser* is used whenever the expression represents a normal situation, a permanent quality, or a permanent condition. *Estar* is used when the condition or situation is temporary, changeable, or has just changed. This difference applies to *all* types of expressions, and is different in several cases from Spanish usage.

If the predicate is a noun or pronoun, the verb will nearly always be *ser.*

É um animal.	It is an animal.
Somos nós.	It is we. (Note that *ser* agrees with its predicate.)

When the predicate is an adjective, the choice is determined by the principle given above.

Ele está doente.	He is ill.
Ele é doentio.	He is sickly.
A água está fria.	The water is cold.
O gelo é frio.	Ice is cold.

In speaking of location, the determining factor is the same—whether or not the location is fixed and permanent.

A cadeira está perto da porta.	The chair is near the door.
A cidade é perto daqui.	The city is near here.

Note: In speaking of permanent location, *ficar* may replace *ser.*

A cidade fica perto daqui.	The city is near here.

Note the following examples:

O livro está rasgado.	The book is torn.
O livro é em inglês.	The book is in English.
A porta está aberta.	The door is open.
A porta é aberta pelo menino.	The door is opened by the boy.

A rua é coberta de asfalto.	The street is covered with asphalt. (passive or not)
Ganhei na loteria; estou rico.	I won in the lottery; I'm rich.
Eu sou rico.	I'm rich.
Os noivos já estão casados.	The bride and groom are now married.
João é casado.	John is a married man.
Ela está bonita.	She looks pretty today.
Ela é bonita.	She is a pretty girl.

24.   Omission of the indefinite article after *ser*. The indefinite article is omitted after *ser* before an unmodified noun or adjective. If the noun is modified, the article is generally used, but may be omitted if the two words are taken to be the expression of one single idea.

Ele é inglês.	He is an Englishman. (*or* He is English.)
Ela é uma professora portuguesa.	She is a teacher from Portugal.
Ele é bom estudante.	He is a good student.

Vocabulary

Nouns

a lição	lesson
o pão, pl. pães	bread, loaf
o cão, pl. cães	dog
o irmão, pl. irmãos	brother
a irmã	sister
a mão, pl. mãos	hand
o órfão, pl. orfãos	orphan
o ônibus	bus
o lápis	pencil
o animal	animal
a tarde	afternoon
o papel /é/	paper
o motel /é/	motel

Prepositions

até	until
antes de	before
depois de	after

Verbs

ser	be (See 23)
jantar	dine, eat dinner
guardar	keep, put away
deixar	let, allow; leave behind, abandon.

Adjectives

alemão, fem. alemã	German
simples	simple
bom, fem. boa /ô/	good
mau, fem. má	bad
fácil	easy
difícil	hard, difficult
aberto /é/	open
doente	sick, ill
rasgado	torn, ripped
casado	married
bonito	pretty
espanhol /ó/	Spanish

Expressions

Boa tarde.	Good afternoon.
Até logo.	So long; good bye.
Até amanhã.	Till tomorrow.

23

Exercise A. Pronounce the following pairs of words, noting similarities and differences:

cara	cada	lira	lida
vira	vida	muro	mudo
cera /ê/	ceda /ê/	Nara	nada
lera /ê/	leda /ê/		

Exercise B. Put all possible words into the plural form:

1. A flor é azul.
2. A voz é boa.
3. O português está doente.
4. O trem é ruim.
5. O espanhol janta em casa.
6. A mão está aberta.
7. O cão do órfão é bom.
8. Lá o café é ruim.
9. O ônibus entra na cidade.
10. O jardim é bonito.
11. O homem é simples.
12. A cidade fica perto.
13. A lição é difícil.
14. Você fala português.
15. O irmão está com a irmã.
16. Eu janto com o amigo.
17. O animal do alemão é mau.
18. Ele guarda o papel na mão.
19. O menino acha que você é mau.
20. A porta é azul.

Exercise C. Replace the underlined word with the words in parentheses and make all other necessary changes:

1. O *irmão* é simples e bom. (irmã, espanhóis)
2. Aqui o *café* é ruim. (leite, água, escolas)
3. O *ônibus* está aberto. (porta, livros, mãos)
4. A *lição* é difícil. (trabalho, português, aulas)
5. *José* é casado. (os alemães, a estudante)
6. O *papel* está rasgado. (lição)
7. O *livro* é difícil. (escola, professores)

Exercise D. Replace the blanks with the correct form of *ser* or *estar*.

1. A porta _____ aberta.
2. A escola _____ na cidade.
3. José _____ um homem rico.
4. _____ frio aqui hoje.
5. O professor _____ um homem.
6. Maria _____ em casa.
7. Nós _____ americanos.
8. A cadeira _____ atrás da porta.
9. O papel _____ rasgado.
10. Ela _____ uma menina bonita.
11. O menino _____ órfão.
12. A casa _____ azul.
13. Maria _____ sentada.
14. O homem _____ jantando.
15. O livro _____ guardado hoje.
16. Você _____ estudando?
17. Nós _____ casados.
18. O livro _____ em português.
19. Os rapazes _____ na escola.
20. A casa _____ na cidade.

Exercise E. Say in Portuguese:

1. The Germans leave the dogs here.
2. The sister is simple and kind.
3. The pencils are with the papers.
4. He lets the orphans stay.
5. I put the books away.
6. The animals are sick.
7. Good evening, Joe.
8. It is warm today.
9. The lessons are easy.
10. The girls are very pretty.
11. The boys are bad.
12. We think he is good.
13. The student is putting away the pencils.
14. He takes the bus in the city.
15. The boy stays near the river.
16. He speaks English badly.

17. Are you finishing the work? Yes.
18. We do not pass the river.
19. Where is the school?
20. I speak slowly.
21. Joe is playing in the classroom.

22. The orphan's hand is cold.
23. He is German, but she is Spanish.
24. The bread is hot.
25. He lets the sister eat dinner.

Lesson V

25. Present indicative forms of the three conjugations. The endings of the infinitive in the three conjugations are respectively *-ar, -er,* and *-ir.* Note that the vowel of the second conjugation infinitive is always /ê/. The forms of the simple present follow.

First Conjugation	*Second Conjugation*	*Third Conjugation*
falar to speak	comer to eat	abrir to open
eu falo	como	abro
você fala	come	abre
ele fala	come	abre
nós falamos	comemos	abrimos
vocês falam	comem	abrem
eles falam	comem	abrem

The progressive forms are as follows:

Eu estou falando, etc.
eu estou comendo, etc.
eu estou abrindo, etc.

26. The imperative: Portuguese possesses imperative forms in the singular and plural. Historically, they were used to give commands with the old second-person subjects *tu* and *vós,* but only in the affirmative. As stated previously, the plural *vós* is no longer used in the spoken language anywhere, and the singular *tu* is comparatively little used in Brazil. But the imperative singular is in common use with the subject *voĉe,* both in the affirmative and the negative. The form, for all regular and most irregular verbs, is the same as the third person singular of the present indicative. As in English, no subject pronoun is used, except for strong emphasis. If used, the subject may precede or follow the verb.

Fala	speak	Fala você. *You* speak.
Come	eat	Você come. *You* eat.
Abre	open	

The verbs *ser* and *estar* have lost this form completely. One uses the subjunctive, respectively *seja* and *esteja.*

The historical imperative plural is completely lost in BF, but a few short indicative plural forms are often used. In most instances, the meaning is expressed in the form of a request or a statement, rather than that of the imperative. The tone of voice in which the words are spoken will often reveal them as a command. One expression so used is the question, *Vocês querem?* followed by the infinitive. The singular, *Você quer,* can also be used thus instead of the imperative singular.

Vocês querem guardar os livros?	Will you put away your books? *or* Put away your books.
Vocês querem falar devagar?	(Please) speak slowly.

25

27. Questions with an interrogative word. In general, when a question begins with an interrogative word, a subject may either precede or follow the verb, although there are cases in which one or the other is more usual.

Para onde vai você?	Where are you going?
Or Para onde você vai?	

Very often, BF uses the interrogative word followed by the phrase *é que*. The following clause is then always arranged with the subject before the verb.

Que é que você está comendo?	What are you eating?
Quem é que parte amanhã?	Who leaves tomorrow?

If the verb consists of more than one word, the subject is always placed before it, either with or without the use of *é que*.

O que você está comendo?	What are you eating?

28. Requesting assent. To ask for agreement with a statement, the question *não é?* is placed after it. In rapid speech, it is often pronounced /né/. In English, the equivalent varies according to the auxiliary of the verb of the statement.

Você lembra João, não é?	You remember John, don't you?
Ele está brincando, não é?	He is kidding, isn't he?

29. Position of adjectives. Adjectives generally follow the noun in Portuguese when they are used to distinguish one type of person or thing from another, i.e., are used objectively. They precede when they express the opinion or feeling of the speaker, or call attention to a known quality, i.e., are used subjectively.

O bom rapaz vai à cidade.	The good fellow is going downtown. (I consider him to be good.)
Os homens bons vão para o céu.	Good men go to heaven. (I am speaking only of the good ones.)

Descriptive adjectives generally follow. Certain common adjectives which usually have a subjective meaning, e.g., good, bad, great, etc., are likely to precede. Demonstrative adjectives (this, that) and adjectives of quantity practically always precede.

30. The formal second-person pronouns. The words *você* and *vocês* are used in informal circumstances. We may judge reasonably well when to use them if we reserve them for persons whom we address by their first names. However, they are used much more widely than the familiar forms are used in Spanish or French.

To address persons more formally—more or less those that we would address by their last names with a title—we use the following: (The pronunciations indicated are those of normal, rapid speech.)

o senhor / u sĩô/	masculine singular	Abbreviation: o sr.
os senhores /u sĩóris/	masculine plural	os sres.
a senhora /a sĩóra/	feminine singular	a sra.
as senhoras /a sĩóras/	feminine plural	as sras.

These words are also used as titles, with the articles omitted when one addresses the person concerned.

Sr. Peres, or sr. álvares está aqui?	Mr. Peres, is Mr. Alvares here?

Note that the title of an unmarried lady is *senhorita* (srta.), but that the pronoun *you* when she is addressed is regularly *a senhora*.

Srta. Peres, como está a sra.?   Miss Peres, how are you?

The verb forms used with the formal modes of address are the same as those used with *você* and *vocês*—the third person singular and plural.

31. Use of the second-person pronouns as objects. All the words used as subjects of verbs with the meaning *you,* except the old forms *tu* and *vós,* may also be used as direct objects of a verb or as objects of prepositions. They are placed in the sentence as if they were nouns. As direct objects, they follow the verb.

Eu não compreendo você.	I don't understand you.
Aqui deixo o senhor.	Here I leave you.
Ele está com você?	Is he with you?
O carro é do senhor?	Is the car yours?
Quem está atrás da senhora?	Who is behind you?

Vocabulary

Nouns

a pena	pen (point)	a carta	letter
João	John	a carne	meat
a xicrinha	demi-tasse	o arroz /ô/	rice
o Brasil	Brazil (use the article)		

Verbs

aprender (a)	learn (to)	usar	use; wear (clothes, long hair, etc.)
escrever[1]	write	abrir	open
partir (de)	depart (from), go away, leave	vender	sell
casar (com)	marry, get married (to)	quer? /é/	will you? (s.)
comer	eat	querem? /é/	will you? (pl.)
compreender	understand		

Note 1. The third person forms of this verb have the vowel /é/ in the stressed syllable.

Expressions

Escrever com pena.	To write with a pen.
Escrever a lápis.	To write with pencil.
Escrever à mão.	To write by hand.
Aprender a falar.	To learn to speak.
Eles casam amanhã.	They are getting married tomorrow.
Ele casa com Maria.	He will marry Mary.
Partimos da cidade hoje.	We are leaving town today.

Exercise A. Put into the progressive form:

1. Nós falamos português.
2. Ele deixa a cidade.
3. Elas escrevem cartas.
4. Eu como carne.
5. Ele usa o lápis.
6. Eles casam.
7. Eu não compreendo você.
8. Ele toma café.
9. Eu abro a janela.
10. Eles vendem carros.

Exercise B. Express with the imperative singular:

1. Speak Portuguese.
2. Study the lesson.
3. Play with the boy.
4. Drink the coffee.
5. Finish the lesson.
6. Remember Mary.
7. Be good.
8. Learn to speak.
9. Eat the bread.
10. Wear the shoes.
11. Work hard.
12. Spend the day at home.
13. Stay here.
14. Come in.
15. Take off the shoes.
16. Think of John.
17. Put away the cups.
18. Write a letter.
19. Open the door.
20. Sell the car.

Exercise C. Give in the singular and the plural:

1. Will you dine with John and Mary?
2. Will you open the door?
3. Will you write a letter?
4. Will you speak to (with) John?

Exercise D. Put in the blanks the correct Portuguese equivalents of the pronoun *you*:

1. Sr. Tavares, _____ quer jantar?
2. Amigo, _____ está estudando muito.
3. Srta. Carvalho, que é que _____ toma?
4. João, _____ aprende depressa.
5. Professora, _____ quer deixar o chapéu aqui?
6. _____ estão aprendendo português, estudantes.
7. Menino, _____ escreve bem.
8. Sr. Gomes e sr. Carvalho, _____ trabalham muito.
9. Hoje eu janto com _____, José.
10. Sra. Gomes, quem está com _____?

Exercise E. Replace the blanks with the correct form of *ser* or *estar:*

1. Onde _____ João?
2. A carne _____ ruim.
3. A lição _____ difícil.
4. A porta _____ sempre aberta.
5. Ele _____ falando português.
6. Os senhores _____ alemães.
7. Os papéis _____ rasgados.
8. O irmão do rapaz _____ um menino.

Exercise F. Put all possible words into the plural form:

1. Eu estou aprendendo alemão.
2. O papel está na mesa.
3. O menino bom não quer abrir a porta.
4. A lição é difícil.
5. A flor bonita fica no jardim.
6. O inglês vende o animal.
7. Eu lembro a voz do rapaz.
8. Ele come pão e toma café.
9. O lápis do irmão é ruim.
10. Ele está com um chapéu na mão.
11. A flor é do órfão.

28

Exercise G. Put all possible words in the feminine form:

1. O rapaz é bom.
2. O homem é alemão.
3. O sr. Gomes é mau.
4. O menino é grande.
5. O professor é português.
6. O estudante é espanhol.
7. O amigo é inglês.

Exercise H. Say in Portuguese:

1. He is eating bread.
2. The man wears a good hat.
3. I eat dinner at home.
4. They don't understand you.
5. Where are the pen and (the) paper.
6. The house is near the school.
7. Eat slowly.
8. Drink the milk.
9. Open the door.
10. He sells flowers.
11. They are playing near the door.
12. John works downtown.
13. The boy is having breakfast.
14. Mary stays at the motel.
15. Put the pencils away.
16. Take off your (the) hat.
17. Write a letter to the girl.
18. The dogs are on the street.
19. Rio is in Brazil.
20. The car is behind the house.

Lesson VI

32. Forms of the irregular verb *ir,* to go.

eu	vou	nós	vamos
você	vai	vocês	vão
ele	vai	eles	vão

33. Uses of *ir*.

a. This verb is used with the meaning *to go* and, as in English, often the present is used as if it were a future tense.

| Ele vai lá todos os dias. | He goes there every day. |
| Eu vou à cidade amanhã. | I'm going downtown tomorrow. |

The progressive form of *ir* is seldom used, and then only in special circumstances.

b. *Ir* is used like the corresponding verb in English, to form an expression which is an equivalent of the future tense. As in English, it may or may not involve actual movement. But it differs from English in that the progressive form is never used. It is not followed by a preposition.

Eu vou comer.	I'm going to eat.
Vou brincar lá no jardim.	I'm going to play out there on the lawn.
Vamos ficar aqui.	We are going to stay here.

c. It is used in inquiring about one's health, and in the answers.

| Como vai você? | How are you? |
| Vou bem, obrigado. | I'm well, thank you. |

d. The first person plural is used to make a suggestion for action—the equivalent of English *let's.*

Vamos comer.	Let's eat.
Vamos trabalhar.	Let's (go to) work.
Não vamos partir hoje.	Let's not leave today.
Vamos!	Let's go!

34. The prepositions *para* and *a*. These prepositions form contractions with the articles. Those of *para* are almost invariably used in speech, but *are not written.*

para + o	pronounced /pru/		para + um	pronounced /prũ/
para + a	/pra/		para + uma	/prũma/
para + os	/prus/			
para + as	/pras/			

The contractions of *a* and the definite article *are* written.

a + o	written ao		pronounced /au/
a + a	à		/a/
a + os	aos		/aus/
a + as	às		/as/

This preposition does not form contractions with the indefinite article.

35. Uses of *para* and *a*.

a. In addition to its meaning of *for, para* is frequently used where English would use *to.* With the verb *ir* and other verbs of motion, *para* is used if the person is going to stay at the place of his destination, or if it is his normal location. If the person is going to be there only temporarily, *a* is used.

O americano vai ao Brasil.	The American is going to Brazil. (He will return.)
O brasileiro vai para o Brasil.	The Brazilian is going to Brazil.

b. Either of these two prepositions may be used to mean *to* with the indirect object, generally interchangeably. *Para* is more frequent in BF.

Escreve para (*or* a) João.	Write to John.

c. *A* is used for *at* with expressions of time. In reference to place, the usual preposition is *em.*

Às duas horas.	At two o'clock.
Ele está em casa.	He is at home.

36. Use and omission of the definite article with the names of languages. The definite article usually accompanies the name of a language.

O português é a língua do Brasil.	Portuguese is the language of Brazil.

But it is omitted when the name of a language follows immediately after the preposition *em* or the verb *falar*. It is usually omitted also after other verbs which denote primarily mental activity, although it is considered acceptable to use it in such cases.

Ele fala português.	He speaks Portuguese.
Eles escrevem cartas em inglês.	They write letters in English.

Eu estou estudando (o) espanhol. I am studying Spanish.
Você fala muito bem o português. You speak Portuguese very well.

Note that in the phrase *um livro de português,* the article is omitted because *de português* is an adjectival modifier. In such cases the article would nearly always be omitted, before any noun.

Vocabulary

Nouns

a hora /ó/	hour; o'clock
o paletó	(suit-) coat
a roça /ó/	cultivated field; the country
a estrada	road, highway

Verb

procurar	look for; try to

Adverbs

pouco	little, very little
mais	more; plus
como	how; as; like
também	also, too
amanhã	tomorrow

Adjectives

americano	American
brasileiro	Brazilian
obrigado	thank you
um, fem. uma	one
dois, fem. duas	two
três	three
ruim (follows noun)	bad, poor
francês	French
branco	white
amarelo /é/	yellow
preto /ê/	black
marrom /õ/	brown, maroom

Expressions

Um pouco.	A little (bit).
Está na hora de comer.	It's time to eat.
Ele também não vai.	He isn't going either.
João é da roça.	John is from the "sticks."
Em casa de José.	At Joe's (house).
À casa de José.	To Joe's.
O trem parte daqui.	The train leaves from here.
Vou partir da cidade.	I'm going to leave town.
Ele está com frio.	He is cold.
Ele está com o chapéu.	He has his hat.
João casa com Maria.	John marries Mary.
João e Maria casam.	John and Mary get married.

Exercise A. Answer affirmatively in Portuguese:

1. O trem parte agora?
2. Você come bem?
3. Vocês falam alemão?
4. Eu escrevo mal?
5. João casa com Maria?
6. Ele compreende a lição?
7. Nós aprendemos protuguês?
8. Ela entra na aula?
9. Você acha o livro difícil?
10. Vocês ficam aqui?
11. Acabamos a lição hoje?
12. Eu guardo o livro?
13. Eles vão estudar?
14. Você quer falar devagar?

Exercise B. Fill in the adjectives in parentheses, in the correct form and location with respect to the noun underlined:

1. (doente) Eu falo com um menino no hospital.
2. (americano) O Mississípi é um grande rio.
3. (dois) As mulheres partem hoje.
4. (preto) Ele está com um chapéu.
5. (aberto) Estamos numa casa com duas janelas.
6. (rasgado) Não guardo um papel.
7. (casado) Ela está com um homem.
8. (bom) José é um menino.
9. (mau) Ele vai casar com uma moça.
10. (ruim) Eu não tomo o café.

Exercise C. Read aloud in Portuguese, at a natural speaking speed:

1. Ele vai para a cidade.
2. São sapatos para um homem.
3. Eu escrevo aos meninos.
4. Ela vai casar com o brasileiro.
5. Vou às duas horas.
6. Eu vou para a rua.
7. Para quem é o chapéu?

Exercise D. Read the sentences, translating the prepositions in parentheses and making contractions where needed:

1. Ele vai (with) você.
2. Let's go (to) o Brasil.
3. Ela parte (for) a cidade.
4. Eles estão (at) a escola.
5. É o irmão (of) o rapaz.
6. Vamos lá (after) amanhã.
7. Ela fica aqui (until) a noite.
8. Eu estudo uma lição (from) o livro.
9. Eu vendo o carro (before) amanhã.
10. João está (at) casa.

Exercise E. Answer questions in complete sentences, in Portuguese:

1. Como vai você, Maria? (or José, etc.)
2. O que você come?
3. Para quem você está escrevendo?
4. Com que você escreve?
5. De que você toma café?
6. Você usa chapéu?
7. Você estuda muito?
8. Você compreende português?
9. Você é casado?
10. O que você acha da lição?

Exercise F. Say in Portuguese:

1. I'm going to drink a cup of coffee.
2. He's going to marry a Spanish lady.
3. He wears two shoes.
4. Who understands the lesson?
5. We are leaving for Brazil.
6. Are you learning much or little?
7. He does not wear a coat.
8. I am going to stay here an hour.
9. Do you eat meat with rice?
10. I write with a pencil.
11. Let's go to (the) class.
12. Let's go home.
13. I'm going to write a letter.
14. He is going to drink water.
15. We are going downtown.
16. They are going to spend the night.
17. We spend two hours studying.
18. I am looking for my (the) hat.
19. Who remembers where it is?
20. Who are they?
21. Two and one are three.
22. [They] are white and yellow flowers.
23. It's time to leave.

24. The car is on the road.
25. The house is in the country.
26. I am going to the city.

27. I don't eat bread, thank you.
28. He drinks black coffee.
29. Tomorrow, let's go in.

Lesson VII

37. The irregular verb *ter,* to have. The present indicative of *ter* is as follows:

eu tenho	nós temos
você tem,	vocês têm
ele tem	eles têm

The third-person form *têm* is pronounced like the singular. Both are used as imperatives.

38. Uses of *ter.* In addition to the literal meaning, *to have, to possess,* this verb has several idiomatic usages.

a. *Ter que* (or *ter de*) = to have to.

Eu tenho que (tenho de) trabalhar.   I have to work.

b. *Ter . . . para,* to have (something) to (be done).

Ele tem uma lição para estudar.   He has a lesson to study.

c. *Tem,* always singular and without an expressed subject, is used in BF to mean *there is, there are.* Note that the noun which follows is the object of the verb, which then does not agree with it.

Tem meninos aqui? Não tem, não.   Are there any boys here? No, there are not.

d. All forms of the verb are used, followed by certain nouns, to denote conditions of the human body or mind. *Ter* may be replaced in these expressions by *estar com,* which is more colloquial in some of them, See the list of such words given in the vocabulary of this lesson.

Tenho frio. (Estou com frio)   I am cold.
Temos calor. (Estamos com calor)   We are warm.
Ele tem muito medo.   He is badly scared.

39. Possessive adjectives and pronouns, first person. The possessive adjectives corresponding to first-person subjects are:

Singular	*Plural*
meu my	meus (agreeing with masc. noun)
minha my	minhas (agreeing with fem. noun.)
nosso /ó/ our	nossos /ó/ (with masc. noun.)
nossa /ó/ our	nossas /ó/ (with fem. noun)
Meu livro.	My book.
Minha casa.	My house.
Nosso amigo.	Our friend.
Nossas amigas.	Our (lady) friends.

The definite article is often used preceding the possessive adjective. It may either be used or omitted, without difference of meaning, except that in two cases it is not used:

a. In direct address.

Meus amigos, como vão?	My friends, how are you?

b. With nouns of relationship, i.e., father, mother, cousin, etc.

Meu pai vai trabalhar.	My father is going to work.
Meu primo é americano.	My cousin is an American.

As pronouns (when not accompanied by nouns), the same words are used, always accompanied by articles, except after forms of *ser.*

o meu, a nossa	mine, ours
A casa de João e a minha.	John's house and mine.

After the verb *ser* there is a slight difference in meaning between the forms with and without the article. The difference is really more of emphasis than of meaning and is not of great importance.

A casa branca é minha.	The white house is mine. (Emphasis on ownership.)
A casa branca é a minha.	(Emphasis on which house is meant.)

40. Possessive adjectives and pronouns, second person. The possessives which refer to *você, vocês,* and also to the more formal subjects, *o senhor, a senhora,* and to their plural forms, are the following (Note that these forms may refer to any of these subjects.):

Singular	*Plural*	
seu	seus	your (with masc. nouns)
sua	suas	your (with femine nouns)

The article is used or omitted with these forms exactly as with those of the first person.

(o) seu livro	Your book
(a) sua casa	Your house
A casa de João e a sua	John's house and yours
A casa branca é sua.	The white house is yours.
A casa branca é a sua.	The white house is yours.

Vocabulary

Nouns

segunda-feira* /si/	Monday	a igreja /ê/	church
terça-feira /ê/	Tuesday	a missa	mass
quarta-feira	Wednesday	a festa /é/	party
quinta-feira	Thursday	a professora /ô/	teacher
sexta-feira /sê/	Friday	o filho	son
sábado	Saturday	a filha	daughter
domingo /du/	Sunday	a prova /ó/	test; proof
a semana	week		

*Feira may be omitted in these words whenever the meaning is clear without it. The plurals of these words are formed by adding -*s* to both parts, e.g., *terças-feiras.*

34

Adjectives

grande	big, large, great
pequeno /pi/	little, small
todo /ô/	all, every

Adverbs

geralmente	generally
só	only
quando	when
aí	there (near you)

Numbers

quatro	four
cinco	five
seis	six
sete /é/	seven

Preposition

em frente de	in front of

Nouns used with *ter*   *Adjective*

o frio	cold	cold
o calor /ô/	heat	hot
o medo	fear	afraid
o sono	sleep	sleepy
a fome	hunger	hungry
a sede /ê/	thirst	thirsty
a sorte /ó/	luck	lucky
o azar	bad luck	unlucky
a razão	reason	right
a raiva	anger	angry
a pressa /é/	haste	in a hurry
a vergonha	shame	bashful, ashamed

a vontade (de)   wish (to)

Expressions

De manhã	In the morning
De tarde	In the afternoon
De noite	At night
Nas segundas-feiras	On (every) Monday (*nas* with fem. days)
Aos sábados	On Saturdays (*aos* with masc. days)
todo (o) homem	Each man, every man
Todos os homens	Every man, all men
Todo mundo	Everybody
Todos	All, everybody
Que é que ele tem?	What's the matter with him?

Leitura

Nós vamos às aulas seis dias da semana. Temos aulas de manhã e de tarde, todos os dias, de segunda até sexta. Aos sábados, só temos aulas de manhã. Nas segundas, quartas e sextas temos aula de português. Vamos à aula com os livros, papel e lápis. Falamos português e escrevemos um pouco. Nas sextas temos uma pequena prova. Nas terças, e nas quintas temos aula de inglês. Lá temos que falar e escrever em inglês. Achamos o inglês mais difícil que o português. Aos domingos muitos vão à igreja.

Exercise A. Use of idioms with *ter* and *estar com:*

1. Você está com frio hoje?   Are you cold today?
2. O francês está com calor.   The Frenchman is warm.
3. Tem muitos brasileiros aqui?   Are there many Brazilians here?
4. Ele tem medo do cão.   He is afraid of the dog.
5. É noite e estou com sono.   It is nighttime and I'm sleepy.
6. Quando estou com fome, como.   When I'm hungry, I eat.
7. Ele está com sede, mas não toma água.   He is thirsty, but he doesn't drink water.
8. Acho que vamos ter sorte hoje.   I think we'll be lucky today.
9. Você tem azar com o professor.   You have bad luck with the teacher.
10. Eu tenho razão, mas você não tem.   I am right, but you are wrong.

11. Acho que ele tem raiva de João.	I think he's mad at John.
12. Estou com pressa, tenho que escrever uma carta.	I'm in a hurry, I must write a letter.
13. Ele tem vergonha do carro.	He is ashamed of his car.
14. O menino tem vergonha.	The boy is bashful.
15. O homem não tem vergonha!	The man is shameless.
16. Tenho vontade de jantar.	I feel like eating.

Exercise B. Answer in Portuguese (possible answers are suggested):

1. Quando é que você acaba o livro?   (hoje, amanhã)
2. Em que dias você tem aulas de português?   (terças, quintas, etc.)
3. O que é que você tem para escrever?   (um livro, uma lição)
4. Que é que tem na mesa do professor?   (uma prova, uma flor)
5. Que dia da semana é hoje?
6. Aonde vai você aos domingos?   (à missa, à igreja)
7. Como é a filha de João?   (pequeno, bonito)
8. Quando temos prova?   (amanhã, quarta)
9. Quem vai ao Brasil?   (eu, você)
10. Para quem é que você está escrevendo?

Exercise C. Answer in Portuguese:

1. Que é que você tem hoje?
2. Em que dias você tem aulas de francês?
3. Onde você toma o café da manhã?
4. O que tem lá atrás da mesa?
5. Você fala depressa ou devagar?
6. Você toma café frio?
7. Onde você guarda os livros?
8. A lição é muito fácil?
9. Os irmãos de José são bons?
10. Com que você escreve a lição?

Exercise D. Repeat the sentence, supplying the correct form for *you*:

1. Sr. Garcia, _____ vai à cidade?
2. Maria, _____ tem festa em casa hoje?
3. Sr. Peres e Sr. Carvalho, _____ vão à festa?
4. Menino, que é que _____ está escrevendo?
5. Irmã, _____ compreende os brasileiros?
6. João, _____ é casado?
7. Srta. Araujo, que é que _____ está estudando?
8. José, eu vou lá e _____ fica aqui.
9. Estudantes, quando é que _____ têm aula?
10. Eu acho que _____, os cães, vão comer agora.

Exercise E. Fill in the correct form of the possessive pronoun or adjective:

1. (mine) A casa branca é _____.
2. (my) _____ irmão é bom.
3. (your) _____ paletó está na cadeira.
4. (yours) O carro marrom é _____.
5. (our) _____ filha vai à escola.

36

6. (my) Não tenho _____ lápis.

7. (your) Vamos a _____ casa.

8. (ours) O ônibus amarelo é _____ .

Exercise F. Say in Portuguese:

1. I am hungry, but he is thirsty.
2. He is afraid, but she is more [afraid].
3. We have to sell our house.
4. Are there good schools there?
5. What do you have to learn tomorrow?
6. What's the matter with you?
7. I haven't [any]water to drink.
8. What do you have in your hand (the hand)?
9. We have yellow flowers in the garden.
10. When do you have breakfast?
11. The house has two windows.
12. They have to go in.
13. I have a lesson to study.
14. You are learning very little from the book.
15. Do you have a coat?

Exercise G. Say in Portuguese:

1. We don't have classes on Thursdays.
2. There are seven days in a week.
3. Saturday (in the) afternoon, we are going downtown.
4. On Sunday I go to church.
5. Mr. Garcia, do you eat in the café?
6. The teacher is a pretty lady.
7. He has two daughters; one is good, but one is bad.
8. We have only meat and rice to eat today.
9. You have to work tomorrow afternoon, boys.
10. I am generally at school in the morning.
11. Who is it in front of the house?
12. Where do you go at night in Rio?
13. He writes a letter every night to his (= the) son at school.
14. He has a sister.
15. We leave for Brazil tomorrow.
16. Who stays at home when you leave?
17. Joe, where are you going?
18. On Saturdays, we study the lessons.

Lesson VIII

41. Forms of the irregular verb *fazer,* to do, to make. Present indicative.

eu faço	nós fazemos
você faz	vocês fazem
ele faz	eles fazem

42. Uses of *fazer*. This verb has most of the uses of the two English verbs mentioned above. However, it is never used as an auxiliary with another verb, and seldom stands for a previously mentioned verb, like English *do*.

Eu faço meu trabalho.	I do my work.
Eu estou fazendo café.	I am making coffee.
Você fala português?	Do you speak Portuguese?
Ele não fala português, mas sim lê.	He doesn't speak Portuguese, but he does read it.

Fazer is used in the third person singular, the infinitive or the present participle, without an expressed subject, followed by the nouns *frio* or *calor,* or by *tempo* and an adjective, to describe the weather. Note that if one speaks of the weather as it is at the moment, the progressive form of the verb is used.

Faz calor no Rio no verão.	It's hot in Rio in summer.
Não está fazendo calor hoje.	It isn't hot today.
Que tempo está fazendo agora?	How's the weather now?
Sempre faz bom tempo aqui.	The weather is always fine here.

43. *Estar* with expressions of weather. *Estar* may be used impersonally, or with the subject *tempo,* in either case followed by *adjectives,* to describe the same conditions of weather, as well as others in which *fazer* is not used. *Estar* does not have a progressive form.

O tempo está bom.	The weather is good.
Está quente hoje.	It's hot today.
Como está o tempo?	How is the weather?
Hoje o tempo está chuvoso.	Today it's rainy.

44. The demonstrative adjectives and pronouns. There are three demonstratives, corresponding to the three persons of the pronouns and verbs. The forms are as follows:

	This (near speaker)	that (near you)	That (far from both)
Singular Masculine	este /ê/	esse /ê/	aquele /ê/
Plural	estes /ê/	esses /ê/	aqueles /é/
Singular Feminine	esta /é/	essa /é/	aquela /é/
Plural	estas /é/	essas /é/	aquelas /é/
Neuter	isto	isso	aquilo

Pronunciation: Note that each gender is distinguished by different vowels, both in the final syllable and the stressed one. The masculine forms all have /ê/ in the stressed syllable, the feminine forms all have /é/, while the neuter forms have /i/.

45. Contractions formed from the demonstratives. The prepositions *de* and *em* form contractions with the demonstratives.

deste	desse	daquele	neste	nesse	naquele
destes	desses	daqueles	nestes	nesses	naqueles
desta	dessa	daquela	nesta	nessa	naquela
destas	dessas	daquelas	nestas	nessas	naquelas
disto	disso	daquilo	nisto	nisso	naquilo

The preposition *a* forms contractions with *aquele* only. These contractions are pronounced like the demonstrative alone:

àquele, àqueles, àquela, àquelas, àquilo

The preposition *para* forms contractions with *aquele* in pronunciation, but *not in writing.*

para + aquele = (pronunciation only) praquele, etc.

46. The negatives. When a negative word is used following a verb, a negative word must precede the verb. If no other negative precedes, then *não* is put before the verb. The position of a negative word in the sentence is determined by its usage. Thus, if it is a subject, it will precede the verb, etc. Adverbs may usually either precede or follow the verb.

Não tenho nada.	I have nothing.
Nunca falo com ele.	I never speak to him.
Não falo nunca com ele.	I never speak to him.
Nem João nem Maria deixa a cidade.	Neither John nor Mary leaves town.

Vocabulary

Nouns

o tempo	weather; time
o ar	air
o sol /ó/	sun
a brisa	breeze
o céu	sky; heaven
a neve /é/	snow
a chuva	rain
a luz	light
a loja /ó/	shop, store
a árvore	tree
a esquina	corner

Verbs

chover	rain
nevar	snow
brilhar	shine
há*	there is, there are

Adjectives

nublado	cloudy
fresco /ê/	cool, fresh
chuvoso /ô/, fem. & pl. /ó/	rainy
brilhante	brilliant, bright
abafado	sultry
tanto	so much

Há means the same as *tem,* but is somewhat more literary.

Negatives

nada (pron.)	nothing
nenhum (adj. & pron.)	no, none
f. nenhuma	
ninguém (pron.)	no one
nunca (adv.)	never
nem (conj.)	nor
nem . . . nem (conj.)	neither . . . nor

Preposition

até	as far as

Adverbs

sempre	always
tão (with adj. or adv.)	so

Expressions

Vou fazer uma viagem.	I'm going to take a trip.
Faz favor de (falar).	Please (speak).
Está ventando.	It's windy.
Não há (tem) pressa.	There's no hurry.
Ele vai com pressa.	He goes hurriedly.
Não está fazendo tanto calor.	It's not so hot.
Não está tão quente.	It's not so hot.

Exercise A. Answer in Portuguese:

1. Que tempo está fazendo na cidade hoje?   (calor, frio, bom tempo, etc.)
2. Onde é que você vai?   (à cidade, à escola, para casa)
3. Onde estão os carros?   (na rua, na cidade, na estrada)
4. O que vendem nas lojas da cidade?   (livros, pão, papel)
5. O que há na esquina da rua?   (uma casa, uma loja, uma àrvore)
6. O que tem perto da estrada na roça?   (roças, casas, àrvores)
7. Onde tem àrvores na cidade?   (perto da rua, na esquina, atrás das casas)
8. Como está o tempo hoje?   (frio, quente, ruim, bonito)

Exercise B. Put the following sentences in the progressive form, as indicated by the words given:

1. Sempre faço meu trabalho.   Agora _____ meu trabalho.
2. Sempre faz calor aqui.   Agora _____ calor.
3. Todo o dia ela faz café.   Agora _____ café.
4. O que é que José faz?   O que José _____ agora?
5. Nós fazemos uma viagem todo ano.   Agora nós _____ uma viagem.

Exercise C. Use *estar* instead of *fazer*, making any other necessary changes.

1. Que tempo está fazendo?
2. Está fazendo calor hoje.
3. Está fazendo mau tempo.
4. Hoje está fazendo frio.
5. Está fazendo um tempo bonito.

Exercise D. Say in Portuguese (*That* may be expressed in two ways in each case, referring to two different locations.):

1. What is that? (neuter)
2. What house is that? (fem.)
3. That is a good boy. Esse é o bom rapaz.
4. What is on that table? Que está nessa mesa?
5. That book is in Portuguese. Esse livro é em
6. This hat is mine. Este chapéu é meu.
7. These tests are easy.
8. This wind is cool.
9. That tree is pretty.
10. I'm going as far as that city.
11. That man's coat is torn.
12. Those doors are white.
13. I'm going to do that tomorrow.
14. Those Frenchmen are going to leave.
15. That light is bright.
16. This chair is for that boy.

Exercise E. Say in Portuguese:

1. The air is cool today.
2. The sun is shining.
3. There is no snow in Rio.
4. The light of the sun is brilliant.
5. The sky is cloudy.
6. Today [it] is rainy.
7. This afternoon it is not so hot.
8. It always snows here.
9. It is raining downtown.
10. There is a cool breeze today.
11. After the rain, it gets (*fica*) sultry.
12. I am not warm now.
13. But we are very hungry!
14. We are going as far as the corner.
15. There are two trees at the corner.
16. These lessons are always so simple.
17. It is windy and snowing today.
18. Please open the door.
19. Let's not leave today.
20. I take off my hat when I come in.

Lesson IX

47. The irregular verb *querer,* to want, to wish; present indicative.

eu	quero /é/	nós	queremos
você	quer /é/	vocês	querem /é/
ele	quer	eles	querem

This verb is followed by an infinitive without a preposition.

Quero ficar.   I want to stay.

48. The preterit tense. The preterit (or simple perfect) tense has the following forms in the regular verbs of the three conjugations.

	falar	*comer*	*abrir*
eu	falei	comi	abri
você	falou	comeu	abriu
ele	falou	comeu	abriu
nós	falamos	comemos	abrimos
vocês	falaram	comeram	abriram
eles	falaram	comeram	abriram

a. The third person plural form of all preterits is often pronounced in Brazil as if the last syllable were *-rom.*

b. All *regular* preterits of the second conjugation have the vowel /ê/ when it is stressed.

c. Note that the first person plural of *regular* preterits is identical with the form of the present tense.

49. Uses of the preterit tense. This tense has retained in Portuguese both of the primary uses of the Latin perfect tense. Thus

a. It refers to a single past action, or to action or condition in the past which is limited in extent of time. It is especially the tense of narration, and therefore of primary importance.

Hoje eu falei com ele.	Today I spoke to him.
Eu fiquei duas horas.	I stayed two hours.
Ele trabalhou muito tempo.	He worked a long time.

b. It is a present perfect tense, referring to an action as recently completed, like the present perfect in English. In this meaning it is frequently preceded by the adverb *já,* which often does not need to be expressed in English. However, the presence or absence of *já* is not necessarily a distinction between the two uses.

Você já falou com o professor?	Have you spoken to the professor?
Você já comeu?	Have you (already) eaten?
Hoje ele trabalhou.	Today he has worked. (*or,* He worked.)

Note: When the verb of a question is accompanied by *já,* an affirmative answer may be simply *já.*

Você já comeu? Já.   Have you eaten? Yes

50. The preposition *por*. /pur/. The final *-r* is always pronounced in this word, with the sound of single *r* between vowels. It forms contractions with the definite article, as follows:

$$por + o = pelo /ê/$$
$$por + a = pela$$
$$por + os = pelos$$
$$por + as = pelas$$

These contractions are obligatory. But no contractions are formed with *por* and any other word.

51. Some uses of *por*.

a. The agent by whom something is done is expressed with *por*.

A porta é aberta pelo menino.	The door is opened by the boy.

b. *Por* = for (the sake of).

Ele faz isso só por fazer.	He does that just for the sake of doing it.
O homem faz isso pelo filho.	The man does that for (the sake of) his son.

c. *Por* = through.

Eu andei pela casa.	I walked (all) through the house.

52. Possessive adjectives and pronouns of the third person. Although historically the adjective *seu* applies to the third person, either singular or plural, and is regularly so used today in the written language, in BF the word *seu* is reserved only for the meaning "your," whether the subject is the familiar *você* or the more formal *o senhor,* or their plurals. The student should not be misled by the fact that "his," "her," "its," and "their" are often expressed by *seu* in literature, including plays, and even in popular songs. Such usage in speaking will be misunderstood. The following constructions are used in speech:

a. If the subject of the clause is the possessor, or the reference is otherwise clear, only the definite article is used.

Ele vendeu o carro.	He sold his car.
Elas estudaram as lições.	They studied their lessons.
Eles deixaram o irmão em casa.	They left their brother at home.
João jantou na cidade; a irmã não jantou.	John ate dinner downtown; his sister has not eaten.

b. If confusion would result from the use of only the definite article, the following contractions are added after the noun:

dele	his	dela	her, hers
deles	their, theirs	delas	their, theirs

Eu vou no carro dele.	I am going in his car.
O irmão delas é alto.	Their brother is tall.
Sua casa e a (casa) dele.	Your house and his (house).

Similar expressions *may* be used for the meanings "your," "yours," but not for the first person possessives.

Este paletó é de você (seu).	This coat is yours.
Este chapéu é meu.	This hat is mine.

42

Vocabulary

Nouns

a avenida	avenue
a calçada	sidewalk
o edifício	building
o cinema	movie
o teatro	theater
o parque	park
o campo	field, open plain
o bairro	district (of city)
o verão	summer
o nome	name
a praça	(city) square

Verbs

querer	wish, want
andar	go, walk
comprar	buy

Adverbs

assim	thus, in this way
enfim	in short; finally
já	already; at once

Conjunction

porque /u/	because

Expressions

De onde?	Where from?
De carro	By car, in a car
De trem	By train, on a train
Onde se acha?	Where is it?
Passar pela rua	To go down (up) the street

Adjectives

estreito	narrow
largo	wide
alto	tall; high
baixo	low; short (stature)
curto	short
comprido	long (space)
longo	long (time)
dividido	divided
cultivado	cultivated
pouco	little (amount)
poucos	few
muito /ũĩ/	much, pl. many

Pronouns

que (rel.)	who, which, that.
tudo (neuter)	all, everything
qual, pl. quais (interrog.)	which; what (of two or more)

Prepositions

por /u/	by; for; through
ao longo de	along

Leitura

As grandes cidades são divididas em muitos bairros, que têm nomes. Assim, Copacabana e Ipanema são bairros da cidade do Rio de Janeiro. Esses bairros têm muitas ruas e avenidas onde passam os carros que vão a outros bairros, ou que vão até as casas e lojas que se acham nas ruas do bairro. As avenidas são largas, mas muitas ruas são estreitas. Ao longo das ruas e avenidas há edifícios grandes e pequenos—lojas, casas, teatros e cinemas. Nas lojas vendem livros, pão, papel, lápis, enfim tudo.

Quando uma rua deixa a cidade e entra na roça, tem o nome de estrada. Na roça há muitas casas, mas poucas lojas e nenhuns edifícios grandes. Ao longo da estrada se acham muitos campos cultivados. Em frente das casas há jardins bonitos com flores e árvores. Vamos fazer uma viagem de carro pela roça, porque é bonita.

Exercise A. Be able to give either language:

1. O senhor está brincando?   Are you kidding?
2. Você quer jantar lá em casa hoje?   Will you have dinner at my house tonight?
3. Não quero vender meu carro.   I don't want to sell my car.
4. Está querendo chover.   It's trying to rain.
5. O senhor quer falar mais devagar?   Will you speak more slowly?
6. Não vou porque não quero.   I'm not going because I don't want to.
7. No inverno as noites são longas.   In winter the nights are long.
8. A longa viagem de volta é difícil.   The long trip back is hard.

Exercise B. Give the form of the preterit which corresponds to the following present tense forms:

1. Ele acha
2. Eu tomo
3. Nós tiramos
4. Eles jantam
5. Eu vendo
6. Ele aprende
7. Nós comemos
8. Eles compreendem
9. Eu abro
10. Ele parte
11. Nós abrimos
12. Eles partem
13. Eu escrevo
14. Ele estuda
15. Eles guardam
16. Eu deixo
17. Ele acaba
18. Você passa
19. Vocês pensam
20. Chove

Exercise C. Answer in the affirmative:

1. Você quer ir à cidade?
2. Nevou na sexta-feira?
3. Você come pão?
4. Há muitas praças na cidade?
5. Vocês já jantaram?
6. A avenida é larga?
7. Tem casas ao longo da rua?
8. Vocês já estudaram tudo?
9. Você comprou um carro?
10. Seu amigo partiu já?
11. Faz calor aqui no verão?
12. Você vai ao cinema?
13. Você andou pelo parque?
14. Vamos passar pela praça?
15. Você faz viagens no verão?

Exercise D. Para responder em português, em sentenças:

1. A avenida é larga ou estreita?
2. O edifício é alto ou baixo?
3. A rua é curta ou comprida?
4. O verão é quente ou frio?
5. O teatro é grande ou pequeno?
6. Qual é um bairro do Rio?
7. Onde fica a calçada?
8. Onde tem estradas?
9. Há mais árvores na cidade ou na roça?
10. Você vai à roça de carro ou de trem?
11. Qual é outro nome de um campo cultivado?
12. Há muitos ou poucos parques nesta cidade?
13. Temos praças nas nossas cidades?
14. Em que são divididas as cidades brasileiras?
15. Você deixou o livro em casa hoje?

Exercise E. Say in Portuguese:

1. A street passes through the city.
2. A road passes throught the country.
3. He does that for John's sake.
4. The fields are divided by the brothers.
5. I'm going to take a trip by car.
6. There are few stores in the country.
7. The name of that city is São Paulo.
8. This avenue is long and wide.
9. He did not remember his coat.
10. I thought of you when I passed your house.
11. Joe married a girl at this church.
12. This district [of the city] has two large squares.

13. The short man is working in the snow.
14. Do you want to sell your car?
15. He passed down the street in his maroon car.
16. My brother is going to write to yours.

17. Your house is tall and white.
18. Is this your car or his?
19. Did he understand his lesson?
20. I went through the park this afternoon.

Exercise F. Say in Portuguese:

1. Through the fields.
2. Along the road.
3. Near the tree.
4. At the movie.
5. In the morning.
6. To Brazil.
7. Of the girls.
8. On the building.
9. After (the) class.
10. Before (the) night.
11. I want the flowers.
12. It rained all night.
13. He looked for his hat.
14. He got married.
15. I used a pencil.
16. He opened the door.
17. He let Joe go.
18. Put away your books.

19. As far as the avenue.
20. Behind the theater
21. In front of the house.
22. With the orphans.
23. At night.
24. By the professor.
25. From the city.
26. Until Sunday.
27. In (the) summer.
28. [Leaving] for Portugal.
29. He sold a car to my brother.
30. It snowed at night.
31. I wrote a letter.
32. They ate the rice.
33. I didn't understand you.
34. He learned (a) write.
35. They ate dinner.

Lesson X

53. The irregular verb *dar*, to give. Present indicative and preterit.

	Present	*Preterit*
eu	dou	dei
você	dá	deu
ele	dá	deu
nós	damos	demos
vocês	dão	deram /é/
eles	dão	deram

54. Uses of *dar*. This verb, in addition to its basic meaning, is used in a great number of idiomatic expressions, in many of which other verbs are used in English.

Dar uma olhada	To take a look
Dar um passeio	To take a walk (drive, ride)
Dar aula	To recite
A janela dá para a rua.	The window faces the street.
Dá nele!	Hit him!
Deram duas horas.	It struck two.
Não dá tempo para ir.	There isn't time to go.
Dar bom dia	To say good morning
Dar para a música	To be good at music
Dar (as) cartas	To deal (the) cards
Dar um grito	To yell

55. Irregular preterits. The following verbs already given have irregular forms in the preterit tense:

	estar	*ser & ir*	*ter*	*fazer*	*querer*
eu	estive	fui	tive	fiz	quis
você	esteve /ê/	foi	teve /ê/	fêz	quis
ele	esteve	foi	teve	fêz	quis
nós	estivemos	fomos	tivemos	fizemos	quisemos
vocês	estiveram	foram	tiveram	fizeram	quiseram
eles	estiveram /é/	foram /ô/	tiveram /é/	fizeram /é/	quiseram /é/

56. Radical-changing verbs, first and second conjugations. The vowels *e* and *o*, when they are the last vowels before the ending of the infinitive, vary in pronunciation in the forms of the present tense according to fixed rules. In the first conjugation, they are open whenever they are stressed, but closed when unstressed. Thus:

	levar	*morar*
eu	levo /é/	moro /ó/
você	leva /é/	mora /ó/
ele	leva /é/	mora /ó/
nós	levamos	moramos
vocês	levam /é/	moram /ó/
eles	levam /é/	moram /ó/

All regular verbs of the first conjugation whose stem-vowels are *e* and *o* show this variation except the following types, which maintain the close vowel in all forms:

a. Verbs in which one of these vowels is followed by a nasal consonant (n, nh, m), e.g., *entrar, contar, tomar, desenhar*.

b. Verbs in which this vowel is part of a diphthong, and is therefore not the last vowel before the ending, e.g., *deixar, poupar*.

c. Verbs which end in *-elhar* or *-ejar*, e.g., *aconselhar, desejar,* However, the verb *invejar* is radical-changing.

d. Verbs in *-oar* and *-ear*. This latter type does have a change, of a kind to be given later. Verbs in *-oar* are completely regular, with the vowel closed in all forms, e.g., *voar*.

e. The verbs *chegar* and *fechar*. *Fechar* is radical-changing in some regions, in others it is not. Thus one may pronounce *fecha* either with /ê/ or with /é/.

In the second conjugation, the vowel remains closed in the first person, but is open in the third.

	conhecer	*correr*
eu	conheço /ê/	corro /ô/
você	conhece /é/	corre /ó/
ele	conhece /é/	corre /ó/
nós	conhecemos	corremos
vocês	conhecem /é/	correm /ó/
eles	conhecem /é/	correm /ó/

All regular verbs of the second conjugation whose stem vowels are *e* or *o* follow this pattern, except those in which the vowel is followed by a nasal consonant, e.g., *aprender, comer*. These maintain the closed vowel throughout. The following verbs already studied have the radical change: *escrever, chover*.

Vocabulary

Nouns

a olhada (para)	look (at)
o passeio	walk, ride, drive (for pleasure)
o pai	father
papai	Daddy
a mãe	mother
mamãe	Mommy
o primo	cousin
a prima	cousin
o tio	uncle
titio	Uncle
a tia	aunt
titia	Aunty
o, a parente	relative
a visita	visit; visitor
os pais	parents
os tios	uncles; uncle and aunt
os primos	cousins

Verbs

dar	give; strike
levar	take, carry
morar	live, dwell, reside
chegar (a *or* em)	arrive, come, get to
fechar	shut, close
conhecer	know (person) be acquainted with, meet, recognize
correr	run; hurry
gostar de	like; love

Adjective

vários	several

Preposition

longe de	far from

Adverbs

depois	afterward (s)
amanhã	tomorrow

Leitura

Amanhã papai e mamãe vão chegar nesta cidade de visita, com meus tios, um primo e meu irmão. Todos estes parentes querem visitar e conhecer a cidade onde eu estou morando. Eu moro numa casa um pouco longe da cidade, num bairro onde há muitos jardins. Amanhã de tarde vamos dar um passeio de carro pela cidade—no carro de meu pai. Vamos ter que correr, porque temos pouco tempo. Uma tarde não dá para andar por todas partes.

Mamãe gosta de ir às lojas fazer compras. Papai quer conhecer os parques e ruas da cidade e depois ir tomar café. Ele não gosta dos passeios que levam muito tempo. Também ele acha que mamãe compra muito quando vai às lojas.

Meus tios moram em outra cidade, não muito longe daqui. Titio é o irmão de minha mãe e titia é a mulher dele. Ela já morou nesta cidade, onde tem muitos parentes. Os tios vão fazer uma visita a estes parentes.

Exercise A. Be able to give either language, from the other:

1. Ele chegou de ônibus.	He came by bus.
2. Mamãe está aqui de visita.	Mother is here on a visit.
3. Ele acaba de chegar.	He has just gotten here.
4. O café não chega para todos.	There isn't enough coffee to go around.
5. Isso chega a dez cruzeiros.	That amounts to 10 cruzeiros.
6. O passeio levou uma hora.	The drive took an hour.
7. Vou visitar um amigo.	I'm going to see a friend.
8. Ela gosta de você.	She likes (loves) you.
9. Eu tenho que correr.	I must hurry.
10. Conheci o João no clube.	I met John at the club.

Exercise B. Change the pronouns and verbs to the plural form:

1. Eu moro nesta cidade.
2. Ele chega em casa.
3. Eu corro para lá.
4. Ele gosta de você.
5. Ele leva você à escola.
6. Eu fecho a porta.
7. Eu conheço sua prima.
8. Ele escreve cartas.
9. Eu deixo você aqui.
10. Ele toma café.

Exercise C. Answer in the affirmative:

1. Você foi à cidade hoje?
2. Seu irmão esteve na aula hoje?
3. José e Maria já partiram para o Brasil?
4. Você ficou em casa sábado?
5. Ele falou português com você?
6. Você já comeu?
7. Eles quiseram partir?
8. Vocês fizeram uma viagem?
9. Você aprendeu português no Brasil?
10. Vocês já tomaram café?

Exercise D. Answer with one of the words in parentheses, or others, forming complete sentences:

1. Por quem a porta foi aberta? (o menino, o alemão, Maria)
2. Por quanto tempo você vai ficar aqui? (três dias, uma semana)
3. Por onde você vai passar na viagem? (A cidade, a roça, o Brasil)
4. Até onde vamos? (a casa de meu tio, o bairro de Ipanema)
5. Como são as ruas de Copacabana? (largo, estreito, bonito)

Exercise E. Give the third-person form corresponding to the first-person form given here:

1. Falo	10. Estou	19. Faço
2. Chego	11. Dou	20. Vendo
3. Fico	12. Vou	21. Levo
4. Tomo	13. Deixo	22. Moro
5. Estudo	14. Como	23. Fecho
6. Acho	15. Parto	24. Corro
7. Entro	16. Escrevo	25. Desejo
8. Acabo	17. Compreendo	
9. Sou	18. Quero	

Exercise F. Give the preterit forms which correspond in person and number to the following forms of the present:

1. Estou	11. Quero	21. Andam
2. Falamos	12. Come	22. Tenho
3. Estudam	13. Escreve	23. Fazemos
4. Trabalha	14. Corro	24. Corremos
5. Passo	15. Dá	25. Comem
6. Fico	16. Como	26. Anda
7. Tomam	17. Corre	27. Têm
8. Sou	18. É	28. Faz
9. Deixo	19. Vamos	29. Levo
10. Vai	20. Querem	30. Somos

Exercise G. Say in Portuguese:

1. Run to the door.
2. Shut the window.
3. I know you.
4. Take this.
5. Wear your coat.
6. Learn this lesson.
7. Take off your shoes.
8. Play in the yard.
9. Be good.
10. Drink your coffee.
11. Do you know my father?
12. Where do you live?
13. He struck the boy with his hand.
14. We took a look at the city.
15. Let's take a walk on the avenue.
16. My aunt's son is my cousin.
17. We have to hurry.
18. I don't like Mr. Garcia.
19. It's going to take a long time.
20. I have several relatives there.

Lesson XI

57. The irregular verb *poder*, can, may, be able. Forms of the present and preterit indicative.

	Present	*Preterit*
eu	posso /ó/	pude
Você	pode /ó/	pôde
ele	pode	pôde
nós	podemos /pu/	pudemos
vocês	podem /ó/	puderam /é/
eles	podem	puderam

Note the difference in pronunciation between *pode*, present tense, and *pôde*, preterit. But *podemos* and *pudemos* are pronounced alike. *Poder* is followed by the infinitive without a preposition.

58. *Poder* in the preterit tense. The uses of the preterit of this verb are limited to situations in which momentary possibilities are indicated. Frequently it expresses a successful or unsuccessful attempt to do something.

Eu quis entrar, mas não pude abrir a porta.

I tried to get in, but I couldn't open the door.

Eu pude ir na semana passada, mas nesta semana não posso.

I managed to go last week, but this week I can't.

59. Use of the simple present for the future. We are already acquainted with the use of the auxiliary verb *ir* to express future action. The simple present tense is often used, especially in BF. If futurity is otherwise expressed, e.g., by an adverb or adverb phrase, or is clear from the context, the simple present is sufficient to give the meaning. The true future indicative is comparatively little used in conversation. But do not use the progressive present for the future, as is often done in English.

Amanhã eu falo com o professor.
Ele vai domingo.
João não fêz o trabalho, mas eu faço.
Ele parte amanhã.

Tomorrow I'll speak to the teacher.
He is going Sunday.
John didn't do his work, but I'll do it.
He is leaving tomorrow.

The progressive present is used for present action.

João não fêz o trabalho, mas eu estou fazendo.   John didn't do his work, but I'm doing it.

60. The personal pronoun objects of the first person. The forms used as either direct or indirect objects of the first person are as follows:

me /mi/   me, to me, myself, to myself
nos /nus/   us, to us, ourselves, to ourselves

Note: Do not confuse *nos* with *nós*, "we."

61. Placing of the object pronouns. The position of these and other object pronouns in relation to the verb varies somewhat, but the following are rules which may be followed, and which permit one to speak colloquially and at the same time in a fashion acceptable in the literary language.

a. Place an object *before* a one-word verb, unless it would become the first word of a clause. If no word precedes the verb in the clause, one may use a subject pronoun first, or may place the object *after* the verb.

Ele me deu um livro.   He gave me a book.
Deu-me um livro.   He gave me a book.

b. Place the object before a one-word verb when it is preceded by a negative word, a relative pronoun, a subordinating conjunction, an adverb, or by an expressed subject.

Aquele é o homem que me deu isto.	That is the man who gave me this.
Não nos deu trabalho.	It gave us no trouble.
Ele me conheceu quando me achou.	He recognized me when he found me.
Sempre nos dão café.	They always give us coffee.
João me escreveu uma carta.	John wrote me a letter.

c. In verb phrases made up of *querer, poder, ir,* etc. and an infinitive, or of *estar* and the present participle, the object precedes the second verb, whether or not the words mentioned in (b) precede the first verb.

Ele está me escrevendo.	He is writing to me.
João não quer me dar o livro.	John won't give me the book.
Você não pode me pegar.	You can't catch me.

d. The object usually precedes the infinitive, unless it would be the first word of a clause. When the infinitive follows a preposition, its object may follow, but more often precedes it in BF.

Pegar-me é o que ele quer.	What he wants is to catch me.
Ele correu para me pegar *or* pegar-me.	He ran to catch me.

Note: When these objects follow a verb form, they are connected with it by a hyphen.

Vocabulary

Nouns

a (sala de) aula	classroom	a caneta /ê/	pen
a turma	class (= people); "the gang"	o quadro-negro /ê/ pl. quadros-negros	blackboard

50

Nouns

o giz	chalk
o, a colega /é/	colleague; classmate
o ano	year
a universidade	university
a faculdade	college, school (of a university)
a vez /ê/	time, occasion
a estação	season; station
a primavera /é/	spring
o verão	summer
o outono	fall, autumn
o inverno /é/	winter
o mês pl. meses	month

Preposition

por /pur/	per

Verbs

pegar	catch
esquecer	forget
chamar	call
preparar	prepare, get (something) ready
freqüentar	attend

Adverbs

ontem	yesterday
ontem à noite	last night
hoje (à noite)	tonight
ainda	still, yet
ainda não	not yet

Adjectives

passado	past, last
presente	present (all senses)
ausente	absent
quanto?	how much?
quantos?	how many?

Expressions

Como se chama você?	What's your name? (What do you call yourself?)
Eu me chamo Pedro.	My name's Pete.
Chamo-me Pedro.	My name's Pete.
Vamos à faculdade.	Let's go over to the University.
Vamos à aula.	Let's go to class.
Freqüentamos aulas de inglês.	We attend English classes.
Duas vezes	Twice
Três vezes	Three times
Uma vez	Once
A semana passada	Last week.
Na semana passada	(At some time in) last week
Peguei no sono.	I fell asleep.
Peguei a gripe.	I caught the flu.

Leitura

Nós freqüentamos a faculdade de filosofia, ciências e letras desta universidade. Temos aulas de inglês, de história, de ciência e de português.

Vamos às aulas de português três vezes por semana—segundas, quartas e sextas. A sala de aula é grande e tem várias janelas que dão para o jardim da universidade. Os estudantes têm cadeiras com um braço onde escrevem. O professor tem uma cadeira e uma mesa. Há quadros-negros onde podemos escrever com giz.

Temos uma boa turma de estudantes. Gosto de todos os meus colegas. Todos querem aprender depressa, preparam bem as lições e dão aula falando português. Poucas vezes estamos ausentes das aulas.

Nos três meses de verão não temos aulas, mas temos no outono, no inverno e na primavera.

51

Exercise A. Answer in Portuguese:

1. Como se chama você?
2. Que foi que você esqueceu esta manhã?
3. A chuva pegou você na rua?
4. Aonde foi você ontem à noite?
5. Que aulas você freqüenta?
6. Você ainda lembra os nomes das estações do ano? Quais são?
7. Que estação temos este mês?
8. Com que você escreve no quadro-negro?
9. Com que escreve no papel?
10. Quando você vai à faculdade?
11. Quantas aulas você tem hoje?
12. Quantas vezes por semana você tem aulas de inglês?
13. Quantos estudantes estão presentes hoje?
14. Quantos estão ausentes?
15. A sua turma é grande ou pequena?
16. Você já preparou a lição de amanhã?
17. Você vai ao cinema hoje?
18. Você quer me comprar um café?
19. Quanto tempo você passa estudando?
20. Que tempo está fazendo agora?

Exercise B. Give the corresponding form of the preterit:

1. Eu posso
2. Ele vai
3. Ele escreve
4. Eu faço
5. Nós somos
6. Eles fazem
7. Ele freqüenta
8. Eu chamo
9. Eles esquecem
10. Ele dá
11. Eles estão
12. Você vai
13. Nós temos
14. Eu quero
15. Eu esqueço
16. Ele guarda
17. Ele compreende
18. Chove
19. Eu ando
20. Ele corre

Exercise C. Exchange subjects and objects of the verbs in the following expressions (Example: I see you. Answer: You see me.):

1. Você me esqueceu.
2. Os senhores nos conhecem.
3. Eu achei vocês em casa.
4. A senhora não me compreende.
5. Eu deixei o João na cidade.
6. Eu chamei o senhor.
7. Eu levo você à festa.
8. Vocês nos pegaram.
9. Eu estou procurando você.
10. Vocês não podem me deixar.

Exercise D. Read the following words, taking care to give the proper value to the stressed vowels:

1. porta
2. professor
3. moça
4. escola
5. flor
6. voz
7. copo
8. órfão
9. arroz
10. hora
11. paletó
12. roça
13. prova
14. calor
15. sorte
16. loja
17. todo
18. nosso
19. chuvoso
20. só
21. hoje

Exercise E. Express the following verbs in the simple present, without the auxiliary verb *ir*:

1. Eu vou esquecer você amanhã.
2. Ele vai pegar o trem ainda hoje.
3. Amanhã vamos jantar em casa.
4. Ele vai me levar à cidade hoje à tarde.
5. Amanhã vou procurar meu colega.

Exercise F. Say in Portuguese:

1. I caught the train at the station.
2. My name is John.
3. I have already gone to class twice.
4. He called us, and we went to his house.
5. How many classmates do you have?
6. Tomorrow I'm going to school.
7. She gets here tomorrow night.
8. We spent last week with my brother.
9. Take your friend to the coffee shop.
10. I couldn't get in through the window.
11. I have forgotten my breakfast.
12. He did that two or three times.
13. (In) last summer, we put away our books.
14. How many times per week do you have class?
15. You will find the bus station on the corner.
16. Are you going to town by car or by bus?
17. He attends classes at the university.
18. He is going to the party tomorrow.
19. He is the friend that you met last week.
20. I caught the rain and it (*ela*) caught me.

Lesson XII

62. The irregular verb *pôr,* to put, place, pour.

	Present	*Preterit*
eu	ponho	pus
você	põe	pôs
ele	põe	pôs
nós	pomos	pusemos
vocês	põem	puseram /é/
eles	põem	puseram

The third plural present form *põem* is usually pronounced exactly like the singular. It may also be pronounced in two syllables, as if written põe-em. Like the singular, the plural is used as an imperative.

63. Uses of *pôr*. This word has a wide variety of uses. For this reason, and because there are some fifteen verbs derived from it, it is very important to master the forms of *pôr*. Some of the situations in which the simple verb is used are illustrated below.

Ele pôs a roupa.	He put on his clothes.
Ele pôs a mão no bolso.	He put his hand in his pocket.
Eu ponho água para você.	I'll pour you some water.
A galinha pôs um ovo.	The hen laid an egg.
Ela pôs a mesa.	She set the table.
Põe a mala aí.	Put the suitcase (down) there.

64. Verbs derived from *pôr*. The many derivatives of *pôr* all have forms like those of the simple verb, preceded by a prefix or prefixes. They correspond in general to English verbs with the root *-pose,* but they often have wider application than these. The accent is not needed on derived infinitives. Some of the derivatives are the following:

propor	suggest, propose	expor	expose; express
repor	put back	impor	impose, be imposing
repor-se	recover (strength)	opor (a)	contrast (with)
compor	compose, make up	opor-se a	oppose
compor-se	compose oneself	descompor	confuse; scold
depor	set down; depose	decompor	cause to decompose
dispor de	have at one's disposal	recompor	recompose, reconcile

65. The future subjunctive. The future subjunctive forms of any verb may be derived by removing the final *-ram* of the third person plural of the preterit, and adding the following endings: -r, -r, -rmos, -rem.

fazer: 3rd plural preterit: fizeram

Future subjunctive

eu   fizer /é/
você   fizer /é/
ele   fizer /é/
nós   fizermos /é/
vocês   fizerem /é/
eles   fizerem /é/

The stressed vowel of the future subjunctive is thus always the same as that of the third person plural of the preterit. It is helpful to become thoroughly familiar with the future subjunctive forms of the verbs which have irregular preterits, so that it will not be necessary to derive them. The following are the singular forms of those irregular verbs we have already studied.

	Future subjunctive		*Future subjunctive*
estar	estiver /é/	querer	quiser /é/
ser	for /ô/	dar	der /é/
ir	for /ô/	poder	puder /é/
ter	tiver /é/	pôr	puser /é/
fazer	fizer /é/		

It will be noted that in regular verbs the singular of this tense will be exactly like the infinitive, e.g., *falar, comer, abrir.*

54

66. Uses of the future subjunctive. In spite of the forbidding sound of the name "future subjunctive," it is one of the simplest forms to master. It is extremely important in colloquial as well as in literary Portuguese. The Brazilian child learns it very early, soon after the preterit, largely because of its frequent use after the basic conjunctions *if* and *when*.

The future subjunctive is used in subordinate clauses following certain, *but not all*, adverbial conjunctions of time, and after some other conjunctions, whenever futurity is implied. The following conjunctions require, or in some cases, permit, the use of the future subjunctive of the following verb, whenever it refers to future action or condition. But remember that we have been using the indicative with *quando,* when futurity was not implied. The following *must* be followed by the future subjunctive when futurity is implied:

se if   enquanto while   quando when

The following *may* be followed by the future subjunctive in such cases, and usually are in BF. The alternative is the present subjunctive.

| logo que | as soon as | assim que | as soon as |
| depois que | after | caso | in case |

There are, however, some conjunctions of time which *may not* be followed by the future subjunctive. For examples of the use of this form, see Exercise A, below.

67. The object pronouns *se, lhe, lhes.*

Se is the reflexive object pronoun used with the new second-person and with the third-person subjects. It is singular or plural, direct or indirect object. It may be translated as *yourself, yourselves, himself, herself, itself, themselves, to yourself,* etc.

Lhe is the indirect object referring to the singular pronouns of the second and third persons, and is translated *to you* (sing.), *to him, to her, to it, for you,* etc. *Lhes* is used in the plural. These pronouns are placed with respect to the verb according to the same principles as *me* and *nos*.

Ele se acha no jardim.	He finds himself (= is) on the lawn.
Como se chama você?	How do you call yourself? (what is your name?)
Eles se deixaram levar.	They let themselves be taken.
Eu lhe escrevi uma carta.	I wrote him (her, you) a letter.
Nós lhes demos café.	We gave them (you) some coffee.

Vocabulary

Nouns

| o casaco | topcoat; lady's coat |
| Deus | God |

Pronouns

se /si/	See above
lhe /li/	See above
lhes /lis/	See above

Verbs

cansar	tire; get tired
cansar-se	get tired
perguntar	ask (question)
parecer	seem, look like, appear
parecer (-se) com	resemble
aparecer	appear (= be visible)
contar	tell (story); count
lembrar-se de	remember, remember to
chamar-se	be called, be named
achar-se	be located

55

Conjunctions

se /si/	if	logo que /ó/	as soon as
se . . . não	if not, unless	assim que	as soon as
enquanto	while	depois que	after
enquanto . . . não	until	caso	in case (that)

Expressions

Perguntei isso a João.	I asked John that.
Perguntamos por você.	We asked for you.

Exercise A. Be able to give either language from the other:

1. Eu vou comer quando chegar em casa. — I'm going to eat when I get home.
2. Vamos gostar da viagem, se formos com José. — We're going to enjoy the trip, if we go with Joe.
3. Queremos estudar esta noite, se tivermos tempo. — We want to study tonight, if we have time.
4. Passa lá em casa, se puder. — Go by the house, if you can.
5. Chove ainda hoje, se Deus quiser. — It'll still rain today, God willing.
6. Eu levo o livro amanhã, se não esquecer. — I'll take the book tomorrow, unless I forget.
7. Eu fico estudando enquanto vocês acabarem o trabalho. — I'll keep on studying while you finish your work.
8. Vamos tomar café enquanto não jantarmos. — Let's have coffee while waiting for dinner.
9. Podemos ficar enquanto não derem quatro horas. — We can stay until it strikes four.
10. Vamos à festa logo que João e Maria chegarem. — We are going to the party as soon as John and Mary come.
11. Não podemos brincar no parque quando fizer frio. — We won't be able to play in the park when it gets cold.

Exercise B. Give the verb forms corresponding to those of the present:

Present	Preterit	Future Subjunctive
1. Eu ponho	ontem eu	se eu
2. Ele está	ontem ele	se ele
3. Nós podemos	ontem nós	se nós
4. Eles acham	ontem eles	se eles
5. Eu tenho	ontem eu	se eu
6. Eles vão	ontem eles	se eles
7. Ele dá	ontem ele	se ele
8. Eu posso	ontem eu	se eu
9. Nós pomos	ontem nós	se nós
10. Eles querem	ontem eles	se eles

Exercise C. Put in the blanks the correct forms of the verbs in parentheses:

1. (abrir) Ele me pegou quando eu _____ a porta.
2. (chegar) Eles vão me levar para lá quando eles _____ .
3. (acabar) Eu lhe conto tudo, depois que você _____ .
4. (pôr) Eu ponho o paletó, se você também _____ .
5. (fazer) Vamos ficar em casa, caso _____ mau tempo.
6. (ir) Vou deixar os livros aqui, enquanto _____ ao café.
7. (dar) Vamos estudar, enquanto não _____ duas horas.

8. (chover) Nunca andamos na rua quando _____ .

9. (ter) Você quer fechar a porta quando _____ que ir?

10. (fechar) Ficou mais quente em casa depois que eu _____ a porta.

11. (querer) Eles podem partir quando _____ .

12. (estar) Você pode fechar a janela se _____ com frio.

Exercise D. Give the second and third persons in the same tense and number as the examples, e.g., I got tired, you got tired, he got tired:

1. Eu me cansei.
2. Nós nos chamamos Carvalho.
3. Eu me oponho a isso.
4. Eu me deixei levar.
5. Eu me expus à neve.
6. Nós nos dispomos a trabalhar.
7. Eu não quero me cansar.
8. Lembrei-me do João.
9. Nós nos preparamos para partir.
10. Eu me comprei um carro.

Exercise E. Change the object pronoun to the third person, e.g., to me—to him:

1. João me deu uma caneta.
2. Você nos fêz uma pergunta.
3. Você me lembrou que tenho que ir.
4. Perguntou-me o nome.
5. Parece-me que vai chover.

Exercise F. Say in Portuguese:

1. He got tired.
2. I told him that.
3. If you want to learn, study hard.
4. His name is Joe.
5. Go there as soon as you can.
6. He is going to buy a house, in case he marries.
7. Write him a letter while you are here.
8. Where is the church located?
9. I can't understand unless you speak slowly.
10. Let me take off my coat.
11. It seems to us that you don't know us.
12. Do you remember that boy?
13. He wears a topcoat in (the) winter.
14. Put on your coat and let's go to the party.
15. You may have coffee now, if you wish.
16. I'll think of you when we go to Brazil.
17. He will arrive by bus, if he can.

Lesson XIII

68. The irregular verb *dizer,* to say, tell.

	Present Indicative	Preterit	Future Subjunctive
eu	digo	disse	disser /é/
você	diz	disse	disser /é/
ele	diz	disse	disser /é/
nós	dizemos	dissemos	dissermos /é/
vocês	dizem	disseram /é/	disserem /é/
eles	dizem	disseram /é/	disserem /é/

69. Uses of *dizer.*

Dizer means *to say* or *to tell* when the statement that follows is a direct or indirect quotation. It also means *to tell to* in the sense of giving an order.

Contar means *to tell* in the sense of *to narrate,* or to tell a lie. *Falar* is *to speak,* with or without an object, or *to talk.* In Rio it may often be heard when one might expect *dizer.*

70. Form of the verb which follows a preposition. With one exception of very limited use, all prepositions in Portuguese require that the following verb form be an infinitive. Note that English often uses the gerund in *-ing.*

Antes de entrar	Before entering
Para dizer	In order to say
Depois de comer	After eating

71. Personal pronoun direct objects, third person. In BF, the direct objects *him, her, them, it* are almost never expressed if they are unstressed. If stress is required for emphasis or contrast, one uses the subject forms *ele, ela, eles, elas.* The neuter stressed object, not referring to a noun, is usually *isso.*

This construction is considered incorrect by grammarians. However, it has existed in the language since the Middle Ages, and has been generally accepted as a normal part of BF. The unstressed forms would be lost in a large percentage of cases in Brazilian speech, because of encounters with like vowels at the beginnings or ends of other words. In the few cases in which clarity would require an object, the sentence is constructed in such a way as to avoid the difficulty. The unstressed forms are used in writing to a limited extent, less than in English, to say nothing of Spanish. In BF they do not exist.

Unstressed forms	Stressed forms	
o	ele	him; it (masculine)
a	ela	her; it (feminine)
os	eles	them (masculine or masculine and feminine)
as	elas	them (feminine)
o	isso	it (neuter)

Unstressed forms are sometimes heard following an infinitive, in some fixed expressions and in the higher levels of speech. In this case, the infinitive drops the final *-r,* the preceding vowel requires an accent in the first and second conjugations, and the object takes a form beginning with *l,* as in the following examples:

Muito prazer em conhecê-lo.	(I'm) very happy to meet you.
Antes de fazê-lo.	Before doing it.
Você quer levá-las?	Will you take them?
Vou abri-los	I'm going to open them.

Actually, only the first example is likely to be heard often. For examples of the use and omission of third person object pronouns, see Exercise A, below.

72. Regular comparison of adjectives and adverbs. The comparative degree of adjectives and adverbs is formed by placing *mais* before them. The superlative degree of adjectives is the same, but preceded by the definite article (which may be replaced by a possessive adjective). With adverbs, the article is used only when a modifying word, phrase or clause follows the adverb.

Positive	Comparative	Superlative
bonito	mais bonito	o mais bonito
frio	mais frio	o mais frio
perto	mais perto	mais perto
		o mais perto possível
devagar	mais devagar	o mais devagar que se possa imaginar

73. Irregular comparison of adjectives and adverbs. The following are irregular:

bom	melhor /ó/	o melhor
mau	pior /ó/	o pior
ruim	pior, mais ruim	o pior, o mais ruim
muito	mais	o mais
grande	maior /ó/	o maior
pequeno	menor /ó/	o menor

(Also *mais pequeno,* in Portugal)

bem	melhor	(o) melhor
mal	pior	(o) pior
pouco	menos	(o) menos

74. Portuguese equivalents of *than. Than* is usually expressed by *que,* but the following must be noted:

a. When it is followed by a number, *de* is used instead of *que.*

b. When the second term of the comparison is a verb, *do que* must be used. It does not change for gender or number. *Do que* may also be used at any time instead of *que* alone.

Tenho mais de três amigos.	I have more than three friends.
Ele é mais alto que (*or* do que) eu.	He is taller than I.
Ele bebe mais do que come.	He drinks more than he eats.

Vocabulary

Nouns

o sapateiro	shoemaker, shoe seller, cobbler
o padeiro	baker
o leiteiro	milkman
a pessoa /ô/	person
duas pessoas	two people (persons)
o médico	doctor, physician
o soldado	soldier
o rei	king
o patrão	employer, "boss"
a patroa /ô/	employer, "boss"
o empregado	employee,
a empregada	employee, maid
a história	story, history
a profissão	profession

Nouns

o prazer /ê/	pleasure
o consultório	office (doctor's)
a manteiga	butter

Adjectives

feliz /fi/	happy
rico	rich
velho /é/	old
doente /du/	sick, ill
possível /pu/	possible
muito	lots of, a lot of, a good deal of, much
nem muito	not much

Verbs

consultar	consult
beber	drink
consertar	repair, mend, "fix"
mandar	order, have (done)
tratar	treat
entregar	hand over; deliver
deixar de	stop (doing something)
deixar	leave alone.

Conjunction

ou . . . ou	either . . . or

Adverbs

menos	less
mal	badly, ill, poorly

Prepositions

entre	between; among
durante	during
para /pra/	in order to

Expressions

Encontrei-me com ele.	I ran into him, I met him.
Mandei consertar o casaco.	I had my coat mended.
Falei com várias pessoas.	I spoke to several people.
Meu irmão mais velho.	My older (oldest) brother.
Trabalho para o sr. Pires.	I work for Mr. Pires.
Ele chamou o João de menino.	He called John a boy.

Leitura

Entre as pessoas que trabalham na cidade se encontram padeiros, leiteiros e sapateiros. O padeiro faz pão durante a noite e vende quente de manhã. Também chamamos de padeiro o homem que entrega pão quente nas casas. Os brasileiros comem pão manteiga com o café da manhã.

O sapateiro ou faz ou vende ou conserta sapatos. Poucas pessoas mandam fazer sapatos agora, mas muitas levam ao sapateiro para consertar.

O nosso médico tem um consultório na cidade. Quando ficamos doentes, vamos consultar o médico. Quando eu estive doente, foi ele que me examinou e tratou.

Muitas pessoas trabalham na cidade como empregados. Trabalham para um patrão ou uma patroa. As empregadas domésticas geralmente trabalham para a patroa e fazem trabalhos de casa. Há homens que chamam a mulher de patroa.

Exercise A. Use of object pronouns.

1. Você me disse que ele lhe escreveu.
2. Disseram-me que José jantou com você.
3. Ele vendeu o carro e não me disse.
4. Ela conhece essa história mas não conta.
5. Eu encontrei o João e levei à cidade.
6. Ele fala português, mas não escreve.
7. Achamos uma casa bonita, que compramos.
8. Eu estudei a lição, mas já esqueci.
9. Disseram que João e Maria estiveram na festa; encontrei ela lá.
10. Quero examinar o livro antes de comprar.
11. Chamei você e ele.
12. Ele guardou as cartas e me deu.
13. Falo um pouco de português, mas nunca estudei.
14. Ele comprou uma flor e deu a Maria.
15. Perguntei-lhe o nome do irmão.
16. Eu vou até achar a estrada.

60

17. Tenho um carro para vender.

18. Depois de jantar, vou ao cinema.

19. Ele é mais alto que você.

20. Por aqui chove mais do que neva.

21. Já comi mais de uma /ũa/ banana.

22. Meu tio também é meu patrão.

23. Levei os sapatos ao sapateiro e mandei consertar.

24. Que é que você tem na mão? Me dá isso!

Exercise B. Be able to give in either language:

1. Meu irmão é maior do que eu.	My brother is bigger than I.
2. Ele não é mais velho.	He is not older.
3. É mais fácil escrever do que falar.	It is easier to write than to speak.
4. Ele está mais doente do que eu.	He is sicker than I.
5. Não tenho mais de seis colegas casados.	I have only six classmates who are married.
6. Hoje está mais nublado do que ontem.	Today it is cloudier than yesterday.
7. Eu gosto mais de café do que de leite.	I like coffee better than milk.
8. Esta xícara é menor que aquela.	This cup is smaller than that one.
9. Ele é ruim, pior que o irmão.	He is bad, worse than his brother.
10. Ela fala bem, mas você fala melhor.	She speaks well, but you speak better.
11. Você está doente; fala o menos possível.	You are sick; speak as little as possible.
12. Se você quiser acabar o curso, tem que estudar mais que todos.	If you wish to finish the course, you'll have to study more than any of the others.

Exercise C. Say in Portuguese:

1. I don't know anyone here.

2. He doesn't do anything.

3. He thinks he as no friends.

4. I know neither John nor Mary.

5. I never told him that.

6. Nothing will catch you out there.

Exercise D. Put in each blank the correct form of the verb used in the first part of the sentence:

1. Ele quer *ir*. Você pode ir quando ele _____.

2. Acho que não *posso* ficar. Fico se _____.

3. Pode *chover*, mas vamos brincar enquanto não _____.

4. Ele diz que me *dá* um lápis. Depois que _____, eu escrevo.

5. Eu *vou* com eles, caso _____ .

6. *Abrem* as portas às seis horas; logo que _____, vou entrar.

Exercise E. Give the plurals of the following nouns and adjectives:

1. O animal

2. O hotel

3. O sol

4. O papel

5. O jornal

6. O motel

7. O espanhol

8. Total

9. Fatal

10. Difícil

11. azul

12. fácil

13. útil

14. geral

15. social

16. nominal

17. numeral

18. possível

19. mundial

20. continental

Exercise F. Say in Portuguese:

1. My boss thinks he is the king.

2. A classmate fixed my shoes.

3. I'm going to have this done.

4. Dr. Pires is the doctor who treats us.

5. We'll deliver this to your house.

6. What is your profession?

7. I met Joe at the party.

8. The house is (situated) among the trees.

9. In order to arrive tonight, you'll have to hurry.
10. Two soldiers are guarding the road.
11. They are older than I [am].
12. We live near the doctor's office.
13. Are the rich happy?
14. Either the lady or her maid will be here tomorrow.
15. We drink lots of milk during the day.

Exercise G.

1. Take this and give it to John.
2. I took the chalk, but I didn't use it.
3. I understand German, but I don't speak it.
4. We have a lesson tomorrow, but we aren't going to study it.
5. Here is your hat; take it.
6. Is my book in this room? I can't find it.
7. That pen is mine; leave it [alone].
8. You are going to speak Portuguese when you learn it.
9. Write me a letter and I'll open it.
10. He speaks well, but I can't understand him.
11. I met him yesterday.
12. Mary went with John; he took her to the station.
13. They didn't call me; I called them.
14. I [will] not forget you.
15. Tell me a story and I'll remember it.

Lesson XIV

75. The irregular verb *ver,* to see.

	Present Indicative	*Preterit*	*Future Subjunctive*
eu	vejo /ê/	vi	vir
você	vê	viu	vir
ele	vê	viu	vir
nós	vemos	vimos	virmos
vocês	vêem	viram	virem
eles	vêem	viram	virem

The third person plural present indicative is pronounced in two syllables, of which the first is *not* nasal.

The preterit (and derived tenses) of this verb is like those of regular verbs of the *third* conjugation.

76. Uses of *ver.* In English, verbs of perception and of predominantly mental activity often do not take the progressive form. In Portuguese, however, these verbs are put in the progressive form in the same situations as any other verbs.

Você explicou isso, e agora eu estou vendo.	You explained it, and now I see.
Estou vendo o João na porta da casa.	I see John in the doorway of the house.
Não estou compreendendo.	I don't understand.

77. Forms of the personal pronouns used as objects of prepositions. A preposition is followed by the *subject* form of the pronoun, except in the first person singular and the third person reflexive. These two have special forms.

a mim	to me	para nós	for us
para você	for you	entre vocês	among you
por ele	by him	com eles	with them
sem ela	without her	sobre elas	about them
But a si	to yourself, himself, themselves, etc.		

a. The preposition *com* combines in special forms with some pronouns.

comigo /kõ/   with me   conosco   with us   consigo   with himself,

b. The prepositions *de* and *em* form contractions with the third-person pronouns as follows:

dele	deles	nele	neles
dela	delas	nela	nelas

78. Prepositional phrase used as indirect object. The indirect object may be expressed as a prepositional phrase in all cases. If the object is a pronoun, it can be emphasized by the use of a phrase instead of the simple pronoun. In other cases, the phrase is optional. Either form, e.g., *lhe* or *a ele,* may be used in any clause containing a verb, but one never uses both, as in Spanish.

To express the meaning "for me," the preposition is *para.* For "to me," either *a* or *para* may be used in most cases, with some preference for *para* in BF.

Note that the prepositional phrase is placed in the same position in the sentence, whether a noun or pronoun is used. In most cases, this is the same position occupied by the phrase in English.

Eu lhe dei o jornal.	I gave him the newspaper.
Eu dei o jornal a ele.	I gave the newspaper to him.
Ele tem um presente para você.	He has a present for you.
Vamos escrever-lhe uma carta.	Let's write him a letter.
Vamos escrever uma carta para (a) ele.	Let's write a letter to him.
Dá isso para mim.	Give it to me.
Conta-nos essa história.	Tell that story to us.

79. *Que* and *qual.* As interrogative pronouns, these two words should be distinguished. *Que* (singular or plural) is used to ask for what amounts to a definition; *qual* (plural *quais*) asks for a selection among individual specimens. The confusion arises purely from English, which is likely to use *what* in either case.

Que é o livro?	What is the book? (a novel, etc.)
Qual é o livro?	Which one is the book?
Qual é o seu nome?	What is your name? (which of the possible names is yours?)

Qual is not properly used as an adjective, although it may be heard in BF in certain situations. *Que* should be used in all cases before a noun.

Que casa é a sua?	Which (what) house is yours?
Qual é a sua casa?	Which one is your house?

Vocabulary

Nouns

o cruzeiro	cruzeiro (Braz. monetary unit)
o jornal	newspaper
o dinheiro	money
a compra	purchase, buy
o presente	present
o largo	square (in city)
a livraria	bookstore
o livreiro	bookseller
o preço /ê/	price
a falta	lack; need; shortage

Adjectives

outro	other, another
um outro	another
noutro (em + outro)	in another
novo /ô/ fem. and pl. /ó/	new, young

Adverb

então	then (expletive), then (at that time)

Nouns

as Lojas Brasileiras	variety stores
o brinquedo /ê/	toy
a diferença	difference

Pronouns

mim	me (after prep.)
si	himself, etc. (after prep.)
comigo /kõ/	with me
conosco /kõ/	with us
consigo	with him (self), etc.

Verbs

explicar	explain
arranjar	get (for one), arrange, fix up with
dever	owe, ought, should
receber	receive, get
saltar	jump, jump down, get off
tentar	try to
ganhar	earn, make (money), get (present), win (game)
voltar	return, go back, come back

Expressions

Esse livro está em falta.	We are out of that book.
Ela está fazendo compras.	She is shopping.
Ele me deu isto de presente.	He gave me this as a gift.
Vocês devem acabar o trabalho	Finish your work. (You must finish your work.)
Devem ser duas horas.	It must be two o'clock.
Ele deve receber mais amanhã.	He should (is to) get more tomorrow.
O pão faz falta.	One needs bread.
Você faz falta na turma.	You are missed in the gang.

Leitura

Ontem fui à cidade fazer compras. Tomei o ônibus na esquina aqui perto e ele me levou até o Largo da Carioca. Lá saltei do ônibus e fui andando até a Rua do Ouvidor. Entrei numa livraria para ver os livros novos. Vendo um livro interessante, perguntei o preço ao empregado. Dei para ele quatro cruzeiros e ele me entregou o livro. Tentei arranjar outro livro novo noutra livraria, mas não pude achar. O livreiro me explicou que esse livro está em falta. Devo ir lá na outra semana, quando o livreiro deve receber mais.

Depois entrei numa Loja Brasileira, onde comprei um brinquedo para levar de presente a meu irmão mais novo. Ele não freqüenta a escola ainda e gosta de passar o tempo com brinquedos. Então tomei outro ônibus para voltar para casa. O preço do ônibus é muito pouco.

Exercise A. Be able to give in either language:

1. Explica esta lição para mim.
Explain this lesson to me.

2. Para amanhã, devem estudar esta lição.
For tomorrow, study this lesson.

3. Você não me deve nada.
You don't owe me anything.

4. Recebemos uma carta dele.
We got a letter from him.

5. Vocês devem estar com muita fome.
You must be awfully hungry.

6. Faz falta aqui um bom livreiro.
A good bookseller is needed here.

7. O café está em falta hoje.
We are out of coffee today.

8. Aqui sempre tem pão, mas agora está em falta.
We always keep bread, but we are out of it now.

9. O senhor pode nos arranjar uma boa empregada?
Can you fix us up with a good maid?

10. Quando vocês chegarem, eu vou à porta recebê-los.
When you arrive, I'll go to the door to receive you.

11. Você recebeu meu presente?
Did you get my present? (Did it arrive?)

12. Ganhei outro do meu amigo.
I got another one from my friend.

13. Fui fazer compras na cidade.
I went shopping downtown.

14. Levei as compras para casa.
I took my purchases home.

15. Qual é a diferença entre "largo" e "praça"? Não tem.
What is the difference between *largo* and *praça*? There isn't any.

16. Você ganha bem no seu trabalho?
Do you make good money at your work?

17. Quantos cruzeiros devemos?
How many cruzeiros do we owe?

18. Os jornais fazem falta quando não temos.
Newspapers are missed when we don't have any.

Exercise B. Be able to give in either language:

1. Estou vendo você lá atrás da porta.
I see you there behind the door.

2. Não podem me pegar se não me virem.
They can't catch me if they don't see me.

3. Se João esteve lá, eu não vi.
If John was there, I didn't see him.

4. Ele vai me ver amanhã.
He is going to see me tomorrow.

5. Quero ver ele correr.
I want to see him run.

6. Não estou vendo meninos na rua.
I don't see any kids on the street.

7. Ele falou para si.
He spoke to himself.

8. João levou o dinheiro.
John took the money with him.

9. Seu amigo deu comigo no cinema.
Your friend ran into me at the movie.

10. Amanhã eu vou lembrar isso a você.
Tomorrow I'll remind you of that.

11. Quais são seus irmãos?
Which ones are your brothers?

12. Que trem chega hoje?
Which train comes in today?

Exercise C. Answer in Portuguese:

1. Quanto dinheiro você tem?
2. Que compras você fez ontem?
3. Que carro você arranjou para ir à festa?
4. De quem você recebeu uma carta hoje?
5. Você ganha bem ou mal no seu trabalho?
6. Você me deve um cruzeiro?
7. Os preços estão altos ou baixos?
8. Com quem você falou ontem?
9. Que presente você ganhou ontem?
10. Tem o nosso livro na livraria, ou está em falta?

Exercise D. Say in Portuguese:

1. What do you see out there?
2. He sees me and I see him.
3. I saw you yesterday in class.
4. If you see me, speak to me.
5. They have never seen this city.
6. Did you see what I see?
7. Explain this to me; I don't see it.
8. He always says "Good morning" when he sees me.
9. We don't see what we saw before.

Exercise E. Say in Portuguese:

1. He is taller than I.
2. It is cooler here than there.
3. It is cloudier today.
4. This street is wider than that [one].
5. He is bigger than his brother.
6. My coffee is blacker than yours.
7. The boss is worse than the employee.
8. I have fewer than three cars.
9. He talks better than he writes.
10. This lesson is easier than the other [one].

Exercise F. Say in Portuguese:

1. Remember me to your uncle.
2. Try to open the door.
3. Get off the bus at the corner.
4. Fix me up with some coffee, please.
5. It's cold today.
6. A shoemaker makes and fixes shoes.
7. There is no difference between these two cups.
8. Let's leave them [alone].
9. The coffee is cold.
10. I'm cold.
11. This town has two newspapers.
12. I bought this present for a cruzeiro.
13. A bookseller works in a bookstore.
14. A milkman delivers milk in the morning.
15. We attend church on Sunday.

Lesson XV

80. The irregular verbs *saber* and *caber*. The present indicative of these two verbs has only one irregular form, the first person singular. All other forms of these two verbs differ only in the first letter. Both verbs are irregular in the preterit and derived tenses.

	Present Indicative		Preterit		Future Subjunative
eu	sei	caibo	soube	coube	souber /é/, etc.
você	sabe	cabe	soube	coube	
ele	sabe	cabe	soube	coube	couber /é/, etc.
nós	sabemos	cabemos	soubemos	coubemos	
vocês	sabem	cabem	souberam	couberam /é/	
eles	sabem	cabem	souberam	couberam /é/	

81. Uses of *saber* and *caber*.

Saber means "to know something factual," "to know how to," "to find out," or "to learn a fact." It must be distinguished from *conhecer,* "to be acquainted with," "to meet" (= get acquainted with).

Eu sei minha lição.	I know my lesson.
Ele sabe acender o fogo.	He knows how to light the fire.
Nós sabemos que você ganhou.	We know you won.
Eu sei quem é mas não conheço.	I know who he is, but I am not acquainted with him.

66

Caber means "to be contained in," "to fit into," "to get into" (find room in). English often looks at the same situation from the opposite point of view, i.e., How many will it hold?

Quantos cabem no seu carro?	How many can get into your car? (How many will it hold?)
Meu pé não cabe neste sapato.	My foot won't go into this shoe.
Ele não cabe em si de contente.	He is beside himself with joy.
Não cabe dúvida.	There is no room for doubt.

82. The imperfect indicative. There are two sets of endings for the imperfect indicative, one used with verbs of the first conjugation, the other with the second and third.

	Falar	*comer*	*abrir*
eu	falava	comia	abria
você	falava	comia	abria
ele	falava	comia	abria
nós	falávamos	comíamos	abríamos
vocês	falavam	comiam	abriam
eles	falavam	comiam	abriam

83. Verbs irregular in the imperfect. There are only four verbs, plus the compounds of some of them, which are irregular in the imperfect indicative.

ter - eu, você, ele tinha; nós tínhamos; vocês, eles tinham

pôr - eu, você, ele punha, nós púnhamos; vocês, eles punham

ser - eu, você, ele era; nós éramos; vocês, eles eram

vir - eu, você, ele vinha; nós vínhamos; vocês, eles vinham.

84. Uses of the imperfect tense. The imperfect is used:

a. To describe a state or condition in past time. The beginning and the end of the condition are not indicated, only that the condition existed at a certain point in the past. Thus, descriptions of past conditions are in the imperfect.

O tempo estava bonito.	The weather was beautiful.
Fazia frio.	It was cold.

The condition may be mental or emotional.

Ele queria comer batatas.	He wanted to eat potatoes.
Cf. Ele quis comer batatas.	He tried to eat potatoes.
Os meninos sabiam os números.	The children knew their numbers.
Não gostávamos dele.	We didn't like him.

b. To denote habitual action in past time. There must be no expressed limitation on the duration of the action.

Quando eu era menino, corria muito.	When I was a boy I ran a lot.
Ele sempre me chamava.	He always used to call me.

c. To express an action in progress at the time of another past action, condition, or point in time. This latter may be a single or limited past action, expressed in the preterit, or it may be another action in progress, expressed in the imperfect.

| Eu comia quando ele telefonou. | I was eating when he called. |
| Escutávamos enquanto ele falava. | We were listening while he talked. |

d. For the conditional in any circumstances: (normally expressed in English by the auxiliary *would*).

| Eu queria ir. | I'd like to go. |
| Ele disse que ia. | He said he'd go. |

85. The progressive form of the imperfect. The progressive is used in the imperfect, as in the present and in all other tenses. But the simple form may at any time replace the progressive form without change of meaning, *in this tense only*. The progressive form makes the expression of the meaning more exact, of course.

| Eu estava falando quando ele chegou. | I was speaking when he arrived. |
| *Or* Eu falava quando ele chegou. | |

Vocabulary

Nouns

o fogo /ô/ pl. fogos /ó/	fire
a luz	light
o pé	foot
a dúvida	doubt
a batata (inglesa)	potato
o número	number
a cafeteira	coffeepot
a carne	meat
o piquenique	picnic
a cama	bed
o lago	lake
a gente	people

Adjectives

contente	pleased, happy
doce /ô/	sweet
cheio	full

Verb

| desligar | turn off |

Conjunction

| de modo que /mó/ | so that, in such a way that, so |

Adjectives

vazio	empty
preciso	necessary
verde /ê/	green

Verbs

caber	fit into, be contained in
saber	know
acender	light (fire); turn on (lights)
botar	put
escutar	listen to, hear
responder (a)	answer
apanhar	pick up, catch; be beaten
assar	roast
apagar	put out (fire, light)
ligar	turn on (light, radio, motor)

Adverbs

| tarde | late |
| não . . . mais | no longer |

Preposition

| sem | without |

Expressions

Ele devia estudar.	He ought to study. (But he doesn't).
Deviam ser duas horas.	It must have been two o'clock.
Eu devia um cruzeiro a ele.	I owed him a cruzeiro.
Vou passar pela casa dele.	I'm going by his house.
Vamos fazer um piquenique.	We're going to have a picnic.
Eu sei lá.	I don't know.
Ele fala língua de gente.	He speaks people's language (i.e., Portuguese)
Ele não gosta da gente.	He doesn't like people (i.e., us).
Que é que a gente faz?	What does one do?
Há pouco.	A little while ago.

Leitura

Vocês não queriam ir à roça hoje? Podemos ir no meu carro, se coubermos todos. Devemos passar pela casa do Luiz para apanhá-lo também. Ele tem um carro grande onde cabem seis pessoas. Podemos ir no carro dele se o meu estiver muito cheio.

Eu sei de um parque onde podemos acender um fogo e fazer café. Já botei uma cafeteira no carro, de modo que podemos tomar café quente.

O Carlos ia conosco, mas chamou há pouco para dizer que não podia mais ir. Parece que o primo ia chegar para passar o dia com ele, e Carlos não queria deixar a casa. Eu respondi que levava o primo também, mas ele não quis ir.

Na semana passada eu fui ao parque com a turma. Era uma noite bonita e fazia um pouco de frio. A luz que tínhamos vinha do fogo que acendemos. Assamos batatas doces e carne. Foi um bom piquenique. Voltamos tarde para casa e eu fui para a cama.

Exercise A. Be able to say in either language on hearing the other:

1. Escuta quando ele fala.	Listen to him when he speaks.
2. Eu não vi você chegar.	I didn't see you come in.
3. O menino apanhou do pai.	The child was whipped by his father.
4. Você gosta de carne assada?	Do you like roast meat?
5. Você já respondeu à carta dele?	Have you answered his letter?
6. A mulher punha carne para assar.	The woman was putting meat on to roast.
7. É preciso saber quando ele chega.	It is necessary to know when he will arrive.
8. A cafeteira está vazia.	The coffeepot is empty.
9. De noite acendemos as luzes.	At night we turn on the lights.
10. O Brasil tem muitas batatas doces e batatas inglesas.	Brazil has lots of sweet potatoes and Irish potatoes.
11. Ele disse que me apanhava às seis.	He said he would pick me up at six.
12. Eu lhe dei tudo o que lhe devia.	I gave him all I owed him.
13. Ele botou o pé na porta.	He put (stuck) his foot in the door.
14. Você vai à aula, não é?	You are going to class, aren't you?
15. Assávamos carne e comíamos sem pão.	We used to roast meat and eat it without bread.
16. Eu escutava sem compreender.	I was listening without understanding.
17. Você está contente de saber que ele deve chegar?	Are you glad (to know) that he is coming?
18. É preciso assar as batatas antes de comer.	It is necessary to roast the potatoes before eating them.
19. Eu lhe disse —Chega para lá.	I said to him, "Move over that way."
20. Apaga a luz e acende o fogo.	Turn off the light and light the fire.

69

Exercise B. Give the imperfect tense in the same person and number as the example given in the present:

1. Eu vou
2. Ele é
3. Nós pomos
4. Eu vejo
5. Eles sabem
6. Nós entramos
7. Eu tenho

8. Ele diz
9. Nós comemos
10. Eles dão
11. Eu ponho
12. Nós vamos
13. Eles têm
14. Ele cabe

15. Nós vemos
16. Ele faz
17. Eu parto
18. Eu sei
19. Eu digo
20. Eu corro

Exercise C. Fill in each blank with the correct form of the imperfect or preterit of the verb in parentheses:

(ir)   1. Naquele tempo eu sempre _____ à casa dele.
(pôr)   2. Antes de ir à escola, eu sempre _____ o paletó.
(ver)   3. Ele não compreendia tudo o que _____ .
(dizer)   4. Ele contou o que você lhe _____ .
(brilhar) 5. O sol _____ durante um mês.
(morar)   6. Nós _____ lá cinco anos.
(saber)   7. Perguntei se ele _____ português
(poder)   8. Não tendo sapatos, ele não _____ andar.
(ir)   9. Ele me disse que _____ jantar.
(caber)   10. No carro dele só _____ quatro.

Exercise D. Write and be able to tell in Portuguese:

It was a warm day and the sun was shining. The sky was blue and beautiful. We took my car and went to the park to have a picnic. There was a small lake in the park. Near it there were many trees, all green. We took the meat out of the car and roasted it over a fire. We walked around in the park, but two remained talking near the fire.

When we used to go to the other park, we always saw many animals. Fewer people went there, so the animals were less afraid. They came (= *chegar*) close to us and ate from our hands. We always took bread to give them. We would like to go back there on Sunday.

Exercise E. Say in Portuguese:

1. How many people can get into this room?
2. I found out that he was looking for me.
3. Did you know who I was?
4. What will they do when they find out?
5. It is John; I know him well.
6. He was putting on his coat when I called him.
7. I was warm because the weather was hot.
8. We used to eat lots of sweet potatoes.
9. You walk [by] putting one foot in front of the other.
10. He always went to bed late.
11. He made good money (= earned well) in that work,
12. You should sell that house and buy a better [one].
13. He answered that he did not know.
14. They had two windows which faced the street.
15. A glass of water is better than an empty glass.

Lesson XVI

The following paragraphs explain the more frequent and basic usages of some of the principal and more difficult prepositions. There are, of course, other uses of most of them.

86. The preposition *a* expresses:

a. *To,* direction to a place, except when the place is the habitual or normal location of a person, and a verb of motion is used. (See §96b).

Vamos à cidade.	We are going downtown.
Eu vou à casa de João.	I'm going over to John's.

b. *At,* with expressions of time.

Ele chegou às duas horas.	He got here at two.
Ela voltou à noite.	She came back at nightfall.
Vamos à igreja aos domingos.	We go to church on Sunday. (used with Saturday and Sunday)

c. *To,* before an indirect object. (But see §96d).

Ele deu um presente a ela.	He gave a gift to her.

d. *To,* following certain verbs, before an infinitive. Each instance must be learned separately.

Ele aprendeu a ler.	He learned to read.
Comecei a trabalhar.	I began to work.

87. The preposition *até* expresses:

a. *As far as,* with reference to space.

Eu vou até a esquina.	I'm going as far as the corner.

b. *Until,* in expressions of time.

Até amanhã.	Until tomorrow.
Fiquei até a meia-noite.	I stayed till midnight.

c. *By,* as the limit of time.

Tenho que acabar até quarta-feira.	I must finish by Wednesday.

d. *Even,* that is, to an unusual degree. (adverbial use).

Até meu irmão mais novo vai comigo.	Even my youngest brother is going with me.
Ele falou até alto.	As a matter of fact, he spoke aloud,

88. The preposition *de* expresses:

a. *Of,* ownership, often put in the possessive case in English.

Este é o carro dele.	This is his car.
A mulher daquele homem é alta.	The wife of that man is tall.

b. *From, of,* origin.

De onde você é?	Where are you from?
Esta música veio do Brasil.	This music came from Brazil.
Este é o sr. Garcia, do Rio.	This is Mr. Garcia, from Rio.

c. *By,* before a means of transportation of persons, except a horse.

Ele viaja de trem.	He travels by train.
De carro, de ônibus, de avião, de navio.	By car, bus, plane, ship.
Ele andava a cavalo.	He was going by horse.

d. The fact that one noun is used as a modifier of another. No article is used with the modifying noun. In English, the modifier is placed immediately before the noun modified. However, if the modifier is a noun denoting a person, it is often in the possessive case. In many instances, in both languages, there is also an adjective which may replace the phrase as a modifier.

Um dia de verão.	A summer day.
Uma vida de cachorro.	A dog's life.
Uma perna de pau.	A wooden leg.

e. *About, of,* on the subject of, concerning.

O que você acha dele?	What do you think of him?
Estão falando de mim.	They are speaking (ill) of me.

f. *To,* after certain verbs, before an infinitive. Each instance must be learned separately.

Não me lembrei de chamar.	I didn't remember to call.
Esqueci-me de ir.	I forgot to go.

89. The preposition *em* expresses:

a. *In,* location in the interior of.

Ele está na cidade.	He is in town.
Eles moram no Brasil.	They live in Brazil.

b. *At,* location which may be in or near.

Ele está na escola.	He is at school.
Ela está em casa.	She is at home.

c. *On,* location on top of.

O copo está na mesa.	The glass is on the table.
Ele está sentado na cadeira.	He is sitting on the chair.

d. *On,* location on the surface of.

O quadro está na parede.	The picture is on the wall.

e. *Into, onto,* movement to the inside or to the surface of.

O cavalo entrou na água.	The horse went into the water.
Ele jogou a roupa no chão.	He threw the clothes on the floor.

f. *In, on,* in a period of time or on an occasion.

Temos festas nas segundas-feiras.	We have parties on Monday (s).
Faz calor aqui no verão.	It's hot here in summer.
Vamos embora no dia primeiro.	We're going on the first.

72

g. *At the house of, at the shop of* with a family name in the plural or with a word denoting a shopkeeper.

Estivemos ontem nos Pereira.	We were at the Pereiras' yesterday.
Eu vou no barbeiro.	I'm going to the barber's (shop).

Vocabulary

Note the following adverbs which may be changed to prepositions by the addition of *de:*

depois	afterwards	depois de	after
antes	before	antes de	before
atrás	back	atrás de	behind
perto /é/	near, nearby	perto de	near
(lá) em cima	up there, upstairs	em cima de	above, over
em frente	in front	em frente de	in front of
dentro	inside	dentro de	inside (of)
em baixo	below, down there	em baixo de	under
fora /ó/	outside	fora de	outside of
diante	ahead, before	diante de	in front of, in the presence of

Nouns

Verb

o lado	side	jogar	play (game); throw; gamble
a meia-noite	midnight		
o meio-dia	noon		
o avião	airplane		
o sanduíche	sandwich		
o quadro	picture, painting		

Expressions

Às vezes	sometimes
O navio joga muito.	The ship pitches a lot.
Joga isso fora.	Throw that out.
Joga a bola para mim.	Throw the ball to me.

Exercise A. Be able to say in Portuguese:

1. The fellow went back to the country.
2. I want to get (= pass) to the other side of the street.
3. I'm coming back to this house tomorrow.
4. He's going to Portugal this summer.
5. I turned off the lights at midnight.
6. We get off the bus here at times. (às vezes)
7. I answered him that I did not wish to go.
8. I write a letter to my mother every week.
9. Here we are going to learn to (*a*) speak Portuguese.
10. I have already told you that.
11. Let's walk as far as the river.
12. They are going to play [ball] until (the) night.
13. You should do this by Thursday.
14. Whose cup is that?
15. John's brother and Mary's sister are here.
16. I like his coat.
17. Where is he from?
18. This word is from our book.
19. I bought these shoes from the shoemaker.
20. She travels on a (by) train.
21. This is a girl's coat.
22. A dog house is needed.

Exercise B. Be able to give either language from the other:

1. O que você pensa de mim?	What do you think of me?
2. Estamos falando de outra pessoa.	We are talking about someone else.
3. Eu gosto de viajar.	I like to travel.
4. Deixa de fazer isso!	Stop doing that!
5. Ele acaba de jantar.	He has just had dinner.
6. João está no teatro.	John is at the theater.
7. Põe o café na mesa.	Put the coffee on the table.
8. Isso foi numa sexta-feira.	That was on a Friday.
9. Aos domingos os parentes passam lá em casa.	On Sunday(s) relatives come by the house.
10. Vamos nos Carvalho(s) amanhã.	Let's go to the Carvalhos' tomorrow.

Exercise C. Say in Portuguese:

1. Afterwards, we eat.
2. I have never seen him before.
3. Who is that fellow back there?
4. Is there a store nearby?
5. My uncle is upstairs.
6. The town is still far away.
7. The house has a yard in front.
8. John is in there (there inside).
9. The kids are playing down there. (lá em baixo).
10. After eating, we go home.
11. We come in before dark.
12. Leave the car behind the house.
13. The church is near here.
14. What is that on top of the table?
15. We live far from the school.
16. Stand (*fica*) in front of the car.
17. The table is inside the house.
18. The dog ran under the table.

Exercise D. Review the position in the sentence of the two sets of object pronouns: (1) *me, nos, lhe, lhes, se* and (2) *você, vocês, o senhor,* etc., *ele, ela, eles, elas.* Place each pronoun in a correct position in the following sentences:

(me)	1. A tia viu.
(você)	2. Meu amigo conhece.
(ele)	3. Eu estou escutando.
(nos)	4. O colega não chamou.
(ela)	5. Pega.
(lhe)	6. Não quero dizer a verdade.
(se)	7. Lembra da Maria?
(o senhor)	8. Esse trabalho vai cansar.
(me)	9. Eu chamo José.
(você e ele)	10. Vamos deixar aqui.

Exercise E. Pronounce the following words, taking care to give the correct value to the stressed vowels:

1. janela
2. mesa
3. café
4. José
5. chapéu
6. igreja
7. medo
8. sede
9. pressa
10. céu
11. neve
12. caneta
13. colega
14. primavera
15. inverno
16. mês
17. vez
18. aberto
19. amarelo
20. preto
21. este
22. esse
23. papéis
24. fresco.

Lesson XVII

90. The irregular verb *vir,* to come

	Present Indicative	Preterit	Imperfect	Future Subjunctive
eu	venho	vim	vinha	vier /é/
você	vem	veio	vinha	vier
ele	vem	veio	vinha	vier
nós	vimos	viemos	vínhamos	viermos
vocês	vêm	vieram /é/	vinham	vierem
eles	vêm	vieram	vinham	vierem

The third person plural of the present has also the form *veem,* both syllables of which are nasal. It is little used.

91. Uses of *vir.* This verb is used without a preposition before an infinitive, except in certain special meanings. *Vir* is very seldom used in the progressive form.

Ele já vem fazer o trabalho.   He is already coming to do the work.

92. Cardinal numbers.

um, fem. uma	1	onze	11	vinte e um	21
dois, fem. duas	2	doze /ô/	12	vinte e dois, etc.	22
três	3	treze /ê/	13	trinta	30
quatro	4	quatorze /ô/ *or* catorze	14	quarenta	40
cinco	5	quinze	15	cinqüenta	50
seis*	6	dezesseis/dizeseis/	16	sessenta	60
sete /é/	7	dezessete /dizeséti/	17	setenta	70
oito	8	dezoito /dizôitu/	18	oitenta	80
nove /ó/	9	dezenove /dizenóvi/	19	noventa	90
dez /é/	10	vinte	20	cem	100

*In giving telephone numbers, house numbers, etc., *meia* is generally used instead of *seis.*

93. Usage of the cardinal numbers. The numbers *one* and *two* have feminine forms which agree with a feminine noun. In larger numbers which end in *one* or *two,* e.g., forty-two, the agreement is also made. If the cardinal numbers are placed after the noun, to take the place of ordinals, however, most speakers do not make the agreement, assuming the word *número* as the basis of agreement.

Quarenta e duas moças.   Forty-two girls.
Lição vinte e dois.   Lesson twenty-two.

The word *cem* is not preceded by *um.* It becomes *cento* when a number from one to ninety-nine is added to it.

Cento e dois. 102
Cento e sessenta e quatro. 164

In theory, the word *e* is always placed between the parts of compound numbers. In practice, some of these are often omitted, in certain large numbers.

94. Time of day. Note the following expressions:

Que horas são?	What time is it?
É uma (hora).	It's one (o'clock).
São duas (horas).	It's two (o'clock).
São três (horas).	It's three (o'clock).
São oito e meia.	It's 8:30.
São quatro e dez (minutos).	It is 4:10.
São cinco e quinze (minutos).	It is 5:15.
São seis e quarenta e oito.	It is 6:48.
Faltam vinte e oito para as sete.	It is 28 to seven.
São vinte e oito para as sete.	It is 28 to seven.
É meio-dia.	It is 12:00 noon.
É meia-noite.	It is 12:00 midnight.
É meia-noite e vinte.	It is 12:20 a.m.
É meia-noite e meia.	It is 12:30 a.m.
É meio-dia e meia (*often* meio)	It is 12:30 p.m.

Hora(s) and *minuto(s)* may be omitted whenever the sense is clear without them.

The numbers *one* and *two* are feminine when they refer to hours, but masculine when they refer to minutes.

The verb *ser* (and any other verb used with the hours, but with no other expressed subject) is singular only when used with *one;* otherwise it is plural.

Eu chegava quando deram duas horas.	I was coming in when it struck two.
Devem ser duas horas.	It must be two o'clock.

Quarto is a masculine noun. *Meia* is an adjective, feminine to agree with *hora.* After *meio-dia* one often hears the masculine form, as if to agree with this noun.

It will be noted that after *ser* the article is not used before the hour. However, it is used after *a* and other prepositions.

À uma (hora)	At one (o'clock)
Às duas (horas)	At two (o'clock)
À quatro e dez.	At 4:10
Às vinte e oito para as sete.	At 28 to seven
Ao meio-dia.	At noon.
À meia-noite.	At midnight.
À meia-noite e vinte.	At 12:20 a.m.
Às oito da manhã.	At 8:00 a.m.
Às cinco da tarde.	At 5:00 p.m.
São dez horas da noite.	It is 10:00 p.m.
Depois da meia-noite.	After midnight.
Até (o) meio-dia.	Until noon.

Vocabulary

Nouns

o meio-dia	noon
a meia-noite	midnight
o minuto	minute
o quarto	quarter
o cento	(group of) 100
janeiro	January
fevereiro	February
março	March
abril	April
maio	May
junho	June
julho	July
agosto /ô/	August
setembro	September
outubro	October
novembro	November
dezembro	December
as férias	vacation
a data	date

Verbs

vir	come
faltar	lack, be lacking, be missing
almoçar	eat lunch, have lunch
levantar	get up, rise; raise
deitar	lie down; go to bed; lay down
acordar	wake up
dar	strike
nascer	be born; come up (sun, plant)

Adjectives

mesmo /ê/	same; self
algum, alguma	some
primeiro	first
inteiro	whole, entire

Adverbs

cedo /ê/	early
cá	here
para cá	here (to this place)

Expressions

da manhã	a.m.
da tarde	in the afternoon, p.m.
da noite	p.m.
Hoje é dia feriado.	Today is a holiday.
Ele veio a saber do que passou.	He found out what happened.
Vem cá.	Come here.
Chega para cá.	Come closer.
Cá nos Estados Unidos não plantamos café.	We don't raise coffee here in the United States.
O sol nasce às seis.	The sun comes up at six.

Leitura

Em casa levantamos cedo. No inverno acordamos antes do sol nascer. Levantamos e tomamos café. Os meninos têm que ir à escola e eu tenho que trabalhar. Alguns vão às sete horas, outros às oito.

Ao meio-dia voltamos para almoçar em casa. Ao meio-dia e meia vamos outra vez ao trabalho ou às aulas. De tarde chegamos em casa a horas diferentes, porque as escolas e o trabalho não acabam na mesma hora. Às seis estamos todos em casa para jantar. Depois os meninos preparam as lições para o outro dia e a gente grande vê o jornal, ou escreve cartas. Mais tarde todos vamos deitar.

Exercise A. Be able to give either language from the other:

1. Hoje é sexta-feira, dia vinte e cinco de outubro. | Today is Friday, Oct. 25.
2. Eu vou à aula às oito da manhã. | I go to class at 8:00 a.m.
3. O dia tem vinte e quatro horas. | A day has twenty-four hours.
4. A semana tem sete dias. | A week has seven days.
5. Temos aulas cinco dias por semana. | We have classes five days per week.
6. Amanhã é o dia vinte e seis de outubro. | Tomorrow is October 26.
7. Ontem só almoçamos às duas horas, porque chegamos tarde. | Yesterday we didn't have lunch till two, because we got in late.
8. Ele nunca deita antes da meia-noite. | He never goes to bed before midnight.
9. Estivemos com ele depois das duas horas. | We were with him after two o'clock.
10. Acordamos cedo de manhã. | We wake up early in the morning.

Exercise B. Answer in Portuguese:

1. A que horas você janta?
2. A que horas acende as luzes?
3. Quais são os meses de verão aqui?
4. Quais são no Brasil?
5. Quantos dias tem setembro?
6. Que dias são feriados?
7. Onde é que você vai estar às dez horas?
8. Que dias da semana temos aula aqui?
9. Qual é a data de hoje?
10. Quanto são dez mais oito?
11. Onze mais onze?
12. Dezesseis menos quatro?
13. Quanto são quatro vezes nove?
14. Que mês vem depois de janeiro?
15. Qual é o mês mais curto?
16. A que horas você almoça?
17. Você acordou cedo ou tarde hoje?
18. Você se levanta sempre à mesma hora?

Exercise C. Put the correct form of *vir* in each blank, in the same person and number as the example in the present:

1. Hoje eu venho.   Ontem eu _____ . Antes eu sempre. _____ .
2. Hoje nós vimos.   Ontem nós _____ . Se nós _____ amanhã.
3. Hoje ele vem.   Ontem ele _____ . Se ele _____ amanhã.
4. Hoje vocês vêm.   Ontem vocês _____ . Antes vocês sempre _____ ?

Exercise D. Read in Portuguese (e.g. 2 + 3 = 5: Dois mais três são cinco.):

1. 7 + 6 = 13.
2. 8 + 4 = 12.
3. 6 + 13 = 19.
4. 11 + 2 = 13.
5. 10 + 5 = 15.
6. 14 + 9 = 23.
7. 25 - (menos) 8 = 17.
8. 33 - 12 = 21.
9. 7 x (vezes) 4 = 28.
10. 6 x 3 = 18.

Exercise E. Fill in the blanks with the correct translations of the words in parentheses:

Ontem nós (went) _____ (to see) _____ o amigo João, que (remained) _____ _____ na cidade quando nós (left) _____ de lá. Quando (we arrived) _____ em casa dele, já (it was raining) _____ . Nós (went in) _____ e (saw) _____ o nosso amigo, que (was working) _____ à mesa. (We knew) _____ que ele (would stop) _____ _____ de (writing) _____ e (would have) _____ (coffee made) _____ para nós. (He called) _____ a empregada e (said) _____ que ele (wanted) _____ café mais tarde. Ele (thought) _____ que ela (would bring) _____ à sala. Nós (stayed) _____ duas horas com o João, (talking) _____ sobre os amigos e colegas (we used to have) _____ e nos tempos em que nós (lived) _____ nesta cidade.

Exercise F. Say in Portuguese:

1. It is 2:30.
2. Come at ten to two.
3. We eat (dinner) at 7:00 p.m.
4. Today is the first of the month.
5. We are going on the 11th of November.
6. We have a vacation in summer.
7. Today is the 13th of June.
8. He used to work at night.
9. We open the doors at ten.
10. We turn out the lights at 5:15.
11. On the sixth of February.
12. On Tuesdays and Thursdays.
13. At ten minutes to four.
14. Before midnight.
15. We leave in the afternoon.
16. I'll do this tonight.
17. December comes after November.
18. There are 31 days in July.
19. Sometimes February has 29 days.
20. When you wake up, come [over] to my house.

Lesson XVIII

95. Verbs irregular in one form only. The following verbs are irregular only in the first person singular of the present indicative. The present subjunctive, as will be shown later, is derived from this form. All other forms of these verbs are regular. Present Indicative of:

	pedir	*ouvir*	*perder*	*valer*
eu	peço /é/	ouço	perco /é/ or /ê/	valho
você	pede /é/	ouve	perde /é/	vale
ele	pede /é/	ouve	perde /é/	vale
nós	pedimos /pi/	ouvimos	perdemos	valemos
vocês	pedem /é/	ouvem	perdem /é/	valem
eles	pedem /é/	ouvem	perdem /é/	valem

96. The preposition *para* expresses:

a. *Toward, for,* movement in the direction of a place, without being specific about arrival.

| Partiram para Portugal. | They set out for Portugal. |
| Vamos para frente. | Let's go forward. |

b. *To,* movement to a place, including arrival, when it is one's normal place or situation, or will become such.

| Eu vou para casa. | I'm going home. |
| Ele se mudou para a cidade. | He moved to town. |

c. *In order to, to,* purpose.

| Vamos entrar para comer. | Let's go in to eat. |
| Para ganhar, é preciso jogar bem. | In order to win, it is necessary to play well. |

d. *For, to,* with the indirect object.

| Ele deu um sanduíche para mim. | He gave a sandwich to me. |
| Eu comprei um presente para ele. | I bought a gift for him. |

e. *For, to,* in comparisons, especially after *muito, bastante,* and similar words.

Isto é muito grande para mim.	This is too big for me.
Eu tenho bastante dinheiro para a viagem.	I have enough money for the trip.
Isto é muito doce para comer.	This is too sweet to eat.

79

f. *For*, before the intended recipient of something, of the benefits of labor, etc.

Tenho uma carta para você.	I have a letter for you.
Eu trabalho para o patrão.	I work for the boss.
Uma xícara para café.	A coffee cup.

97. The preposition *por* expresses:

a. *By*, the agent of an action.

A terra é cultivada pelos filhos.	The land is cultivated by the sons.
Um livro escrito por Veríssimo.	A book written by Veríssimo.

b. *For*, to get and take away.

Vamos passar por você.	We'll come by for you.
Foram pelo médico.	They went for the doctor.

c. *For*, in exchange for.

Paguei muito pela experiência.	I paid a lot for the experience,
Dei um cruzeiro pela caneta.	I gave a cruzeiro for the pen.

d. *For*, in place of.

Quer ir à aula por mim?	Will you go to class for me?
Vou trabalhar por ele.	I'm going to work in his place.

e. *For* the sake of.

Arte pela arte.	Art for art's sake.
Eu faço isso por você.	I'll do that for you.

f. *Per, a.*

Comemos três vezes por dia.	We eat three times a day.
Vinte por cento.	Twenty percent.

g. *By*, by way of.

Viajei por mar.	I traveled by sea.
Mandei a carta por avião.	I sent the letter by plane.

h. *Through, up, down, along*, movement through space.

O vento entrou pela janela.	The wind came in through the window.
Ele está passando pela rua.	He is going up (down, along) the street.
Andei pelo país inteiro.	I went all over the country.

i. *Around, through*, location or movement in a more or less vague area.

Não tem ninguém por aqui.	There is no one around here.

j. *Around, about*, near the time mentioned.

Lá pelo meio-dia.	Along about noon.
Por então não tinham carros.	Back then they didn't have cars.

Vocabulary

Nouns

o mundo	world
o sorvete /ê/	ice cream
a televisão	TV
o rádio	radio (set)
a música	music
a pena	trouble; pity
a pergunta	question
a mala	suitcase
a cerveja /ê/	beer
o barulho	noise

Verbs

pedir	ask for, beg
ouvir	hear
perder	lose, miss
valer	be worth

Prepositions

sem	without
segundo	according to
sobre /ô/	on; concerning
além de	besides

Adverb

atrás (See expressions)	ago

Adjectives and adverbs

muito	too, too much
bastante	enough, quite a bit
alto	loud, aloud

Expressions

Dez dias atrás.	Ten days ago.
Todo (o) mundo.	Everybody.
Tomar sorvete.	To eat ice cream.
Ver televisão.	To watch TV.
Ouvir (o) rádio.	To listen to the radio.
ouvir música.	To listen to music.
Valer a pena.	To be worth while (the trouble).
Ter pena de . . .	To be sorry for . . .
Ouvir dizer que . . .	To hear that . . .
Perder o trem.	To miss one's train.
Pedir para ver a casa.	To ask to see the house.
Fazer uma pergunta.	To ask a question.
Fazer as malas.	To pack one's bags.

Exercise A. Be able to give in either language:

1. Tem trem para São Paulo?	Is there a train to São Paulo?
2. Os brasileiros voltaram para o Brasil.	The Brazilians went back to Brazil.
3. Volto (muito) tarde para jantar.	I'm coming back too late to eat.
4. Você vai consertar os sapatos ou mandar consertar?	Are you going to fix your shoes or have them fixed?
5. Eu disse para ele que devia ficar.	I told him he should stay.
6. Escreve para mim.	Write to me.
7. Para quem você escreve este papel?	For whom will you write the paper?
8. Chamei pelo médico.	I called for the doctor.
9. João não pode ir trabalhar; eu vou por ele.	John can't go to work; I'm going in his place.
10. Mandei uma carta por avião.	I sent an airmail letter.
11. Vocês não podem passar por aqui.	You can't get through here.
12. Acho que ele está aqui perto.	I think he's close by.

Exercise B. Give the plurals of the following nouns and adjectives:

1. o ônibus
2. o lápis
3. o pires
4. simples

5. o cão
6. o pão
7. o alemão
8. o irmão

9. a lição
10. o verão
11. a mão
12. o órfão

Exercise C. Words which end in -*vel* /vél/ in Portuguese usually correspond to English words in -*ble*. Give the English for the following words, and note small differences in the spelling of some:

1. possível
2. provável
3. impossível
4. indelével
5. móvel
6. solúvel
7. estável

8. dirigível
9. utilizável
10. potável
11. incorrigível
12. terrível
13. horrível
14. intangível

15. indestrutível
16. passável
17. inevitável
18. filtrável
19. desejável
20. legível
21. comível

Exercise D. Say in Portuguese:

1. Prepare the meat for a picnic.
2. We have enough bread for everybody.
3. No (without) doubt, you are going to the country.
4. According to John, the man is going to talk about Brazil.
5. Those shoes are Mother's.
6. There were several women there, besides the children.
7. I have lots of friends around here.
8. He can't catch me without running.
9. I have bought you some flowers.
10. We meet at the movies.
11. They spent the night at a motel.
12. He talks on "Today's College."
13. It looks good enough to eat.
14. He hurried to arrive before night.
15. I'm going to bed.
16. Go to the store for bread.
17. Will you give me a cruzeiro for this?
18. We went by plane, because I don't like to travel by sea.
19. There he comes down the street.
20. They are worth twenty cruzeiros a hundred.

Exercise E. Say in Portuguese:

1. He asked me for [some] paper. — Ele me pediu papel.
2. We asked to listen to the radio. — Pedimos para ouvir o rádio.
3. Speak louder; I don't hear well. — Fala mais alto, não ouço bem.
4. Speak up; I don't hear you. — Fala alto, eu não estou ouvindo.
5. I have lost his letter. — Perdi a carta dele.
6. It's not worth while looking for it. — Não vale a pena procurar.
7. He will give it to you if you ask for it. — Ele dá se você pedir.
8. He missed the bus and had to walk. — Ele perdeu o ônibus e teve que andar (a pé).
9. I am worth as much as the next one. — Valho tanto como o outro.
10. Everybody eats ice cream. — Todo mundo toma sorvete.
11. We watch TV every night. — Vemos televisão todas as noites.
12. He lived there thirty years ago. — Ele morava lá trinta anos atrás.

82

13. I'm sorry for him.	Tenho pena dele.
14. I asked his name.	Perguntei o nome dele.
15. Don't ask that question.	Não faz essa pergunta.
16. Will you drink beer or water?	Você quer tomar cerveja ou água?

Lesson XIX

98. The irregular verbs *ler,* to read, and *crer,* to believe.

	Present Indicative	*Present Indicative*
eu	leio	creio
você	lê	crê
ele	lê	crê
nós	lemos	cremos
vocês	lêem	crêem
eles	lêem	crêem

The other tense forms are regular.

99. Forms of the present subjunctive. There are two sets of endings in the present subjunctive. The first conjugation has the vowel *e,* the second and third have the vowel *a.*

	falar	*comer*	*abrir*
que eu	fale	coma	abra
que você	fale	coma	abra
que ele	fale	coma	abra
que nós	falemos	comamos	abramos
que vocês	falem	comam	abram
que eles	falem	comam	abram

The present subjunctive of any verb which has a first person present indicative form ending in -*o* (except *querer*) can be found by removing this final -*o* and adding the endings of the conjugation. This method will give the irregular stems used in the present subjunctive, and also the quality of the vowel in forms stressed on the stem. The student should become familiar with the following subjunctive forms of verbs that have been studied:

Infinitive	*1st singular present indicative*	*Present Subjunctive, singular*
caber	caibo	caiba
crer	creio	creia
dizer	digo	diga
fazer	faço	faça
ler	leio	leia
ouvir	ouço	ouça
pedir	peço /é/	peça /é/
perder	perco /é/ or /ê/	perca /é/ or /ê/
pôr	ponho	ponha
poder	posso /ó/	possa /ó/
ter	tenho	tenha
valer	valho	valha

83

Infinitive	1st singular present indicative	Present Subjunctive, singular
ver	vejo /ê/	veja /ê/
vir	venho	venha
levar	levo /é/	leve /é/
dever	devo /ê/	deva /ê/

The other personal endings are added to the same stem. Open vowels close when they occur in unstressed syllables.

100. The subjunctive of will. Any verb or phrase which expresses the imposing or the attempt to impose the will of one person or group on another requires that the dependent verb be in the subjunctive. Among the verbs which require the subjunctive in such circumstances are the following:

querer, desejar	wish, want, desire
mandar	order
dizer	tell to
pedir	ask to
proibir	forbid, prohibit
aconselhar	advise to
deixar, permitir	let, allow to, permit to
preferir	prefer

Note that if the logical subjects of the two verbs are the same, there can be no imposition of the will of one subject on another. In that case, the infinitive is used.

The verbs mentioned above are always followed by *que* before the clause that contains the subjunctive.

In many, but not all cases, there are alternate ways to construct a sentence with these verbs, without using the subjunctive. Since these constructions vary from verb to verb, however, it is better to learn first the subjunctive, which is uniform for all. For examples of the present subjunctive, see Exercise A, below.

101. Note on spelling. Certain regular and predictable changes in spelling are made in verb forms, so that the pronunciation of the stem will be correctly indicated in all forms. Thus

a. Verbs whose infinitive ends in -*car* change *c* to *qu* before *e*.

    ficar: present subjunctive fique, fiquemos, fiquem
         preterit   fiquei, *but* ficou,

b. Verbs whose infinitive ends in -*gar* change *g* to *gu* before *e*.

    chegar: present subjunctive chegue, cheguemos, cheguem
         preterit   cheguei, but chegou, etc.

c. Verbs whose infinitive ends in -*cer* require a cedilla under the letter *c* before *a* or *o*.

    Conhecer: present indicative conheço, but conhece, etc.
         present subjunctive conheça, conheçamos, conheçam

d. Verbs whose infinitive ends in -*çar* drop the cedilla before *e*.

    começar: present subjunctive comece, comecemos, comecem
        preterit indicative comecei, but começou, etc.

Vocabulary

Nouns

		Verbs	
o garçom	waiter	desejar	want, wish, desire
a garçonete /é/	waitress	mandar	order, command
o embrulho	package	dizer	tell to, order to
a verdade	truth	pedir	ask to
a maçã	apple	proibir	forbid, prohibit
		aconselhar	advise to
		permitir	permit, allow
		preferir	preferir, like better
		ajudar (a)	help (to)

Expression

Eu preferia ficar.   I'd rather stay.

Note the use of written accents on the forms of *proibir*.

Present Indicative	*Present Subjunctive*
proíbo	proíba
proíbe	proíba
proibimos	proibamos
proíbem	proíbam

Exercise A. Examples of the use of the present subjunctive:

1. O sr. quer que eu ajude?	Do you want me to help?
2. O que deseja que eu faça?	What do you want me to do?
3. Ele manda que fiquemos aqui.	He orders us to stay here.
4. João diz que jantemos com ele.	John tells us to have dinner with him.
5. Peço que me levem à cidade.	I ask you take me downtown.
6. Proíbo que você fale com ela.	I forbid you to speak to her.
7. Aconselhamos que vocês usem chapéus.	We advise you to wear hats.
8. Não deixo que ele beba cerveja.	I don't let him drink beer.
9. Permitimos que vejam televisão.	We let them see TV.
10. Preferimos que não chamem o garçom.	We'd rather you didn't call the waiter.

Exercise B. Replace the underlined verb with each of the verbs in parentheses, in the same person and number:

1. Eu quero que você *acabe* o trabalho.

> (entregar) o embrulho.
> (arranjar) uma empregada.
> (ouvir) a música.
> (compreender) a lição.
> (dizer) a verdade.

2. Ele manda que os meninos *brinquem* no jardim.

> (fechar) as janelas.
> (correr) para casa.
> (levantar) cedo.
> (beber) leite.
> (vir) para casa.

3. Nós permitimos que vocês *almocem* conosco.
   (escrever) para eles.
   (vender) as maçãs.
   (abrir) a porta.
   (pôr) o chapéu.
   (freqüentar) a escola.
4. Eles pedem que eu *responda* às perguntas.
   (apagar) a luz.
   (não perder) a caneta.
   (voltar) para casa.
   (fazer) uma visita.
   (explicar) a pergunta.
5. Ele prefere que nós *esqueçamos* a história.
   (estudar) a lição.
   (poder) ir com ele.
   (ver) televisão.
   (aprender) português.
   (assar) a carne.

Exercise C. Give the other tenses of the following verbs in the same person and number as those given in the present indicative:

Present Indicative	Preterit	Imperfect	Present Subjunctive	Future Subjunctive

1. falo
2. pedimos
3. ouve
4. perdem
5. valemos
6. ouço
7. tem
8. põem
9. cabe
10. deve
11. vem

Exercise D. Pronounce the following forms, taking care with stressed *e* and *o*:

1. Aconselho	11. veja	21. chega
2. deixa	12. entregue	22. more
3. desejam	13. consertam	23. levem
4. almoça	14. bebo	24. neve
5. acordo	15. esqueça	25. chove
6. botam	16. pegue	26. come
7. acendam	17. possa	27. escreve
8. volto	18. corra	28. vieram
9. recebe	19. conheçam	29. perderam
10. deva	20. fecha	30. corre

Exercise E. Say in Portuguese:

1. It is 3:00 p.m.
2. Today is November first.
3. It's a quarter to midnight.
4. We go at 8:20 a.m.
5. He is coming on Tuesday the twenty-second.
6. I tell him to do the work.
7. I let my classmates listen to the radio.
8. He asks me to get off the bus with him.

9. John's father forbids him to play with Joe.
10. I don't want you to miss your train.
11. I order John to help his brother.
12. He prefers for us to tell him.
13. We advise you to think of this.
14. The boss doesn't permit me to ask questions.
15. Everybody is eating ice cream.
16. The waiter took that package [with him.]
17. Tell me the truth.
18. We used to listen to music every day.
19. Is it worth while to buy apples?
20. He asks to meet the young lady.
21. I missed my lunch.
22. I find the noise [to be] very loud.
23. This ice cream is not very cold.
24. Let's help him.
25. Let me help you.

Lesson XX

102.   The irregular verb *trazer,* to bring.

	Present Indicative	Preterit
eu	trago	trouxe /trosi/
você	traz	trouxe
ele	traz	trouxe
nós	trazemos	trouxemos /trusẽmus/
vocês	trazem	trouxeram /trusérõ/
eles	trazem	trouxeram

Present subjunctive traga, tragamos, etc.
Future subjunctive trouxer, etc.

103.   Radical-changing verbs of the third conjugation. There are several types of radical changes in this conjugation. The situation is quite different from that of the other conjugations, in that it is not possible to predict which verbs will change by noting the spelling of the infinitive. Each of the verbs which change must be learned. Sometimes verbs which are compounds of the same root are conjugated differently. Note that there are changes in spelling, as well as in pronunciation. Note also the influence of a stressed *i* on the pronunciation of a preceding *e* or *o*.

a. The most frequent change is that which affects most verbs of this conjugation whose stem-vowel is *e* or *o*. Thus:

	vestir		*engolir*	
	Present Indicative	Present Subjunctive	Present Indicative	Present Subjunctive
eu	visto	vista	engulo	engula
você	veste /é/	vista	engole /ó/	engula
ele	veste	vista	engole	engula
nós	vestimos /vi/	vistamos	engolimos /gu/	engulamos
vocês	vestem /é/	vistam	engolem /ó/	engulam
eles	vestem	vistam	engolem	engulam

When the stem-vowel *e* is followed by *m* or *n*, the change takes place in the first person singular, but the vowel is closed in the third person forms. There are no verbs of this type with *o* followed by *m* or *n*.

	Present Indicative	Present Subjunctive
eu	sinto	sinta
você	sente	sinta
ele	sente	sinta
nós	sentimos /sĩ/	sintamos
vocês	sentem	sintam
eles	sentem	sintam

b. A second type has the stem-vowel *u*, which changes to *o* in certain forms. If it is followed by *m* or *n*, the vowel remains closed.

	subir	*sumir*
	Present Indicative	Present Indicative
eu	subo	sumo
você	sobe /ó/	some /õ/
ele	sobe	some
nós	subimos	sumimos
vocês	sobem /ó/	somem /õ/
eles	sobem	somem
	Present subjunctive suba, etc.	soma, etc.

Verbs of the type of *vestir* are quite numerous. One should generally assume that a verb of the third conjugation whose stem vowel is *e* will belong to this type, although there are some exceptions. There are only a few verbs like *engolir*, since there are not many whose stem vowel is *o*. But several of these are words of high frequency in the spoken language. There are few more than a dozen of the type of *subir*, but some are quite important.

Vocabulary

Nouns

o correio	mail; post office
o vestido	dress
o cheiro	smell, odor
a escada	stair; ladder
a camisa	shirt
a volta /ó/	turn: return; stroll
a sala (de estar)	(living) room
a saúde	health
o esporte /ô/	sport

Nouns

o maiô	(woman's) bathing suit
o calção	(men's) trunks

Adverbs

cadê (colloq.)	where is, where are
lá fora	out there, outside
de volta	back

Verbs

trazer	bring, wear
vestir (eu visto)	put on; dress
vestir-se	dress
despir (eu dispo)	take off; undress
despir-se	undress
seguir (eu sigo)	follow; go on, keep on
engolir (eu engulo)	swallow

Verbs

dormir (eu durmo)	sleep; go to sleep.
subir (ele sobe)	go up; come up
sumir (ele some)	disappear; be gone
sentir (eu sinto)	feel; be sorry
ir (-se) embora	go away

Expressions

Eu vou (-me) embora.	I'm going away.
Nós vamos embora.	We're going away.
Dei uma volta.	I took a stroll.
Ela pôs um vestido.	She put on a dress.
Ela se vestiu.	She got dressed.
Bastante bem.	Rather well.
De uma vez.	Once and for all; all at once.
Sentir pena de.	To feel sorry for.
Sentir-se bem (mal, doente, etc.)	To feel well (bad, sick, etc.)
Sentir um barulho.	To hear (sense) a noise.
Sentir um cheiro.	To smell an odor.
Meu lápis sumiu.	My pencil is gone.
Ontem eu dormi tarde.	I went to sleep late last night.
Hoje eu dormi até tarde.	I slept late this morning.
Eu sinto falta dele.	I miss him.
Uma passagem de ida e volta.	A round-trip ticket.
Andar a pé.	To walk.

Hoje à noite João me leva a uma festa e depois vai me trazer de volta. Eu não sei que roupa eu devo vestir. Os rapazes usam camisa esporte em algumas festas, mas as moças geralmente vestem uma roupa mais elegante.

Na semana passada fui a outra festa na casa de um colega. Lá pelas oito horas peguei um ônibus que ia até aquele bairro e saltei perto da casa onde ele mora. Depois subi uma escada que leva da rua até a porta da casa. Como fazia calor, as janelas estavam abertas e o vento entrava pelas salas trazendo o cheiro das flores to jardim.

Exercise A. Be able to say in either language from the other:

1. Eu vou à sua casa e você me traz de volta.
   I'll go over to your house and you'll bring me back.
2. Por que você não veste o maiô?
   Why don't you put on your bathing suit?
3. A Adélia está se vestindo para ir fazer compras.
   Adelia is dressing to go shopping.
4. Levanto cedo e visto-me antes de tomar café.
   I get up early and dress before breakfast.
5. Vamos ver se tenho uma carta dele, quando trouxerem o correio.
   We'll see whether I have a letter from him, when they bring the mail.
6. Não toma esse café quente tão depressa.
   Don't drink that hot coffee so fast.
7. Você deve tomar devagar e não engolir tudo de uma vez.
   You should drink it slowly and not swallow it all at once.
8. Como é que você está se sentindo?
   How do you feel?
9. Eu me sinto bastante bem nesta cidade.
   I feel rather well in this town.
10. Estou ouvindo o barulho de vozes.
    I hear the sound of voices.
11. Podemos sentir o cheiro das flores que estão na mesa.
    We can smell the flowers that are on the table.
12. Ele subiu a escada correndo.
    He ran upstairs.
13. Vou subir ao quarto.
    I'm going up to my room.
14. Temos que subir a pé.
    We must walk up.
15. Os preços estão subindo.
    Princes are rising.
16. Esta estrada sobe a serra.
    This road goes up the mountain.
17. Ele subiu no ônibus e foi embora.
    He got on the bus and left.

18. Cadê meu livro? Sumiu.	Where's my book? It's gone.
19. Some daqui!	Get out of here!
20. Segue aquele carro.	Follow that car.
21. Despe-se antes de dormir.	Undress before you go to bed.
22. Ele tirou o paletó e ficou de camisa.	He took off his coat and went in his shirt sleeves.

Exercise B. Give the third-person form in the same tense and number as the form given:

1. Dispo-me.	6. Engulo	11. Peço	16. Despimos
2. Durmo	7. Trago	12. Ouço	17. Dormimos
3. Visto	8. Subimos	13. Perco	18. Sentimos
4. Sinto	9. Preferimos	14. Sei	19. Sumimos
5. Sumo	10. Valho	15. Vejo	20. Sigo

Exercise C. Fill blanks with the correct forms of the verbs in parentheses:

1. (seguir) Eu mando que ele me _____ .
2. (trazer) Permitem que eu _____ um amigo.
3. (subir) Aconselho que você _____ ao quarto.
4. (dormir) Eu quero que você _____ logo.
5. (pedir) Preferem que você _____ outro.
6. (engolir) Ele proíbe que os meninos _____ o chocolate.
7. (vestir) Ele manda que nós _____ os paletós.
8. (despir) Vocês permitem que eu me _____ nesse quarto?
9. (sumir) Não quero que vocês _____ .
10. (sentir) Não queremos que vocês _____ pena de nós.

Exercise D. Say in Portuguese:

1. It is 6:30 p.m.
2. He came at midnight.
3. I leave at 20 to 8:00 tomorrow morning.
4. 22 women came to see me this evening.
5. It snowed on the 15th of November.
6. It was raining at 3:00 p.m., when I came in.
7. My hat is gone.
8. I put a letter in the mail.
9. I can hear the noise of the train.
10. He went up the ladder and entered by the window.
11. $42 + 26 = 68$.
12. $65 - 12 = 23$.
13. $73 - 33 = 40$.
14. $3 \times 5 = 15$.
15. Good night. Sleep well.

Exercise E. Fill in each blank with the correct form of the verb in parentheses:

1. (poder) Vocês devem dormir logo que _____ .
2. (pedir) Eu dou isto para eles quando me _____ .
3. (brilhar) Vai ficar bonito enquanto o sol _____ .
4. (voltar) Vamos falar com ele logo que _____ .
5. (dizer) Eu não deixo que vocês joguem, se não me _____ a verdade.
6. (fazer) Ele volta para casa, assim que _____ o trabalho.

7. (pôr) Vocês vão sentir frio, se não _____ os casacos.

8. (querer) Vocês podem tomar café quando _____ .

9. (caber) Vamos levar dois carros, caso não _____ num.

10. (passar) Vai ficar bonito, depois que a chuva _____ .

Exercise F. Say in Portuguese:

1. She dresses well.
2. I feed bad today.
3. He slept late this morning.
4. He brought his friend.
5. Take this book, if you are going up.
6. Go on up the street.
7. I can smell the apples on the fire.
8. She put on a white dress.
9. He swallows his beer too fast.

10. It's quite cold outside.
11. Take off your coat.
12. Go around in your shirt [sleeves].
13. Where's the waiter?
14. I want him to bring coffee.
15. Tonight I'm going to sleep late.
16. I feel sick.
17. He feels sorry for me.
18. Get a round-trip ticket.

Lesson XXI

104. The reflexive verbs. A reflexive verb is one whose object is the same person or thing as the subject. A verb is made reflexive by the use of the reflexive object pronouns. Thus:

Chamo-me José *or* Eu me chamo José.   My name is Joe.
Chama-se Maria *or* Ela se chama Maria.   Her name is Mary.

105. Use of the reflexive verbs. The reflexive construction is used in various ways, some with very different meanings from others.

a. The action which the subject performs upon itself may be literal.

Ele se viu no espelho.   He saw himself in the mirror.

b. If the subject is inanimate, singular or plural, the reflexive form of the verb may be used instead of the passive voice. While this usage is fairly frequent, it should be remembered that the real passive is much more used in BF and limits the reflexive usage considerably.

Falam-se várias línguas na Suiça.   Several languages are spoken in Switzerland.
Fêz-se o trabalho num minuto.   The work was done in a minute.

c. If the verb is in the third person singular, the reflexive *se* is used in many expressions almost as if it were an impersonal, unidentified subject, more or less equal to *one* in English. But see the use of the impersonal subject *a gente,* below.

Como é que se pode não gostar de café?   How can one help liking coffee?
Vai-se à cidade de ônibus.   You go (one goes) downtown by bus.

d. The reflexive pronoun objects may have a reciprocal meaning (each other) in the plural.

Eles se escrevem de vez em quando.   They write to each other from time to time.
Nós nos vemos com freqüência.   We see each other often.

Since in many cases it would be difficult to distinguish whether or not the reflexive pronoun should be understood as reciprocal, the situation may be clarified by the use of *um ao outro,* either as a direct or as an indirect object. If this expression is used, the reflexive pronoun is omitted.

If *all* persons or things included in the expression *um ao outro* are feminine, both words become feminine—*uma à outra*. Otherwise, both are masculine. If more than two individuals are involved, both words become plural.

João e Maria escrevem cartas um ao outro. John and Mary write each other letters.
As três mulheres vêem umas às outras. The three women see each other.

106.　Omission of the reflexive object. In many cases, the use of the reflexive object simply maintains the transitive character of the verb, where English would use it intransitively. But BF, like English, is no longer much concerned with maintaining the distinction between transitive and intransitive verbs. In such cases the reflexive object is very often omitted, as in English.

Ele (se) deita. He lies down.
Eu (me) levanto. I get up.

The reflexive pronoun *nos* is never used in BF following the verb, It is either omitted or placed before the verb.

Nós nos levantamos *or* Levantamos. We get up.

Some verbs have alternate expressions, one with a noun or pronoun object, the other with a reflexive pronoun followed by a preposition.

Eu lembro isso. I remember that.
Eu me lembro disso. I remember that.

107.　Equivalents in Portuguese of the impersonal subject "one." In English there are several subjects which may be used to denote that the subject is a vague, unidentified person or persons—one, people, you, they, etc. The subject most frequently used in Portuguese is *a gente*.

A gente estuda muito e aprende pouco. One studies a lot and learns little.

A second construction uses the third person singular of the verb and the reflexive pronoun *se*.

Estuda-se muito e aprende-se pouco.

When action is attributed to unknown persons, the verb may be expressed in the third person plural, without an expressed subject.

Dizem que não vai haver Carnaval. They say there won't be a Carnival.

Note: The word *um* as a subject is always a number, never an indefinite pronoun.

Um vai e outro vem. One goes and another comes.

108.　Cardinal numbers above 100.

duzentos, -as	200	mil	1,000
trezentos, -as	300	um milhão	1,000,000
quatrocentos, -as	400	um milhar	1,000 (group)
quinhentos, -as	500		
seiscentos, -as	600		
setecentos, -as	700		
oitocentos, -as	800		
novecentos, -as	900		

duas mil e duzentas casas	2,200 houses
um milhão de casas	1,000,000 houses
milhares de pessoas	thousands of people
milhões de pessoas	millions of people
dois milhões de pessoas	two million people
Um milhão duas mil e três casas	1,002,003 houses

The hundreds from 200 to 900, and the numbers *one* and *two* agree with feminine nouns except when they precede *milhão,* which is a masculine noun. In theory, the word *e* is placed before any number which is *added* to the preceding number. In BF, it is generally used in the following cases, but omitted in others.

a. Before tens and units, and before *cem* and *cento.*

Oitenta e seis	86
Cento e dez	110
Trezentos e quarenta e três	343
Um milhão e cem	1,000,100

b. After *milhão* and *mil,* before a multiple of *cem,* if no smaller number follows the latter.

mil e quinhentos	1,500
Um milhão e seiscentos	1,000,600

Note that in writing numbers the use of the comma and period is exactly reversed from the use in English.

14.392,28	Fourteen thousand three hundred ninety-two and twenty-eight hundredths.

The period is implicit in the reading of the numbers; the comma is read *vírgula.*

3,5	três vírgula cinco	three point five

109. Ordinal numbers. The ordinals from first to tenth are as follows:

primeiro	first	sexto /ê/	sixth
segundo /si/	second	sétimo	seventh
terceiro	third	oitavo	eighth
quarto	fourth	nono	ninth
quinto	fifth	décimo	tenth

Above tenth the ordinals are little used, doubtless because they are long and complex. The cardinal numbers may be used as ordinals by placing them after the noun, using the word *número* when needed.

Capítulo 23	Chapter 23

With the names of kings, etc., the ordinals are used up to tenth, but the cardinals thereafter. No article is used.

Carlos Quinto	Charles V
Luiz Quatorze	Louis XIV

With days of the month, only *primeiro* is used. All other dates are expressed by cardinals.

Vocabulary

Nouns

o telefone	telephone
a palavra	word
o relógio	watch; clock
o caderno /é/	notebook

Adjectives

útil	useful
cego /é/	blind
coitado	poor, pitiful
certo /é/	certain; correct, right
errado	incorrect, wrong
fraco	weak
leve /é/	light (weight)
pesado	heavy
escuro	dark

Adverbial and Prepositional Phrases

para cá	this way, in this direction
para cá de	on this side of
para lá	that way
para lá de	on the other side of, beyond
do lado de lá	on the other side
do lado de cá	on this side
do lado de fora	on the outside
do lado de dentro	on the inside
desta vez	this time
quanto tempo	how long
em breve /é/	soon
de leve /é/	lightly

Verbs

enxergar	catch sight of, manage to see
mudar	change; move
encher (de)	fill (with)
atravessar	cross
atrasar	delay; get behind
demorar	delay; be long
emprestar	lend
convidar (para)	invite (to)
chamar	call
chamar-se	be called, be named
lavar (-se)	wash (one's self)
despedir (like pedir)	discharge, fire (an employee)

Verbs

despedir-se (de)	take leave (of), say good-bye (to)
divertir	amuse
divertir-se (eu me divirto)	have a good time

Other expressions

Eu queria saber.	I wonder. (I'd like to know)
Não presta atenção a ele.	Don't pay any attention to him.
Coitado do Pedro!	Poor Pete!
Eu vou me mudar.	I'm going to change clothes; I'm going to move.

Exercise A. Use of idiomatic expressions:

1. Está muito escuro; não posso enxergar o telefone.
It's very dark; I can't see the telephone.

2. Quanto tempo você vai demorar para aprender essa palavra?
How long will it take you to learn that word?

3. O telefone é útil para chamar as pessoas.
The telephone is useful for calling people.

4. O coitado é cego.
The poor fellow is blind.

5. Parece um pobre coitado.
He looks like a pitiful fellow.

6. Já enchi o caderno de apontamentos.
I've filled my notebook with notes.

7. Temos que mudar de roupa antes da festa.

We must change clothes before the party.

8. Você já mudou de casa?

Have you moved yet?

10. É fácil atravessar esta rua estreita.

It is easy to cross this narrow street.

11. Tenho uma coisa atravessada na garganta.

I have something stuck in my throat.

12. Você está certo.

You are right.

13. Estou certo que ele vem atrasado.

I'm sure he'll come late.

14. Meu relógio atrasou dez minutos.

My watch got ten minutes slow.

15. Você quer me emprestar o caderno?

Will you lend me your notebook?

16. Desta vez não me convidaram para a festa.

This time they didn't invite me to the party.

17. Há um carro do lado de cá

There's a car on this side.

18. A loja fica do lado de lá da rua.

The shop is one the other side of the street.

19. Chega mais para cá.

Come closer.

20. Ele anda de lá para cá e de cá para lá.

He paces back and forth.

21. Este café está para lá de ruim.

This coffee is awful. (worse than bad)

22. A casa está acabada do lado de fora.

The house is finished on the outside.

23. Quero convidar você para jantar lá em casa.

I want to invite you to eat dinner at my house.

24. Vou ao correio, mas não demoro.

I'm going to the post office, but I won't be long.

25. É difícil enxergar na chuva.

It's hard to see in the rain.

26. O menino lavou as mãos.

The child washed his hands.

27. Não prestei atenção à lição.

I paid no attention to the lesson.

Exercise B. Read in Portuguese:

1. In the year 1892.
2. In 1972.
3. 1,372,431.
4. 1,426

5. 1,500.
6. 2,438 persons.
7. 562 houses.
8. 851 women.

Exercise C. Use of reflexive verbs:

1. Ele se chama Jorge.

His name is George.

2. Chama Jorge para almoçar.

Call George for lunch.

3. Levantamos às oito.

We get up at eight.

4. Não demoro para me deitar.

I won't be long in going to bed.

5. Você se diverte na praia, ou diverte os outros?

Do you enjoy yourself at the beach, or do you amuse the others?

6. Você se esqueceu disso, não é? Esqueci.

You forgot that, didn't you? Yes.

7. A mãe dele lava para fora.

His mother takes in washing.

8. Uma mão lava a outra.

One hand washes the other. (We help each other out.)

9. Agora despeço-me de vocês.

Now I say good-bye to you.

10. Despedi a empregada.

I fired the maid.

11. João e Maria (se) casaram.

John and Mary got married.

12. Maria (se) casou com João.

Mary married John,

13. Eu vou me vestir.

I'm going to dress.

14. Vestiram a menina de azul.

They dressed the girl in blue.

15. Veste a roupa.

Put on your clothes.

16. Eles se encontraram na aula.

They met in class.

17. Proíbe-se tomar banho nesta praia.

It is forbidden to bathe at this beach.

18. Perdeu-se um cachorro.	Lost: a dog.
19. Procura-se empregada.	Wanted: a maid.
20. A luz se acendeu.	The light was lit.
21. Ganha-se muito neste trabalho.	You make a lot at this job.
22. Uma boa casa se arranja.	You can get a good house.
23. Consertam-se relógios.	Watches repaired.
24.Nós nos conhecemos.	We know each other.
25. Não nos falamos mais.	We don't speak to each other any more.

Exercise D. Say in Portuguese:

1. (the) King Louis X
2. Charles XII
3. Henry II (Henrique)
4. Leo XI (Leão)
5. The first of May

6. The tenth of August
7. The third (= second) floor
8. The fourth year of school
9. The tenth number
10. The forty-third person

Exercise E. Say in Portuguese:

1. He moved to another town.
2. The poor fellow is weak after being sick.
3. I'm sure you're wrong.
4. We'll take a long time to move this heavy table.
5. Please pay more attention.
6. The town is beyond the mountains.
7. He filled his glass with water.
8. My watch is ten minutes slow.
9. I was invited to spend the night.
10. I can't see well in the dark.
11. These clothes are too light for winter.
12. He called me to the house.
13. Those things are called blackboards.
14. Get up and follow me.
15. She washes clothes for me.

16. I have been fired.
17. We are going to say good-bye to Aunty.
18. I have forgotten everything I learned.
19. Did you have a good time?
20. He wonders who you are.
21. The package has words on the outside.
22. How long are you going to be gone (= *fora*)?
23. We are going to cross [over] soon.
24. This is a very useful word.
25. The poor fellow lost his coat.
26. The street is narrow and dark at night.
27. He touched me lightly.
28. The school is on this side of the post office.
29. He filled my glass with beer.
30. This time get (= prepare) your lessons.

Lesson XXII

110. The personal infinitive. Thus far, the impersonal infinitive only has been used in this text. It is invariable in form and has no subject. There is also a personal infinitive, i.e., one possessing personal endings, which are added to the impersonal infinitive. The translation of this form varies with the usage. The forms of the personal infinitive are as follows:

Impersonal Infinitive
falar

Personal Infinitive
eu falar
você falar
ele falar
nós falarmos
vocês falarem
eles falarem.

There are also endings for the old second person forms. It will be noted that, in verbs which are are regular in the preterit, the personal infinitive coincides in its forms with the future subjunctive. But future subjunctive forms of verbs whose preterits are irregular have a different stem. Thus *fazer:*

> Future subjunctive fizer, fizermos, fizerem
> Personal Infinitive fazer, fazermos, fazerem

111. Use of the personal infinitive. There are no rules governing the use of the personal infinitive which have not been violated by the best authors of the language. And there is not a single idea which cannot be expressed correctly in Portuguese without the use of this form. However, it is in constant and frequent use both by writers and by speakers of all levels of speech, and it is therefore very important. Its use in BF is rather clearly defined, basically as follows:

The infinitive is personal when its logical subject has not yet been mentioned in the sentence, either as subject or direct object of the preceding verb. It may occasionally be heard in these circumstances also if the infinitive is separated from the preceding verb by several words. A pronoun used as the subject of the infinitive is always in the subject (nominative) form. It may be expressed whenever it is emphasized, or merely for clarity, especially in the singular.

The personal infinitive may very often replace the subjunctive, and sometimes the indicative. At other times it is used instead of the impersonal infinitive, for greater clarity. When it replaces the subjunctive, the construction varies from verb to verb, so that it is necessary to learn the constructions which follow each verb. Thus, we may use either the subjunctive or the personal infinitive after *dizer,* to tell to.

> Ele diz que façamos o trabalho.　　　　He tells us to do the work.
> Ele nos diz para fazermos o trabalho.　　He tells us to do the work.

In this instance, the indirect object may be used or omitted. The preposition *para* must be used.

Also after *pedir* the same construction is used.

> João pede que ajudemos na loja.　　　　John asks us to help at the store.
> João pede para ajudarmos na loja.

Whenever a conjunction requiring the subjunctive is paralleled by a preposition having the same meaning, we may replace the conjunction and the subjunctive by the preposition and the personal infinitive.

> Vão jantar depois que nós chegarmos.　　They will dine after we arrive.
> Vão jantar depois de nós chegarmos.

112. Radical-changing nouns and adjectives. Some nouns and adjectives which end in *o* in the masculine singular have the stem vowel /ô/ in that form, but have /ó/ in all others. This applies to adjectives and to nouns in which the difference in gender is shown by changing final *o* to *a.* It should be remembered that most nouns and adjectives keep the vowel of the masculine singular in all forms, whether it is /ô/ or /ó/. Those which change must be learned.

Vocabulary

Nouns

o avô	grandfather
pl. avós	
a avó	grandmother
pl. avós	
o fogo /ô/	fire
pl. fogos /ó/	
o olho /ô/	eye
pl. olhos /ó/	
o ovo /ô/	egg
pl. /ó/	
a horta /ó/	garden
o legume	vegetable
a couve	kale
o quiabo	okra
o pomar	orchard
a laranja	orange
a laranjeira	orange tree
a manga	mango (fruit)
a mangueira	mango tree
a jaca	jack fruit
a jaqueira	jack fruit tree

Adjectives

novo /ô/	new, young
pl. and fem. /ó/	
castanho	brown (hair, eyes)
feio	ugly
frito	fried
mexido	stirred, scrambled
doméstico	domestic

Nouns

o cavalo	horse
a vaca	cow
a cabra	goat
a galinha	chicken; hen
o pato	duck
o cachorro /ô/	dog
a fazenda	farm; ranch
o fazendeiro	farmer; rancher
a família	family
o aniversário	birthday
o dente	tooth
a lua	moon
a planta	plant
a parte	part
o lugar	place
o cabelo /ê/	hair
o milho	corn
a coisa	thing

Verbs

calçar	put on (shoes, gloves)
olhar (para)	look (at)
cozinhar /ku/	cook
plantar	plant; raise
existir	exist
criar	raise (animals)
montar	ride (horse)

Adverbs

ali	right there
quase	almost
também não	not . . . either

Expressions

Toda parte	Everywhere
Outra parte	Elsewhere
Alguma parte	Somewhere
Fazer anos	To have a birthday
Fazer 29 anos	To have one's 29th birthday
Olha o carro!	Look at the car. Look out for the car.
Olha para o carro.	Look at the car.
Montar a cavalo	To ride horseback
A maior parte de	Most of
A fazenda mesma	The farm itself

Leitura

Meus avós moram na roça. Meu avô tem uma pequena fazenda em Minas Gerais. Tem muitos fazendeiros naquele estado. Algumas fazendas são grandes, mas muitas são mais ou menos pequenas.

Meu avô planta milho e tem uma pequena horta onde planta legumes como couve e quiabo. Existe também na fazenda um pomar, com laranjeiras, mangueiras e jaqueiras. Ele cria também animais domésticos, como cavalos, vacas e cabras. Os cavalos são de montar. As vacas e cabras dão leite e carne para a família. Meus avós criam também galinhas e patos que põem ovos. E meu avô tem um cachorro que anda sempre com ele pela fazenda e guarda a casa de noite.

A maior parte do que a família e os empregados comem é da fazenda mesma. Há uma empregada que cozinha tudo para a casa.

Exercise A. Learn to say the following, using either the subjunctive or the infinitive:

1. Ele (nos) diz que sigamos atrás dele. — Ele diz para seguirmos atrás dele.
2. Eu peço que vocês me tragam um sorvete. — Eu lhes peço para trazerem um sorvete para mim.
3. Você permite que eu acenda a luz? — Você me permite acender a luz?
4. Nós aconselhamos que eles acordem cedo. — Nós lhes aconselhamos acordarem cedo.
5. Ele deixa que abramos a janela. — Ele nos deixa abrir a janela.
6. Nossos pais proíbem que tomemos cerveja. — Nossos pais nos proíbem tomar cerveja.
7. Ele manda que voltem amanhã. — Ele manda voltarem amanhã.
8. Eu prefiro que vocês brinquem lá fora. — (subjunctive only)
9. Queremos que eles calcem os sapatos. — (subjunctive only)
10. Desejo que guardem os livros. — (subjunctive only)
11. Ele manda que venhamos com você. — Ele nos manda vir com você.

Exercise B. Use of the infinitive:

1. Vocês não podem ir embora até tocarmos esta música. — You can't leave until we play this music.
2. Temos medo de entrar na loja. — We are afraid to enter the store.
3. Não queremos pagar até saber que a coisa é boa. — We don't want to pay until we know the article is good.
4. Antes de criarmos vacas, vamos plantar milho. — Before we raise cows, let's raise some corn.
5. Olhamos para a rua antes de atravessar. — We look at the street before we cross.
6. Depois de lermos este livro, vamos saber mais sobre o Brasil. — After we read this book, we are going to know more about Brazil.
7. Para ganharmos dinheiro, é preciso trabalhar. — In order to earn money, we must work.
8. Não gosto destes cachorros, por serem feios. — I don't like these dogs, because they are ugly.
9. Eles partiram sem sabermos. — They left without our knowing.
10. Quero saltar nesta esquina. — I want to get off at this corner.
11. Não aconselhamos fazer isso. — We don't advise doing that.
12. Prefiro não ficar. — I prefer not to stay.

Exercise C. Word usage. Be able to give in English from hearing the Portuguese:

1. Você tem razão quando diz que ele é feio.
2. Se ele nasceu nesta data, hoje é o aniversário dele.
3. Comemos laranjas, mangas e jacas.
4. A que horas a lua nasce hoje?
5. Este menino tem um dente nascendo.
6. Meu irmão tem cabelo castanho.
7. Existe muita coisa feia neste mundo. (Note sing. *muita coisa*)
8. Tenho que calçar os sapatos.
9. Essa moça tem olhos azuis.
10. Creio que aquele está olhando para mim.
11. Eu creio que sim. Você não acha?
12. Olha o cachorro!
13. Uma árvore é uma planta grande.
14. Ele não gosta deste lugar e eu também não gosto.
15. Em que dia você faz anos?
16. Quantos anos você faz hoje?
17. Alguma coisa não está no lugar.
18. Eu não nasci aqui; eu sou de outra parte.
19. Você gosta de montar a cavalo?
20. Ela cozinha sobre o fogo.

Exercise D. Say in Portuguese:

1. This hen laid an egg.
2. My grandparents live in the country.
3. I like fried eggs.
4. They cooked (= prepared) scrambled eggs on the fire.
5. My grandmother has brown hair.
6. Put on your shoes and come with us.
7. What do you eat for (= with) breakfast?
8. My plants have come up.
9. The sun has come up.
10. The moon rises at 9:30 p.m.
11. He says for us to come up.
12. Before dressing, we must take a bath. (tomar banho)
13. After hearing this, they called me.
14. He asks (for) you two to get him a dog.
15. Without finishing our work, we can't go.
16. I was able to leave without their forbidding it.
17. He said for us to keep the money.
18. We prefer to stay alone.
19. In order for me to read this book, a light is needed.
20. I heard the boys talking in the store.

Exercise E. Fill in blanks with the correct forms of the verbs in parentheses:

1. (olhar) Não querem que nós _____ para elas.
2. (calçar) Ele manda que eu _____ os sapatos.
3. (existir) Não permitem que essas coisas _____ .
4. (montar) O médico aconselha que você _____ a cavalo.
5. (criar) Proíbem que nós _____ cabras na cidade.

100

6. (cozinhar) Desejo que você _____ para nós.

7. (despedir-se) Prefiro que eles _____ de nós.

8. (demorar) Pedimos que eles não _____ .

9. (encher) Queremos que a garçonete _____ nossas xícaras,

10. (dormir) Não deixam que nós _____ .

Exercise F. Fill in blanks with the correct forms of the verbs in parentheses:

1. (ter) Mandaram-nos para cama antes de [nós] _____ sono.

2. (fazer) Era bom [nós] _____ uma viagem ao Rio.

3. (encontrar) Temos vontade de nos _____ com vocês lá.

4. (desligar) Pedi-lhes para _____ o rádio.

5. (nascer) Fica bonito de manhã depois do sol _____.

6. (vir) Tenho medo de eles _____ muito cedo.

7. (trazer) Eu já disse para vocês _____ os calções de banho.

8. (cansar) Estudamos até os olhos se _____ .

9. (ganhar) Para eu _____ , é preciso você me ajudar.

10. (poder) Na chuva ficamos sem _____ nos enxergar.

Exercise G. Say in Portuguese:

1. People don't do that.
2. He lives beyond the river.
3. We must move to another house.
4. They go (to) everywhere.
5. The sun always shone.
6. The boy is looking at the moon.
7. His eyes are black.
8. Were you born in this place?
9. When is your birthday?
10. His hair is ugly.

11. You are right and I am wrong.
12. He is [right over] there.
13. I don't believe it either.
14. He doesn't either.
15. Look at me!
16. I am [standing] between you.
17. It is [lying] on the table.
18. She has brown eyes and black hair.
19. He raises corn and okra.
20 The cows give us milk and meat.

Lesson XXIII

113. Irregular present subjunctives. The rule for forming the present subjunctive states that we use the first person singular of the present indicative and remove the final *o*, to find the stem of the present subjunctive. However, there are six verbs which do not have a final *o* in this form. In addition, the verb *querer* does not follow this rule. The present subjunctive of these seven verbs must be learned separately. Note further irregularities in the third person plural in two verbs, *dar* and *ir*.

	ser	estar	ir	dar	saber	querer
eu	seja /ê/	esteja /ê/	vá	dê	saiba	queira
você	seja	esteja	vá	dê	saiba	queira
ele	seja	esteja	vá	dê	saiba	queira
nós	sejamos	estejamos	vamos	demos	saibamos	queiramos
vocês	sejam	estejam	vão	dêem	saibam	queiram
eles	sejam	estejam	vão	dêem	saibam	queiram

The seventh verb is *haver*, which has not yet been studied.

114. The subjunctive of emotion. Any verb, or a combination of a verb with a noun or adjective, which expresses emotion, is followed by the subjunctive if the dependent verb has a subject which is different from that of the main verb. If the logical subject of the two verbs is the same, the impersonal infinitive is used, although it is often possible to use the subjunctive in these cases also.

Eu sinto que ele não possa ir.	I'm sorry he can't go.
Eu sinto não poder ir.	I'm sorry I can't go.
Eu sinto que eu não possa ir.	I'm sorry I can't go.

Some of the more frequently used expressions of emotion are the following:

sentir (que)	to be sorry (that), feel sorry (that), regret (that)
esperar (que)	to hope (that)
tomara (que)	I hope (that), would (that)
temer (que)	to fear (that
surpreende (-me) (que)	(I am) surprised (that), it surprises (me) (that)
ter pena (que)	to be sorry (that)
ter medo (que)	to be afraid (that)
É pena (que)	it's too bad (that)
estar contente (que)	to be glad (that)

The future subjunctive is *not* used after expressions of emotion; the present is used instead.

115. The past participle. Regular past participles are formed by adding *-ado* to stems of verbs of the first conjugation, *-ido* to those of the second and third conjugations.

falar	falado	spoken
comer	comido	eaten
ouvir	ouvido	heard

Unless used as part of a perfect tense, the past participle agrees with the noun or pronoun it modifies.

Essa língua é falada lá.	That language is spoken there.
É uma conversa ouvida na rua.	It's a bit of gossip heard on the street.

116. Irregular past participles. The following verbs already studied have irregular past participles:

vir	vindo	come
ganhar	ganho	won, earned
ver	visto	seen
entregar	entregue /é/	delivered
dizer	dito	said, told
pôr	posto /ô/ pl. and fem. /ó/	put, placed
fazer	feito	done, made
abrir	aberto /é/	open, opened
escrever	escrito	written

117. The passive voice. The passive voice is formed by the use of the auxiliary verb *ser*, followed by the past participle. The participle agrees with the subject in number and gender.

João foi chamado.	John was called.
A carta foi recebida.	The letter was received.
As bananas foram entregues.	The bananas were delivered.

Portuguese differs from other Romance languages in that the passive voice is used almost as frequently as in English. It is also important to remember that the auxiliary *ser* may be used with the past participle whenever the state denoted by the participle is permanent, without necessarily forming the passive voice.

There is a second construction which corresponds closely with the use of "get" in English with the past participle. The verb used in Portuguese is *ficar*.

Fiquei perdido.	I got lost.
Meu amigo ficou cansado.	My friend got tired.

Vocabulary

Nouns

a língua	tongue; language
a selva /é/	jungle
o mato	brush, low forest
a serra /é/	range (hills or mountains)
o morro /ô/	hill
o Rio	Rio
o Rio de Janeiro	Rio de Janeiro
o Rio Amazonas	Amazon River
o distrito	district
a capital	capital (city)
o centro	center
o leste /é/	east
o oeste /é/	west
o norte /ó/	north
o sul	south
a costa /ó/	coast
o mar	sea
o interior /ô/	interior
a planície /ísi/	plain
o país	country

Adjectives

federal	federal
nenhum, nenhuma	no
contente	glad, happy
grosso /ô/ pl. and fem. /ó/	thick

Nouns

a mata	forest
a geografia /jiu/	geography
a montanha	mountain

Verbs

cobrir (eu cubro p.p. coberto /é/	cover
crescer	grow
variar	vary
estender-se	extend
sentir	be sorry, regret
esperar	hope
tomara (*from* tomar)	I wish; would that
temer	fear
surpreender	surprise; be surprising to

Preposition

por causa de	because of

Adverbs

antigamente	formerly
até	even
daí	from there, from then on, thence

Expressions

ao norte daqui.	north of here
ao sul da cidade	south of town
a oeste da serra	west of the mountains
a leste do Paraná.	east of the Paraná
Ele está variando.	He's delirious.
Espera por ele.	Wait for him.
Tomara que chova.	I hope it rains.
Isso foi antigamente.	This was in the old days.
E daí?	So what?

Leitura

O Brasil tem vinte e dois estados, além de quatro territórios e um distrito federal. A capital, Brasília, fica no centro do país, no Distrito Federal. A leste da capital se acha o estado de Minas Gerais, que tem muitas montanhas. Algumas destas são mais ou menos altas, mas nenhuma está coberta de neve. A maior parte do estado era antigamente coberta de mato. Uma parte do sul é chamada a Zona da Mata, por causa das árvores altas que cresciam lá. Não tem selvas nesta parte do Brasil. A selva se encontra nos vales do rio Amazonas, do Paraná e do Paraguai. O Amazonas passa pelo norte do país, mas o Paraná e o Paraguai ficam no oeste e vão para o sul.

A geografia do Brasil é muito variada. Mesmo no Rio de Janeiro existem muitos morros e até uma serra. A Serra do Mar se estende ao longo de uma grande parte da costa do país. Longe no interior há planícies cobertas de mato. Daí vem o nome do estado de Mato Grosso. O rio Paraná passa entre este estado e São Paulo.

Exercise A. Read and repeat aloud:

1. No Rio tem muitas pessoas vindas de outros estados.
2. Há até muita gente de outros países.
3. Muitos deixam o Norte e vão morar no Sul.
4. Temos que subir a serra para ir do Rio a Minas.
5. Você conhece o Morro da Babilônia no Rio?
6. A serra não fica muito longe do mar.
7. Mata é mais alta do que mato.
8. A mata do vale do Amazonas se chama selva.
9. São Paulo fica a oeste do Rio.
10. Temos que estudar geografia.
11. A planície se extende pelo sul de Mato Grosso.
12. Antigamente o Rio era a capital do país.
13. Os territórios têm pouca gente.
14. Eu quero que você dê uma olhada no mapa do Brasil.
15. A mata não cobre todo o vale do Amazonas.

Exercise B. Be able to give either language from the other:

1. Uma pessoa vem. Espero que seja João.	Somebody's coming. I hope it's John.
2. Eu sinto que ele esteja doente.	I'm sorry he's sick.
3. Tomara que ele venha.	I hope he comes.
4. Ele teme que vamos embora.	He fears we'll leave.
5. Quero que você saiba isto.	I want you to know this.
6. É pena que ele não queira ajudar.	It's a shame he won't help.
7. Surpreende-me que eles ainda estejam aqui.	I'm surprised they are still here.
8. É pena que eles não saibam quem você é.	It's too bad they don't know who you are.

9. Estou contente que vão me dar café.　I'm glad they're giving me coffee.
10. Tenho medo de não ganhar.　I'm afraid of not winning.
11. Ele sente não poder ir amanhã.　He's sorry he can't go tomorrow.
12. Tomara que eu possa dormir bem.　I hope I can sleep well.
13. Eu sinto muito não conhecer o médico.　I'm very sorry I don't know the doctor.
14. Espero que não tenha muita gente lá.　I hope there won't be many people there.
15. Surpreende-me que não dêem para você　I am surprised they don't give you what they
　　o que lhe devem.　　owe you.

Exercise C. Past participles:

1. O português é a língua falada no Brasil
2. Tudo foi comido.
3. A voz de Maria foi ouvida por muita gente.
4. Conheci muitas pessoas vindas do Norte.
5. Este dinheiro foi ganho com o meu trabalho.
6. Dito e feito. (No sooner said than done.)
7. Não quero ser visto por ele.
8. Aquele embrulho já foi entregue?
9. Vi uma mesa posta para seis pessoas.
10. Uma porta aberta deixou a gente entrar.
11. Comprei uma coisa feita à mão. (by hand)
12. Ouvi uma coisa dita em voz baixa.

Exercise D. Fill blanks with correct forms of verbs in parentheses:

1. (ter) É pena que você _____ medo.
2. (seguir) Não quero que ele me _____ .
3. (cobrir) Temo que a neve _____ a serra até amanhã.
4. (trazer) Tomara que ele _____ o carro.
5. (ver) Esperamos que ele não nos _____ .
6. (pedir) Surpreende-nos que ele ainda _____ mais.
7. (vestir) Preferem que nos _____ de branco.
8. (subir) Proíbem que nós _____ o morro.
9. (caber) Sentimos que alguns não _____ no carro.
10. (surpreender) Temos medo que o frio nos _____ muito cedo.

Exercise E. Replace each of the underlined verbs with the correct form of each of the other verbs listed:

1. Ele sente que você não *ouça* a voz dele.
　　　　　a. (conhecer)　　o amigo dele.
　　　　　b. (olhar)　　para a gente.
　　　　　c. (responder)　　às perguntas.
　　　　　d. (almoçar)　　com ele.
　　　　　e. (fazer)　　uma viagem.

2. Eu espero que vocês *calcem* os sapatos.
　　　　　a. (vestir)　　os paletós.
　　　　　b. (crer)　　minha história.
　　　　　c. (ler)　　a lição.
　　　　　d. (trazer)　　os livros.
　　　　　e. (subir)　　a escada.

3. Tomara que ele *me diga* quem é.
          a. (perder)   o trem.
          b. (permitir)   que vão.
          c. (preferir)   ficar.
          d. (acordar)   na hora.
          e. (vir)   de avião.

4. Tememos que eles *nos apanhem* aqui.
          a. (entregar)   a roupa tarde.
          b. (ver)   Maria na rua.
          c. (não caber)   na sala.
          d. (não pôr)   a mesa
          e. (não poder)   ir.

5. Surpreende-lhe que você não *parta* cedo.
          a. (abrir)   a porta.
          b. (ir)   à igreja.
          c. (ser)   rico.
          d. (estar)   doente.
          e. (dar)   dinheiro.

6. É pena que nós não *falemos* português.
          a. (beber)   café.
          b. (saber)   tocar piano.
          c. (receber)   cartas dele.
          d. (ter)   dinheiro.
          e. (valer)   mais.

Exercise F. Say in Portuguese, using the subjunctive:

1. I prefer that you give me a glass of water.
2. He permits me to go.
3. He tells us to know the lesson.
4. We advise the children to be good.
5. We order him to listen to the radio.
6. I ask you to be there.
7. We want you to sleep late.
8. He is sorry we don't want [to].
9. I hope you (plural) will give him the pen.
10. We fear you will tell him.
11. It's too bad you prefer that [one.]
12. I am sorry you have to study.
13. Let me do that.
14. Tell him to put on his coat.
15. I'm surprised he doesn't miss his train.

Exercise G. Say in Portuguese, using the infinitive:

1. Tell him to do that.
2. I ask them to have lunch with me.
3. I want to see the boys before they go away.
4. He regrets our having to fix it.
5. They let me live with them.
6. We forbid their keeping the money.
7. He advised us to arrive early.
8. It is necessary for us to write [some] letters.
9. It was a pity they didn't get off the bus.
10. We came home after being at the theater.

Exercise H. Say in Portuguese:

1. Do you know a man named Pires?
2. This language is spoken in Brazil.
3. These books are written in Portuguese.
4. I have a chair made from a tree.
5. He had a coin won from a friend.
6. This book is called *The United States Seen by a Brazilian.*
7. She found three eggs laid by her hens.
8. The open door let them enter the house.
9. Here are two packages delivered by the boy.
10. I found the chalk covered by a paper.

Lesson XXIV

118. Verbs with infinitives in *-air*. The verb *sair* may serve as a model for all verbs whose infinitives end in *-air*, of which there are some fifteen.

	Present Indicative	*Preterit*	*Imperfect Indicative*	*Present Subjunctive*
eu	saio	saí	saía	saia
você	sai	saiu	saía	saia
ele	sai	saiu	saía	saia
nós	saímos	saímos	saíamos	saiamos
vocês	saem	saíram	saíam	saiam
eles	saem	saíram	saíam	saiam

Past participle: saído

With the exception of written accents, the only irregularities are found in the present indicative singular.

119. The subjunctive with impersonal expressions. There are very many impersonal expressions, generally formed with an impersonal verb and a noun or an adjective, expressing necessity, importance, inevitability, probability, etc. The impersonal verb is most frequently *ser* in the third person singular. Such expressions, whether affirmative or negative, regularly take the subjunctive in the following clause, if there is a subject that is not impersonal. If the impersonal expression indicates certainty, however, the *indicative* is used in a following clause.

É preciso que ele vá.	It is necessary that he go.
É necessário que eu saiba.	It is necessary for me to know.
É provável que eles cresçam.	It is probable that they will grow.
É seguro que eu vou.	It is certain that I'm going.
É preciso trabalhar.	It is necessary to work.

120. The infinitive with impersonal expressions. Most of these same impersonal expressions may be followed by the personal infinitive which becomes the logical subject of the third-person verb. The person of the infinitive may be clarified or emphasized by the use of a subject pronoun.

É preciso ele ir.	It is necessary for him to go.
É necessário eu saber.	It is necessary for me to know.
É possível encontrarmos com ele.	It is possible for us to run into him.
É urgente acharmos os meninos.	It is urgent for us to find the boys.

121. The subjunctive of doubt or disbelief. Any verb or other expression of doubt or disbelief is followed by a subjunctive. This includes expressions of belief if they are negative. In the affirmative, expressions of belief are followed by the indicative.

Eu creio que ele sabe.	I think he knows.
Achamos que eles tomam café.	We think they drink coffee,
Acredito que é verdade.	I believe it is true.
Não creio que ele saiba.	I don't think he knows.
Não acredito que seja verdade.	I don't believe it is true.

In practice, the subjunctive is often avoided by transferring the negative to the subordinate verb.

      Creio que ele não sabe.   I don't think he knows.

Expressions of doubt are followed by the subjunctive, whether they are affirmative or negative.

      Duvido que seja ele.   I doubt it is he.
      Não duvido que seja ele.   I don't doubt it is he.

In questions containing expressions of belief, the subjunctive may be used to express the *speaker's* doubt.

      Você crê que ele faz isso?   Do you believe he does that?
      Você crê que ele faça isso?   Do you really believe he does that?

Vocabulary

Nouns

a comida	food
o bife	steak
a carne de porco /ô/ pl. /ó/	pork
a vitela /é/	veal
o presunto	ham
a fruta	fruit
a maçã	apple
o pêssego	peach
o mamão	papaya
o morango	strawberry.
o abacaxi	pineapple
o açúcar	sugar
o sal	salt
a refeição	meal (dinner, etc.)
o prato	plate, dish
a faca	knife
o garfo	fork
a colher /é/	spoon
o chá	tea

Adjectives

incrível	incredible
(in) justo	(un) just
lamentável	lamentable, unfortunate
(im) possível	(im) possible
(im) provável	(im) probable

Nouns

o feijão	beans
a cozinha	kitchen; cuisine

Verbs

sair	go out, come out
sair (de)	leave
cair	fall
atrair	attract
acreditar (em)	believe (in)
duvidar	doubt
viver	live (be alive)
fritar	fry
haja (*subj. of* há)	there is, there are

Adjectives

necessário	necessary
inevitável	inevitable
(in) desejável	(un) desirable
difícil	unlikely
fácil	likely
importante	important
aconselhável	advisable
urgente	urgent
seguro	certain, sure
cozido	boiled, stewed
mal passado	rare
bem passado	well done

Leitura

No Brasil, como em outros países, a gente geralmente come três vezes por dia. Pela manhã a gente toma café com leite e come pão com manteiga. Algumas pessoas preferem frutas, que lá são muito boas. Há frutas em todos os meses do ano, porque não faz frio na maior parte do país. Há sempre frutas tropicais, como a laranja e a banana. Durante uma parte do ano há também abacaxis, morangos, pêssegos e mamão. As maçãs geralmente vêm de outros países.

Ao meio-dia a gente almoça. Esta refeição também é uma parte importante da comida brasileira. Os que trabalham na cidade podem comer um bife com batatas fritas e legumes. Mas em casa o almoço geralmente é mais variado. O bife é a carne que os brasileiros preferem, mas comem bastante carne de porco também. O presunto e a vitela se encontram mais nos restaurantes do que em casa.

Exercise A. Be able to give the Portuguese at a natural speaking pace:

1. Eu saí de casa às oito.	I left the house at eight.
2. Sai daí!	Get out of there!
3. O trem sai da estação.	The train leaves the station.
4. Vi muita gente entrando e saindo.	I saw lots of people going in and coming out.
5. Se este livro sair bem, vai ser publicado.	If this book turns out well, it will be published.
6. Seu filho saiu bem no exame?	Did your son pass the examination?
7. João não está; já saiu.	John isn't here; he has gone out.
8. A maçã caiu da árvore.	The apple fell off the tree.
9. Uma coisa caiu lá de cima.	Something fell from up there.
10. Os meninos caíram em cima do sorvete.	The kids fell on (ate up) the ice cream.
11. Vamos cair na água.	Let's take a dip.
12. Nessa eu não caio.	I won't fall for that one.
13. É uma coisa que não me atrai.	It's something that doesn't attract me.
14. Isto não atrai os olhos da gente.	This doesn't attract attention.
15. O professor distraído esqueceu a aula.	The absent-minded professor forgot his class.

Exercise B. Give the following using the infinitive:

1. É preciso que você espere.
2. Acho necessário que eles se conheçam.
3. É inevitável que você seja chamado.
4. É desejável que ele mande consertar o carro.
5. É possível que encontremos visita em casa.
6. É importante que vocês saibam isto.
7. É incrível que meu primo não responda à minha carta.
8. É improvável que jantemos em casa.
9. É urgente que eu arranje um médico.
10. É lamentável que ele esteja doente.

Exercise C. Give the following, using the subjunctive:

1. É preciso estarmos em casa hoje.
2. É injusto termos que trabalhar sem ganhar.
3. É fácil explicarem a licão, se quiserem.
4. É desejável os meninos ficarem em casa.
5. É provável acharmos o jantar preparado.
6. É necessário fazermos o trabalho.
7. Não é importante eu tomar este trem.

Exercise D. Use of reflexives:

1. No inverno a terra se cobre de neve.
2. Cozinham-se arroz e feijão.
3. Os sapatos devem calçar-se.
4. Os morangos se compram barato.
5. Ganhava-se muito dinheiro nesse trabalho.
6. Onde se acham flores para comprar?
7. Isso não se deve comer.
8. A que horas se abrem as portas?
9. Perdeu-se um chapéu.
10. A carne se vende pelo quilo.

Exercise E. Fill in the correct form of the verb in parentheses:

1. (compreender) Tomara que João _____ .
2. (almoçar) Esperamos que você _____ conosco.
3. (chegar) Temem que nós _____ tarde.
4. (beber) Sinto que você não _____ leite.
5. (andar) Preferem que eu _____ por aqui.
6. (apanhar) Temos medo que a chuva nos _____ .
7. (ouvir) Peço que você me _____ .
8. (conhecer) Surpreende-me que ele não _____ você.
9. (cobrir) Aconselho que vocês _____ a mesa.
10. (ficar) É pena que eles não _____ .

Exercise F. Fill in blanks with the past participles of the verbs in parentheses, making necessary changes for agreement:

1. (falar) Uma língua _____ .
2. (dizer) Palavras _____ em voz alta.
3. (deitar) Pessoas _____ no chão.
4. (crescer) Um menino _____ .
5. (cobrir) Pratos _____ .
6. (tocar) Música _____ na vitrola.
7. (crer) Histórias _____ pelo povo.
8. (escrever) Livros _____ em português.
9. (pôr) Mesas _____ na sala de jantar.
10. (fazer) Sapatos _____ à mão.
11. (entregar) Embrulhos _____ para casa.
12. (ganhar) Tempo _____ .
13. (ver) Luzes _____ ao longe.
14. (dar) Andando de mãos _____ .
15. (cair) Neve _____ durante a noite.

Exercise G. Say in Portuguese:

1. He left the house early.
2. When is the book coming out?
3. Let's get into the water.
4. This street used to attract people.
5. It is impossible for us to go.
6. It is urgent that we get home.
7. It is incredible that he would sell it.
8. Do you believe it is worth the trouble?
9. We doubt he'll miss dinner.
10. Lots of potatoes are eaten in this country.
11. I came out well on the exam.
12. Go in and don't come out.
13. I fell on the sidewalk.
14. A well-set table attracts the kids.
15. It is likely he will find us.
16. It is important to know this.
17. There is no doubt he will ask for it.
18. I don't think he'll do it.
19. It's unlikely he'll catch it.
20. This is the money that was owed to John.

Exercise H. Say in Portuguese:

1. I want pork for (= *no*) dinner.
2. She put a knife, a fork and a spoon at each plate.
3. I like pineapples better than oranges.
4. We live well, eating meat, beans, rice, and fruit.
5. He prefers fried potatoes.
6. Did you put salt on your vegetables?
7. In Bahia the food is very good.
8. Today we have apples, peaches, and bananas.
9. This coffee has too much sugar.
10. Brazilian cooking uses lots of rice and beans.
11. We eat three meals a day.
12. The rice is better than the bread.
13. I doubt that you will like this veal.
14. These strawberries came from São Paulo.
15. We are going to have coffee in the living room, if you wish.

Lesson XXV

122. The irregular verbs *rir* and *sorrir*.

	Present Indicative	Preterit	Imperfect Indicative	Present Subjunctive
eu	rio	ri	ria	ria
você	ri	riu	ria	ria
ele	ri	riu	ria	ria
nós	rimos	rimos	ríamos	riamos
vocês	riem	riram	riam	riam
eles	riem	riram	riam	riam

All forms are regular except the present indicative. *Sorrir* is conjugated exactly like *rir*, with *sor-* prefixed to each of its forms.

123. The imperfect subjunctive. The forms of the imperfect subjunctive of *any* verb may be derived from the third person plural of the preterit. The letters *-ram* are removed, and the endings *-sse, -ssemos,* and *-ssem* are added. The vowel before the ending is always that of the preterit form. The first person plural requires a written accent on this vowel.

	falar	*comer*	*abrir*	*ser*
singular form (eu, você, ele)	falasse	comesse	abrisse	fosse /ô/
nós	falássemos	comêssemos	abríssemos	fôssemos
vocês, eles	falassem	comessem	abrissem	fossem

124. Use of the imperfect subjunctive. This tense is used instead of either the present or future subjunctive whenever the verb of the main clause is in any past tense. The choice of the imperfect is purely a matter of the sequence of tenses.

a. If the main verb is in the present or future tense, or in the imperative, the subjunctive in a dependent clause will be in the present (or in the future in the cases previously given).

111

b. If the main verb is in any past tense (including the conditional), the subjunctive of the dependent clause will be in the imperfect.

c. In certain cases the expression of emotion, although put in the present tense may be the result of a condition which existed in the past. In such cases, the imperfect subjunctive may follow a present tense.

Eu quero que você vá comigo.	I want you to go with me.
Eu queria que você fosse comigo.	I wanted you to go with me.
Ele sente que você esteja doente.	He's sorry you are ill.
Ele sentia que você estivesse doente.	He was sorry you were ill.
Ele sente que você estivesse doente.	He is sorry you were ill.

125. Subjunctive in adverbial clauses. The subjunctive is used in many dependent adverbial clauses (those introduced by an adverbial conjunction).

a. Following adverbial conjunctions of time, the subjunctive is used if the dependent clause refers to future action or condition. The futurity may be either in relation to present time or to the time of the main verb.

It must be remembered that, following certain of these conjunctions, the future subjunctive is used. Following others, the present must be used. Some conjunctions permit the use of either, but in these cases BF prefers the future. The following conjunctions are regularly followed by the future subjunctive, after a main verb in the present or future, if futurity is implied.

quando	when
enquanto	while, as long as

The following may be followed by either the present or the future, but BF usually prefers the future.

logo que	as soon as
assim que	as soon as
depois que	after

The following may only be followed by the present.

antes que	before
até que	until

b. Following an adverbial conjunction of concession (*although, even if*), the present subjunctive (never the future) must be used, whether or not the statement of the following verb is factual. The main conjunctions of this type are:

embora	although, even if
ainda que	although, even if
posto que	although, even if

c. Following an adverbial conjunction of purpose, the present subjunctive is used, after a present or future tense.

para que	in order that, so that, so
a fim de que	in order that

d. Following an adverbial conjunction of result, the subjunctive is used only if purpose is also implied. Otherwise, the verb is in the indicative.

de maneira que	so that, in such a way that, so
de modo que	so that, in such a way that, so
de jeito que	so that, in such a way that, so

In all cases, following a past tense, a subjunctive in the dependent clause will be in the imperfect tense.

Vocabulary

Nouns

o jeito	way, manner
a espécie	kind
a pedra /é/	rock, stone
o futebol /ó/	soccer
o time	team
o pássaro	bird
a cana (de açúcar)	cane
o pedaço	(broken) piece
a terra /é/	land, earth
a foto (grafia)	photo (graph)
o chão	ground; floor
o dedo /ê/	finger; toe

Conjunctions

antes que	before
até que	until
embora /ó/	although
ainda que	although
posto que /ô/	although

Adjectives

seguinte /si/	following
próximo (x = /s/)	next
passado	past, last
juntos	together
só or sozinho /ó/	alone

Conjunctions

para que	in order that, so that
de maneira que	so that, in such a way that
de modo que /ó/	so that
de jeito que	so that

Verbs

rir	laugh
sorrir	smile
cortar	cut
pagar	pay
sentar (-se)	sit down
descer	come down, go down
começar (a)	begin (to)
chupar	suck

Adverb

só	only, just

Expressions

Domingo passado	last Sunday
No ano seguinte	the next year
No ano que vem	next year
Ele começa a estudar.	He begins to study.
Tomara que eu pudesse.	I wish I could.
Tirei uma foto.	I took a picture.
Tiraram a mesa.	They cleared off the table.

Exercise A. *Rir* and *sorrir:*

1. Ela tem olhos que riem.   She has laughing eyes.
2. Ela está (se) rindo de mim.   She is laughing at me.
3. Ela (se) ri destas idéias.   She laughs at these ideas.
4. Ele falou sorrindo.   He spoke smiling(ly).
5. Meu amigo sorria da minha simplicidade.   My friend smiled at my simplicity.
6. O menino sorriu para mim.   The child smiled at me.

Exercise B. Note the constructions in the following sentences:

1. Os meninos gostam de chupar cana de   The kids like to suck sugar cane.
   açúcar.
2. Vocês comem laranjas, mas nós chupamos.   You eat oranges, but we suck them.
3. Os rapazes estão jogando futebol.   The boys are playing soccer.
4. O meu time ganhou.   My team won.
5. Tirei uma foto de vocês.   I took a picture of you.
6. Um pedaço de papel caiu no chão.   A piece of paper fell on the floor.
7. Você não sente frio sentado lá no chão?   Don't you feel cold sitting there on the floor?
8. Vou mandar cortar o cabelo.   I'm going to have my hair cut.
9. Senta aqui e espera até que ele venha.   Sit here and wait until he comes.
10. Vamos andando, embora ainda tenhamos   Let's be going, although we still have time.
    tempo.
11. Vamos juntos à festa?   Shall we go to the party together?
12. Ou você prefere ir sozinho?   Or do you prefer to go alone?
13. Você quer outra coisa? —Não. É só.   Do you want something else? No, that's all.
14. Vou lá na quinta e volto no dia seguinte. I'm going there Thursday and I'll come back
                                                  the following day.
15. Já estive lá no ano passado.   I was there last year.

Exercise C. Give the imperfect subjunctive in the same person and number as the following present subjunctives:

1. Que ele peça.   11. Que eu leia.
2. Que nós durmamos.   12. Que nós saiamos.
3. Que eu almoce.   13. Que ele viva.
4. Que eles permitam   14. Que vocês tragam
5. Que você valha   15. Que eu saiba.
6. Que ele ouça.   16. Que eles vejam.
7. Que eu diga   17. Que nós ponhamos
8. Que nós venhamos   18. Que ele dê.
9. Que eles prefiram.   19. Que você queira.
10. Que você cresça.   20. Que eles vão.

Exercise D. Put in the blanks the correct forms of the words in parentheses:

1. (falar) Eu lhe disse que [ele] _____ português.
2. (querer) Ele não acreditou que eu _____ ir.
3. (ter) Ele pedia que nós _____ pena dele.
4. (ser) Ele preferia que eles _____ amigos.
5. (fazer) Deixávamos que ele _____ o trabalho.
6. (estar) Eu sentia que você _____ doente.
7. (morar) Tomara que você _____ perto de mim.
8. (ler) Esperávamos que você _____ o jornal de hoje.

114

9. (escutar) Eu temia que ele me _____ .
10. (conhecer) Surpreendia-me que ele me _____ .
11. (chegar) Era preciso que você _____ cedo.
12. (vender) Era importante que eles _____ a casa.
13. (deixar) Era urgente que nós _____ a cidade.
14. (divertir-se) Era provável que vocês _____ nas férias.
15. (sentar-se) Foi necessário que eu _____ no chão.
16. (vir) Eu disse que esperava enquanto ele não _____ .
17. (querer) Ele sabia que podia sair quando _____ .
18. (voltar) Eu pedi que me chamasse logo que _____ .
19. (chover) Ele me disse que ia à cidade, embora _____ .
20. (poder) Abri a porta para que eles _____ entrar.
21. (cair) Puseram a água em cima da porta, de maneira que _____ sobre ele.
22. (querer) Ele não pôde vir, posto que _____ .
23. (estar) Eu disse a você que não devia chamá-lo quando _____ falando.

Exercise E. Change the following sentences to past time (Note: some sentences may not remain in the subjunctive):

1. Você pode ir quando quiser.
2. Vocês vão ficar aqui enquanto formos à cidade.
3. O inverno fica feio enquanto não nevar.
4. Eu vou deitar assim que subir ao quarto.
5. Ele vai abrir a porta depois que ouvir as vozes de fora.
6. Você deve se vestir antes que desça à sala.
7. Vamos sair antes que ele chegue.
8. Não podemos sentar até que os senhores se sentem.
9. Ele não é muito novo, embora jogue futebol.
10. Dou dinheiro aos meninos para que se divirtam.

Exercise F. Idiomatic usages:

1. Ele janta comigo na sexta que vem.	He has dinner with me next Friday.
2. Sábado passado foi dia de chuva.	Last Saturday was a rainy day.
3. Aquelas duas andam sempre juntas.	Those two are always together.
4. Ele jogou uma pedra em mim.	He threw a rock at me.
5. Cortei o dedo com uma faca.	I cut my finger with a knife.
6. Paguei o almoço dos dois.	I paid for lunch for the two of them.
7. Paguei vinte cruzeiros por isto.	I paid Cr$20,00 for this.
8. Senta aqui, por favor.	Sit down here, please.
9. Não acho lugar para (me) sentar.	I can't find a place to sit.
10. Você quer descer com este embrulho?	Will you take this package down?
11. Ele está descendo a escada.	He is coming downstairs.
12. Diverte-se na feira.	Have fun at the market.
13. Isto é bom de chupar o dedo.	This is finger-licking good.
14. Não tem jeito de fazer isso.	There's no way to do that.
15. De jeito nenhum!	Not at all! (No way!)
16. Temos que dar um jeito para arranjar um carro.	We must find a way to get a car.
17. Ele ficou sem jeito.	He was embarrassed.
18. Meu tio é muito jeitoso.	My uncle is very skillful.
19. O nosso mundo é a Terra.	Our world is the earth.

20. Este rapaz é da minha terra.
21. Isto é uma espécie /spés/ de brinquedo.
22. Que espécie de carro você tem?
23. Meu livro está caindo aos pedaços.

This fellow is from my part of the country.
This is some kind of toy.
What kind of car do you have?
My book is falling to pieces.

Exercise G. Say in Portuguese:

1. Let's find a way to (= de) speak to them before they leave.
2. He took off his hat and smiled at her.
3. Don't laugh at me just (= só) because I am ugly.
4. She smiled at (de) my story, but she didn't smile at (para) me.
5. He threw his shoe on the floor.
6. Cut the bread so we can eat it.
7. We can leave if you will pay for the coffee.
8. Come down the hill to see our team play.
9. There were pieces of paper on the ground.
10. I took a picture of a bird on the house.
11. He lives in a kind of stone house.
12. The boy was sucking his thumb. (= dedo)
13. Have a good time while you are here.
14. Won't you sit down and wait a bit?
15. He loves to suck sugar cane.
16. What kind of book are you reading?
17. Are you beginning to learn?
18. I can't find a way to fix this.
19. He ate (tomou) his ice cream with a spoon.
20. What is the difference between smiling and laughing?

Exercise H. Say in Portuguese:

1. Catch him before he goes up [stairs].
2. If I miss the bus, I'll have to walk.
3. We are not going to give it to him until he asks us [to].
4. He feels well, although he fell off the ladder.
5. I told (falei) him about it in such a way that he could not understand it.
6. We are going in my car, even though we don't fit [into it] very well.
7. He works so that his children can eat.
8. Next year we are going to travel, even if we don't have much time.
9. (In) last year, he played soccer.
10. So you don't want to get married?
11. I gave him a present so he would think of me on his birthday.
12. Sit down so that you can rest.

Lesson XXVI

126. The irregular verb *haver*.

	Present Indicative	Preterit	Present Subjunctive
eu	hei	houve	haja
você	há	houve	haja
ele	há	houve	haja

nós	havemos	houvemos	hajamos
vocês	hão	houveram /é/	hajam
eles	hão	houveram /é/	hajam

The imperfect indicative is regular. The future and imperfect subjunctive may be derived from *houveram.*

127. Uses of *haver.* Although it is derived from the Latin verb meaning "to have," this verb never has that meaning in BF.

The third person singular forms in the various tenses of the indicative and subjunctive are used to mean "there is (are)," "There was (were)" etc. In addition, all forms of the present and imperfect may be used as auxiliaries of the future and conditional as explained below. Only the third person singular of the preterit is used nowadays.

The word *há,* when followed by a noun or expression of a period of time, means "ago."

Há dois anos   Two years ago

128. The expression of futurity in Portuguese. We have already taken up two methods of expressing the future—the use of the auxiliary *ir,* and the simple present. There are two others. All are used in the colloquial as well as the literary language.

The simple future tense is formed by adding the endings *-ei, -á -emos, -ão* to the full infinitive of the verb. The same endings are used in all three conjugations.

	falar	*comer*	*abrir*
eu	falarei	comerei	abrirei
você	falará	comerá	abrirá
ele	falará	comerá	abrirá
nós	falaremos	comeremos	abriremos
vocês	falarão	comerão	abrirão
eles	falarão	comerão	abrirão

Three verbs add these endings to shortened forms of the infinitive.

fazer	farei, etc.
trazer	trarei, etc.
dizer	direi, etc.

The present tense of the verb *haver,* followed by *de* and the infinitive, forms a periphrastic future tense. This form may have the meaning "He is to speak, he is supposed to speak," etc., but is often exactly equivalent to the simple future. The forms are as follows:

	falar
eu	hei de falar
você	há de falar
ele	há de falar
nós	havemos de falar
vocês	hão de falar
eles	hão de falar

The least used in BF is the simple future. The verbs which have only one syllable preceding the ending—*serei, 'starei, terei, irei, farei,* etc.—are heard fairly frequently; longer verbs are used much less in this form. But all the four constructions are perfectly natural in BF. See exercises for examples.

129. The conditional tense. The conditional represents two quite different meanings, both in English and in Portuguese. For example, it may represent futurity after a verb in past time. Compare:

> He says we will do it.
> He said we would do it.

On the other hand, it is essentially a different mood of the verb in conditional sentences, such as

> If I were you, I wouldn't do it.

There are four ways to express the conditional in Portuguese, similar to those expressing futurity.

a. The imperfect indicative. This is by far the most frequent way, and can be used in all cases.

Ele disse que vinha.	He said he would come.
Se eu fosse você, não fazia isso.	If I were you, I wouldn't do that.

b. The imperfect of *ir* with the infinitive may be used, if the conditional stands for the future in sequence after a verb in a past tense, but not elsewhere. This usage corresponds to English.

Ele diz que vai voltar.	He says he is going to return.
Ele disse que ia voltar.	He said he would (was going to) return.

c. The simple conditional tense. This tense is formed by adding the endings *-ia, -ia, -íamos, -iam* to the infinitive (with the same three short forms mentioned above).

	falar	*comer*	*abrir*
eu	falaria	comeria	abriria
você	falaria	comeria	abriria
ele	falaria	comeria	abriria
nós	falaríamos	comeríamos	abriríamos
vocês	falariam	comeriam	abririam
eles	falariam	comeriam	abririam

d. The imperfect indicative of *haver,* followed by *de* and the infinitive, forms a conditional tense. The meaning may be simply the conditional or there may be also connotations of of expectation, previous agreement, etc., as with the similar construction of the future.

falar	havia de falar, etc. I would speak
dizer	havia de dizer, etc. I would say.

The simple conditional (*falaria,* etc.) is very little used in BF, except in those verbs which have only one syllable before the ending. Even in these the imperfect is used more or less as often as the conditional. The construction *eu ia falar* is used in practically the same way as in English. *Eu havia de falar* is used quite frequently, but often carries connotations in addition to the basic meaning of the conditional.

130. Placing of personal pronoun objects with the future and conditional. Formerly the pronoun objects were in many cases placed between the infinitive and the endings in the simple future and conditional.

Falar-me-á	He will speak to me.
Di-lo-ei.	I shall say it.
Ver-se-iam.	They would see each other

118

This construction is becoming rather unusual even in literary style. In BF it is totally absent. In fact, it is practically unintelligible to Brazilians, if used in speech. The objects *me, nos, lhe, lhes,* and *se* should always be placed before the future and conditional. A subject pronoun may be used in order to avoid beginning the clause with an object pronoun.

Ele me falará.	He will speak to me.
Eles se veriam.	They would see each other.

The object pronoun may follow the infinitive in those constructions in which the infinitive is a separate word. However, it is more usually placed between the forms of *ir* and the infinitive.

Eles haviam de ver-se.	They would see each other.
Eles vão me dizer.	They are going to tell me.

The other object pronouns —*você, o senhor. ele,* etc. —are placed after all verb forms, as if they were nouns.

Eu disse que levaria você.	I said I would take you.

Vocabulary

Nouns

a rede /ê/	net; network; hammock
o quarto	(bed) room
a cor /ô/	color
o trabalhador	worker
o sotaque /su/	(foreign) accent
o garoto /ô/	boy
o jogo /ô/	game
pl. jogos /ó/	

Adjectives

japonês	Japanese
forte /ó/	strong
carioca (m. and f.) /ó/	from Rio
limpo	clean
sujo	dirty
alegre /é/	jolly, cheerful
pobre /ó/	poor
moreno	dark (complexion)
profissional	professional
simpático	nice, agreeable

Preposition

apesar de	in spite of

Nouns

o lixo	trash
o escândalo	loud talk, quarrel
o bicho	animal
o ar	air

Verbs

haver	(see above)
mexer	stir, mix
escolher	choose, pick, select
caçoar (de)	tease
armar	set up
conversar	chat
procurar	look for; try to
cantar	sing
custar	cost
queimar	burn
tocar	play (music); ring (bell); touch

Adverbs

primeiro	first
aliás	besides; or rather

Expressions

Armar uma rede.	To put up (hang) a hammock.
Armar um escândalo.	To raise a fuss.
Custa-me crer.	It's hard for me to believe.
Alto, moreno e simpático.	Tall, dark, and handsome.
Tocar piano.	To play a (the) piano.

Leitura

Amanhã irei à casa de meus tios, que moram numa fazenda. Primeiro telefonarei para eles para dizer a que horas chegarei lá. Quando eu chegar, escolherei uma rede das várias que eles têm em casa, para armar num dos quartos da casa. Depois de conversar com os tios e primos, sairei para procurar os lugares bonitos que eu lembro das outras visitas. Espero que tudo esteja como era, porque eu gosto de ver os pássaros de cores brilhantes que cantam nas árvores da fazenda.

Há vários trabalhadores que moram na fazenda. Um deles é um japonês que planta legumes. Apesar dos muitos anos que mora no Brasil, ele ainda fala português com um forte sotaque. Aliás, meus tios sempre caçoam do meu sotaque carioca, que é diferente do jeito de falar deles.

Custa-me crer que há dez anos eu jogava futebol aqui com os outros garotos. Saíamos de casa limpos e alegres e, depois do jogo, voltávamos para casa sujos e cansados. Geralmente perdíamos, porque os filhos dos trabalhadores são fortes e jogam muito bem. Havia um deles, um moreno, que ficou conhecido nos jogos profissionais.

Exercise A. Study the following examples of constructions expressing the future and conditional and their equivalents:

1. Mexerei a sopa para que não se queime.   I'll stir the soup so it won't burn.
   Vou mexer a sopa para que não se queime.
   Hei de mexer a sopa para que não se queime.
   Mexo a sopa para que não se queime.

2. Eles escolherão os lugares logo que chegarem. They will pick their places as soon as they arrive.
   Eles vão escolher os lugares logo que chegarem
   Eles hão de escolher os lugares logo que chegarem.

3. Armarão uma rede em baixo de uma árvore.   They will put up a hammock under a tree.
   Vão armar uma rede, etc.
   Hão de armar uma rede, etc.

   (No clue to futurity would permit *armam,* unless the context of the conversation makes it clear.)

4. Ele achava que choveria de tarde.   He thought it would rain in the afternoon.
   Ele achava que havia de chover.
   Ele achava que chovia.
   Ele achava que ia chover.

5. Se eu estivesse no seu lugar, jogaria isso no lixo.   If I were in your place, I'd throw that in the trash.
   eu jogava isso no lixo.
   eu havia de jogar isso no lixo.
   (*ia jogar* would mean "I would go and . . .")

120

6. Ela não faria isso nunca.   She would never do that.
  Ela não fazia isso nunca.
  Ela não havia de fazer isso nunca.

7. Só queria era ver a cara dele.   I'd just like to see his face.
  (only imperfect used here).

8. Se quisesse, eu teria uma rede.   If I wanted to, I'd have a hammock.
  Se quisesse, eu tinha uma rede.
  (*Havia de ter* implies insistence.)

9. Eu gostaria de viajar.   I'd like to travel.

(In this meaning, "I'd like," only the conditional is used *with this verb*. But the imperfect is usual if the verb is *querer*.)

Exercise B. Idiomatic usages:

1. A mulher armou um escândalo.   The woman raised a fuss.
2. Não mexe nas minhas coisas.   Don't bother my things.
3. Põe açúcar no café e mexe.   Put sugar in the coffee and stir it.
4. Por que está se mexendo na cadeira? Why are you fidgeting in the chair?
5. Queimei um dedo no fogo.   I burned my finger in the fire.
6. Todo mundo caçoa de mim.   Everybody teases me.
7. Custa crer que você seja ruim.   It's hard to believe you are bad.
8. Estou procurando meus sapatos.   I'm looking for my shoes.
9. Ele procura sempre estar limpo.   He always tries to be clean.
10. Mostra a mão!   Show (stick out) your hand.
11. Antes de haver gente no mundo, havia Before there were people in the world, there
  bichos.   were animals.
12. Muitos brasileiros gostam do jogo do Many Brazilians like the animal lottery.
  bicho.
13. Tem bichos do ar, bichos da terra e There are animals of the air, the land, and
  bichos do mar.   the sea.
14. Tem até bichos tão pequenos que não There are even creatures so small they can't
  se vêem.   be seen.
15. Ele é alto, moreno e simpático.   He is tall, dark and handsome.
16. Em garoto, eu jogava pedras nos As a boy I threw stones at the birds.
  pássaros.
17. Vocês conhecem a canção "A Garota Do you know the song "The Girl from Ipa-
  de Ipanema"?   nema"?
18. Eu tenho dois, aliás três bons amigos. I have two, or rather, three good friends.
19. Apesar de ser pobre, ele está sempre In spite of being poor, he is always cheerful.
  alegre.
20. Você tem um pouco de sotaque americano. You have a little bit of American accent.
21. Esta maçã está bichada.   This apple is wormy.

Exercise C. Change the underlined verb to an appropriate past tense and make any other necessary changes:

1. Eu *quero* que você ria.
2. *Mando* que vocês venham da escola ao meio-dia.
3. Ele *proíbe* que joguem futebol na rua.
4. Ela *diz* que trará o filho quando vier.
5. Eu *peço* que me dêem uma hora para estudar.

121

6. *Aconselhamos* que sorriam mais quando falarem com ele.

7. *Prefiro* que me paguem logo.

8. *Espero* que nos divirtamos enquanto estivermos lá.

9. *Temo* que você caia dessa árvore.

10. Ele não *fala* muito, embora saiba muito para falar.

11. *Sinto* que você não escolha os melhores livros.

12. *Vamos* procurar o colega antes que ele suma.

13. Ele nos *vende* laranjas quando houver.

14. *Arranjaremos* um quarto para o senhor logo que pudermos.

15. Ela *canta* aqui hoje, se chegar a tempo.

Exercise D. Give the future and imperfect subjunctives corresponding to the present subjunctives which follow, in the same person and number:

	Future Subjunctive	*Imperfect Subjunctive*

1. Haja

2. Vocês mexam

3. Você caçoe

4. Nós queimemos

5. Eu arme

6. Eu desça

7. Ele jogue

8. Eles riam

9. Eu me divirta

10. Você viva

11. Ele caia

12. Eu sinta

13. Vocês leiam

14. Ele siga

15. Ele traga

Exercise E. Pronounce the following, giving special care to the stressed vowels:

1. Joga	10. Eles conversam	19. A pedra
2. O jogo	11. Houvesse	20. O leste
3. os jogos	12. Que eu mostre	21. O oeste
4. Eles cortam	13. Que ele caçoe	22. A costa
5. Ele desça	14. Alegre	23. O pêssego
6. Eu começo	15. Carioca	24. A vitela
7. Eles se divertem	16. Forte	25. Os olhos
8. Eu mexo	17. Avó	
9. Vocês escolham	18. Espécie	

Exercise F. Say in Portuguese:

1. Tomorrow I'll speak to him.

2. There will be a lot of people at the party.

3. He is going to live on a little farm.

4. I'm afraid they'll laugh at my accent.

5. If I were you, I'd play soccer.

6. I hope you aren't going to burn your hand on that fire.

7. He raised a ruckus because he lost the game.

8. It would be very hard (= *custar*) to choose between the two.

9. If you put up a hammock here, it will be very hot.
10. He is a native of Rio. (Say in two words.)
11. She is very happy; she met a tall, dark and handsome man.
12. After searching for a long time, the boys found the paper in the trash.
13. I will learn a lot, in spite of the professors.
14. He will begin working there tomorrow.
15. They will enjoy themselves when they go to the beach.
16. I hope it won't be very cold tomorrow.
17. When he was a boy he would play a lot.
18. Would you do something for me?
19. He believed I would explain this to him.
20. If I could, I would (do it).
21. We wanted to see him before he saw us.
22. I thought you would light a fire.
23. When you get back, our Japanese friend will be living here.
24. We'll be fixing the cars when you get here.
25. He will always be poor, but he is very happy.

Lesson XXVII

131. Verbs formed on the stem *-duzir*. This root does not exist in Portuguese as a verb, but numerous compounds of it do exist. They all have one irregular form; the third person singular of the present indicative has lost the final *e*. All other forms are regular.

Ele produz.	He produces.
Ele reduz.	He reduces.
Você induz.	You induce.

Other verbs formed on this root are given in the vocabulary, below.

132. The perfect tenses. The perfect tenses are formed by using the simple tenses of the verb *ter* as auxiliaries of the past participle. The verb *haver* may be used theoretically, and it occurs in literary style, especially in the imperfect. But BF always uses *ter*. The participle is invariable when used with *ter* or *haver*.

	Present Perfect Indicative	*Pluperfect Indicative*	*Future Perfect Indicative*
eu	tenho falado	tinha falado	terei falado
você	tem falado	tinha falado	terá falado
ele	tem falado	tinha falado	terá falado
nós	temos falado	tínhamos falado	teremos falado
vocês	têm falado	tinham falado	terão falado
eles	têm falado	tinham falado	terão falado

Conditional Perfect: teria falado, etc.

The preterit of *ter* is not used as an auxiliary.

		Present Perfect subjunctive	*Pluperfect Subjunctive*	*Future Perfect Subjunctive*
eu		tenha falado	tivesse falado	tiver falado
você		tenha falado	tivesse falado	tiver falado
ele		tenha falado	tivesse falado	tiver falado
nós		tenhamos falado	tivéssemos falado	tivermos falado
vocês		tenham falado	tivessem falado	tiverem falado
eles		tenham falado	tivessem falado	tiverem falado

Perfect infinitive:

impersonal	ter falado	to have spoken
personal	(eu) ter falado	(for me) to have spoken,
	(você) ter falado	etc.
	(ele) ter falado	
	(nós) termos falado	
	(vocês) terem falado	
	(eles) terem falado	

Perfect active participle: tendo falado

133.   English equivalents of the perfect tenses. Most of the perfect tenses correspond rather closely to the tenses of the English verb. But one must distinguish in some cases.

a. The present perfect in English is usually expressed by the preterit in Portuguese.

Eu (já) falei.   I have spoken.

The compound tense is used in Portuguese when the action or condition is either *continuous* or *continual* in the recent past. It comes up to, but does not specifically include, the present. There is no general equivalent in English, but often the best means of expressing the meaning is the progressive form of the present perfect.

Como é que você tem estado	How have you been?
Que é que ele tem feito?	What has he been doing?
Tenho ido à cidade com freqüencia.	I have been going downtown frequently.
Temos viajado na Europa.	We have been (for some time) traveling in Europe.

But note:

Eu já viajei na Europa várias vezes.	I have traveled in Europe several times.
Ele mora nesta cidade há sete anos.	He has been living in this city for seven years. (and still does.)

b. The pluperfect or past perfect is used as in English,

Eu já tinha acabado o trabalho.   I had already finished my work.

c. The future perfect tense has the same meaning as in English, but is used somewhat more, and also more than the simple future indicative in Portuguese.

Até segunda-feira terei acabado.   By Monday I will have finished.

d. The conditional perfect is used somewhat more than the simple conditional in Portuguese, but is often replaced by the pluperfect indicative.

Se eu tivesse visto o João, teria falado
   com ele. (tinha falado com ele.)

If I had seen John, I'd have spoken to him.

e. The three perfect tenses of the subjunctive in Portuguese are usually expressed in the indicative in English. Since the future perfect is seldom used in English, the meaning is usually expressed by the present perfect. But if futurity is implied, after certain conjunctions, the form *must* be the future perfect in Portuguese.

Espero que ele já tenha chegado.	I hope he has already arrived.

Você não deve sair antes que tenha
   acabado de jantar.
	You shouldn't go out before you have
	   finished eating.

Sentimos que ele tivesse perdido a festa.	We were sorry he had missed the party.

Vamos sair quando você tiver acabado o
   jantar.
	We are going out when you have finished
	   eating.

Ele irá conosco assim que se tiver vestido.	He will go with us as soon as he has dressed.

Note that all three perfect tenses of the subjunctive are in current use in BF.

134.   Verb forms used after the conjunction *se*.

a. If the verb following *se* expresses habitual action or state (the most usual meaning of the simple present indicative), the present indicative is used in Portuguese. The present subjunctive is *not* used after *se*.

Se ele dá com um amigo, sempre fica
   conversando.

If he runs into a friend, he always stops to
   talk.

b. In the past, if the verb following *se* expresses an admitted fact or a possible fact, the indicative is used.

Se ele dava com um amigo, sempre
   ficava conversando.
	If he ran into a friend, he always stopped to
	   to talk.

Se ele esteve em casa ontem, ninguém
   viu.
	If he was at home yesterday, nobody saw
	   him.

c. A contrary-to-fact supposition is expressed in the imperfect subjunctive.

Se desse tempo, eu iria.	If there were time, I'd go.
Se ele fosse rico, gostaria de viajar.	If he were rich, he'd like to travel.

d. An assumption or supposition concerning possible future action may be expressed in the imperfect subjunctive, following *se*. The main clause is in the conditional or imperfect indicative.

Seria (era) gozado se ele nos apanhasse aqui.	It would be funny if he caught us here. (were to catch, should catch)
Se eu fosse à Europa, visitava (visitaria) Portugal.	If I were to go to Europe, I'd visit Portugal.

e. If the verb following *se* refers to action or condition which will or may exist in indefinite future time, the future subjunctive is used, if the main verb is in the present or future.

Você pode ir amanhã, se quiser.

You may go tomorrow if you wish.

125

f. When *se* is followed by alternatives, one or the other of which is true (the meaning of "whether"), only the indicative is used.

Não sei se ele foi ou ficou.	I don't know whether he went or stayed.
Ainda não me disseram se ele vai ou não vai.	They haven't told me yet whether he is going or not.

Vocabulary

Nouns

o namorado	boy friend
a namorada	girl friend
o coração	heart
o noivo	fiancé; groom
a noiva	fiancée, bride
os Estados Unidos	United States
a máquina	machine
a perna /é/	leg
a dor /ô/	pain; grief
a chave	key

Adjectives

louro	blond
lindo (*superlative of* bonito)	beautiful
firme	firm, steady
último	last (of all)

Adverb

ultimamente	lately

Nouns

o curso	course
a encrenca	difficulty; "mess"
a arquitetura	architecture
a companhia	company
o contrato	contract

Verbs

produzir	produce
reduzir	reduce
conduzir	conduct, lead
reproduzir	reproduce
introduzir (em)	lead into, introduce (into)
induzir (a)	induce (to)
pertencer (a)	belong (to)
apresentar	present (play); introduce (man)
namorar	"go with," "date"
gastar pp. gasto	spend (money)
quebrar	break
faltar	be lacking
sonhar (com)	dream (about)
agüentar	stand (pain); hold firm; endure
formar	form; graduate
formar-se	be graduated

Expressions

Ficaram noivos.	They got engaged.
Em fins do mês	About the end of the month
Ele se formou em filosofia.	He graduated in liberal arts.
Ela faltou à aula.	She missed class.
Ela matou a aula.	She cut class.
Pelo menos	At least

Leitura

Meu amigo Waldemar tem uma namorada loura e linda. Quando se viram pela primeira vez, ele lhe deu logo o coração. Como não conhecia a família da moça nem pertencia ao grupo de amigos da casa, pediu que eu fosse lá com ele e apresentasse. Depois eu introduzi o Waldemar na roda que os amigos da família formavam.

Acho que Waldemar sonhou com a moça depois desse primeiro encontro. Pelo menos, sei que os dois começaram a namorar. Dentro de poucos meses ficaram noivos. Dizem que vão casar logo que ele acabar o curso na universidade e se formar. Deve formar-se em fins deste ano, se não houver encrencas.

Waldemar é estudante de arquitetura. Depois de formado vai trabalhar para uma companhia de arquitetos que tem contratos em Mato Grosso. Os noivos vão morar em Cuiabá, capital do estado. É uma cidade pequena, mas uma que deve crescer muito nos próximos anos. Só que fica muito longe dos grandes centros culturais do país.

Exercise A. Verbs in -*duzir*. Give each sentence with the verb in the preterit tense:

1. Estas terras produzem muito café.
2. Por que você não introduz a música brasileira aqui?
3. Ele me induz a falar aos estudantes.
4. De tudo isso, deduzimos que ela é sua namorada.
5. Meu dinheiro se reduz a muito pouco.
6. Eu conduzo este grupo pela escola.
7. Esta máquina reproduzirá o que você escreveu.

Exercise B. Uses of the perfect tenses of the indicative:

1. O João tem contado esta história em toda parte.
   John has been telling that story everywhere.
2. Ele tem ganho e gasto bastante dinheiro.
   He has been making and spending quite a bit of money.
3. Tem feito um tempo bonito ultimamente.
   The weather has been pretty lately.
4. Você tem visto o Luiz?
   Have you seen Louis (lately)?
5. Quantas horas você tem dormido nestas últimas semanas?
   How many hours have you been sleeping these last few weeks?
6. Você tem passeado no carro de seu pai?
   Have you been going driving in your father's car?
7. Tenho sonhado com você todas as noites.
   I have dreamed about you every night.
8. Ele quebrou a perna e tem sentido muita dor.
   He broke his leg and has been feeling a lot of pain.
9. Há quanto tempo você está estudando?
   How long have you been studying?
10. Nós já nos encontramos muitas vezes.
    We have already met many times.
11. Quando procurei o João, ele já tinha saído.
    When I looked for John, he had already gone out.
12. Terei entrado em casa antes da chuva cair.
    I will have gone into the house before the rain comes down.
13. Ele vai trabalhar no ano que vem, quando já se terá formado.
    He is going to work next year, when he will have graduated. (definite future time.)
14. Se tivéssemos gasto o dinheiro, não teríamos podido comprar isto.
    If we had spent the money, we couldn't have bought this.
15. Eu já teria feito essa viagem, se tivesse tido tempo.
    I would have taken that trip already, if I had the time.

Exercise C. The perfect tenses of the subjunctive:

1. Eu espero que não tenha faltado nada a você.
   I hope you have lacked nothing.
2. Sentimos que você tenha perdido o livro.
   We are sorry you have lost your book.
3. Ele não quer crer que eu tenha ganho tanto.
   He doesn't want to believe that I have earned so much.

127

4. Era importante que você tivesse recebido a carta a tempo.

It was important that you had received (should have received) the letter on time.

5. Eu não achava que ele tivesse aprendido português.

I didn't think he had learned Portuguese.

6. Era possível que eles tivessem visto você.

It was possible they had seen you.

7. Fiquei com pena que Maria tivesse quebrado a caneta.

I was sorry Mary had broken the pen.

8. Quando você tiver jantado, vamos sair.

When you have eaten, let's go out.

9. Irei a sua casa depois que tiver entregue este embrulho.

I'll go to your house after I have delivered this bundle.

10. Leva esta chave, caso tiverem fechado a porta.

Take this key in case they have locked the door.

Exercise D. If-clauses and conditional sentences:

1. Se você está com fome, come isto.

If you're hungry, eat this.

2. Se eu deito tarde, fico com sono no dia seguinte.

If I go to bed late, I'm sleepy the next day.

3. Eles podem se casar, se quiserem.

They can marry if they wish.

4. Se você não agüentar firme na escada, cai.

If you don't hold on to the ladder, you'll fall.

5. Se você pertencesse à turma, podia entrar.

If you belonged to the gang, you could come in.

6. Se nevasse nesta terra, tudo era diferente.

If it snowed in this country, everything would be different.

7. E se fôssemos assar esta carne?

What if we were to roast this meat?

8. Se eu arranjasse um café, você tomava?

If I got some coffee, would you drink it?

9. Nós morávamos lá se pudéssemos.

We'd live there if we could.

10. Até amanhã terei recebido a carta dele, se me mandou.

I'll have gotten his letter by tomorrow, if he sent it to me.

11. Se João falou sobre isto, eu não ouvi.

If John spoke about this, I didn't hear him.

12. Se eu respondesse assim, meu pai não gostava.

If I answered like that, my father wouldn't like it.

13. Se tivéssemos sabido disso, não teríamos falado.

If we had known about that, we wouldn't have spoken.

14. Se fossem pedir uma coisa dessas, ninguém dava.

If they were to ask for one of those things, nobody would give it.

15. Se o cinema já tiver começado, vamos esperar.

If the movie has already begun, let's wait.

16. Não pode sair enquanto fizer frio.

You can't go out while it's cold.

Exercise E. Say in Portuguese:

1. He induced me to reduce the cost (*custo*).
2. I want to introduce this music into the United States.
3. It is necessary for this farm to produce more.
4. He conducted me to the living room and introduced me to his mother.
5. I have reproduced the photograph you gave me.
6. Reduce the number of pages we are to study.
7. I have been missing class during the past week.
8. This school has graduated many doctors.
9. Have you already spent your money?
10. Those two have been going together, and now they are going to get engaged.

11. He has a steady (*firme*) girl friend.
12. What have you been doing lately?
13. He had broken his leg and had to endure the pain.
14. The last time (that) we saw him, he had produced a new book.
15. I'll have finished it before you can say two words.
16. If he belongs to that family, he is your cousin.
17. If he graduates next year, he is going to get married.
18. The bride and groom are going to live here, if they can buy the house.
19. If I had this contract, I'd begin work next month.
20. If you were to miss class, I'd have the lesson reproduced for you.
21. What did you graduate in?
22. Who(m) do you work for?
23. This job is hard, but we have to stand it.
24. I hope there won't be [any] difficulties with this company.
25. I don't believe he has learned [very] much.

Lesson XXVIII

135. Forms of verbs in *-ear*. Verbs whose infinitive ends in *-ear* add an *i* following stressed *e*. The affected forms of *passear* are

	Present Indicative	*Present Subjunctive*
eu	passeio	passeie /êyi/
você	passeia	passeie
ele	passeia	passeie
nós	passeamos /siã/	passeemos /siẽ/
vocês	passeiam	passeiem
eles	passeiam	passeiem

The verb *odiar* is conjugated similarly.

Indicative: odeio, odeia, odiamos, odeiam.
Subjunctive: odeie, odiemos, odeiem.

All verbs in *-ear*, but only a few others in *-iar* are conjugated in this way. Only the present indicative and subjunctive and the imperative are affected.

136. Verbs in *-uir* and *-oer*. Verbs whose infinitives end in these spellings (except those like *seguir*, in which the *u* does not represent a sound) have an orthographic irregularity in the third person singular of the indicative. The vowel of the ending is written *-i*, to indicate that it forms a diphthong with the preceding vowel.

instruir: ele instrui
doer: isso dói

Note that *construir* and *destruir* are radical changing and therefore have the forms *constrói* and *destrói* respectively:

137. Position of object pronouns with verbs in the perfect tenses. The object pronouns are placed with respect to the auxiliary *ter* in the perfect tenses. They are not connected with a hyphen when they follow *ter*. In BF there is also a strong tendency to place the object between the two parts, even when a negative or conjunction precedes.

Têm me dito.	They have told me.
Não lhe tinha dado.	He had not given to him.

138. The relative pronouns.

a. *Que* is the most frequently used relative pronoun. It may refer to persons or things, singular or plural, and may be subject or object.

b. *Quem* as a relative pronoun is most often used to include its antecedent. It may be translated "he who," "anyone who," "the one who." In this usage it is always singular.

Quem pergunta aprende.	He who asks learns.
Ele anda como quem tivesse se perdido.	He walks like someone who got lost.
Quem pedir receberá.	He who (whoever) asks will get.
Quem deve ganhar sou eu.	I'm the one who should win.

Quem is also used as a simple relative pronoun when it is the object of a preposition, always referring to a person or persons. This usage is generally avoided in BF. In some cases, the idea is expressed in a different form. Frequently the preposition is omitted and *que* is used. This construction is not approved by normative grammar, but is very frequent in BF. *Quem* used in this way may be either singular or plural, but *without change of form.*

Aquele é o senhor com quem eu jantei.	That is the gentleman with whom I ate dinner.
É uma pessoa que eu gosto. (*Literary:* de quem)	He's a person I like.
Aqui vem o homem que eu dei o dinheiro. (*Literary:* a quem)	Here comes the man I gave the money to.

c. *O que (a que, os que, as que)* is properly a combination of a demonstrative pronoun, *o* (the one, that), with the relative *que*. The singular is sometimes equivalent to *quem*, but generally refers to a more specific person or thing. The form *o que* is also used as a neuter, equal to the English relative *what.*

Aqui está seu carro, mas não estou vendo o que deixei aqui.	Here's your car, but I don't see the one I left here.
Os que vão embora pensam voltar.	Those who go away intend to return.
Quero ver o que você tem.	I want to see what you have.

d. *O qual (a qual, os quais, as quais)* is practically limited to literary usage, often after prepositions, sometimes for clarity when the antecedent is not the last noun mentioned.

Há uma casa velha lá, em frente da qual se acha um chafariz.	There is an old house there, in front of which there is a fountain.
Encontrei com a mãe de João, a qual tem estado doente.	I met John's mother, who has been ill.

139. The subjunctive in relative clauses. The subjunctive is used in relative clauses whenever the antecedent of the relative pronoun is not a known, predetermined person or thing, but any one which may fit the conditions stated in the sentence. It is also used if the antecedent is negative or otherwise shown to be nonexistent.

Eu não gostaria de um homem que fizesse tal coisa.	I wouldn't like a man who did (might do, would do) such a thing.
Quero arranjar um carro que não me dê encrencas.	I want to get a car that won't give me trouble.
Não tem ninguém que possa fazer isso.	There isn't anyone who can do that.

If the relative pronoun may refer to *any or all* of the individuals named by the antecedent, and the action refers to the future, the future subjunctive is used. Otherwise, one uses the present. The future is more or less equivalent to the meaning expressed in English by *whoever, whichever, whatever,* etc.

Quem quiser comer terá que trabalhar.	Whoever wants to eat will have to work.
O homem que tiver este número ganha o prêmio.	The man (whoever) who has this number wins the prize.
A moça que casar com ele terá sorte.	The girl that marries him will be lucky.

In any of these sentences, if a past tense is used in the main clause, the present or future subjunctive will be replaced by the imperfect.

Ele disse que quem quisesse comer teria que trabalhar.	He said that anyone who wanted to eat would have to work.

Vocabulary

Nouns

a criança	child
o prêmio	prize
o chafariz	fountain
o restaurante /tô/	restaurant
a toalha	towel
a toalha de mesa	tablecloth
a areia	sand
a praia	beach
o castelo /é/	castle
o fato	fact
a peteca /é/	a game (with a bird struck with the hand)

Adjectives

tal *pl.* tais	such (a)
apinhado (de)	crowded (with)
antigo	ancient; former

Adverb

lá de cima	from above

Nouns

a piscina	swimming pool
a ceia	supper
a bicicleta /é/	bicycle

Verbs

passear	drive, ride, walk, etc. for pleasure
odiar	hate
pentear	comb
nadar	swim
parar (ele pára)	stop
espalhar	spread, scatter
dirigir	direct; drive (car)
dirigir-se a	go to

Prepositions

feito[1]	like
segundo[2]	according to
como[3]	like

131

Expressions

Passear de carro.	Go driving.
Passear a pé.	Go walking
Passear de bicicleta.	Take a bike ride.
Passear a cavalo.	Go horseback riding.
Eu gostaria que (gostava *not used*)	I'd like for . . .
Eu queria que (quereria *little used*)	I'd like for . . .
De fato.	In fact.
Um antigo patrão meu.	A former boss of mine.
Uma cidade antiga.	An ancient city.
Feito (um) gato.	Like a cat.
Como um gato.	Like a cat.

Notes on prepositions:

[1] *Feito* is in origin a past participle and should agree. But it is used in BF as a preposition, without agreement. It is followed by the subject forms.

[2] *Segundo* may only be followed by *subject* forms which may accompany a verb in the third person.

[3] *Como* is a conjunction. It is used like the English preposition *like,* but is followed by the subject form of a pronoun.

Leitura

Amanhã vamos dar um passeio na praia. Eu gostaria de passear de bicicleta, porque podíamos parar onde quiséssemos. Vou vestir o calção de banho para ver se achamos um bom lugar para nadar. Eu gosto de nadar numa piscina, mas prefiro a praia. Se encontrarmos amigos, pode ser que fiquemos até de noite.

Você acha bom jantarmos perto da praia? Um pouco para cá da avenida que se estende ao longo do mar há um bom restaurante. Fica em frente daquele chafariz na praça. Segundo o Pedrinho, a comida é boa lá. Espero que tenhamos sorte.

Durante a parte da manhã tem muitas crianças na praia. De fato, as praias do Rio ficam apinhadas de gente. É até difícil às vezes encontrar um lugar para cair na àgua. A gente estende toalhas na areia e deita para tomar o sol. As crianças constroem castelos e cidades na areia, correm pela praia, ou jogam peteca. Às vezes é até difícil atravessar a praia para chegar até a água.

Exercise A. Examples of usage:

1. Os cariocas passeiam no parque.	The *cariocas* stroll in the park.
2. Vamos passear a pé ao longo da praia.	Let's walk along the beach.
3. Eu penteio o cabelo antes de sair.	I comb my hair before I go out.
4. Ele odeia as cobras.	He hates snakes.
5. Por que você não nada feito eu?	Why don't you swim like me?
6. O ônibus pára aqui.	The bus stops here.
7. Não tivemos a sorte de ganhar o prêmio.	We weren't lucky enough to get the prize.
8. Deita na areia como os outros.	Lie down on the sand as the others (do).
9. Segundo você, esse deve ser um bom restaurante.	According to (what) you (say), that must be a good restaurant.
10. Ela viu um homem alto e louro, como eu.	She saw a tall blond man, like me.
11. Você sabe dirigir?	Do you know how to drive?
12. Eu gostaria que você me ajudasse.	I'd like for you to help me.

132

Exercise B. Relative pronouns:

1. Quais são os homens que você viu?
2. Foi alguma coisa que caiu lá de cima.
3. Eram fatos que tínhamos esquecido.
4. Quem vai fazer isso sou eu.
5. Ele olha para fora como quem quer sair.
6. Estou numa encrenca sem quem me ajude.
7. Quem partiu foi o João.
8. Encontrei o Carvalho, por causa de quem (BF= e por causa dele) estou chegando tarde.
9. Os que nunca estudam nunca aprendem muito.
10. Fui apanhado pela chuva, o que me fez esperar.
11. Não sei o que ele tem na mão.
12. Ele casou com a irmã de Pedro, a que estudou nos Estados Unidos.

Exercise C. Fill each blank with an appropriate relative pronoun:

1. Conheci um homem baixo＿＿＿＿＿＿ não sabia inglês.
2. João assou uma galinha ＿＿＿＿＿＿ ficou deliciosa.
3. A moça com ＿＿＿＿＿＿fui ao cinema mora em Ipanema.
4. O meu antigo patrão para＿＿＿＿＿＿ trabalhei deixou a cidade.
5. ＿＿＿＿＿＿ passeou de carro foi Davi.
6. ＿＿＿＿＿＿ quiser nadar pode.

Exercise D. Express the following sentences in such a way as to avoid the use of literary relative pronouns:

1. É uma encrenca difícil, apesar da qual temos que continuar.
2. Você está vendo aquela serra, atrás da qual fica a cidade?
3. O homem com quem encontrei hoje é meu primo.
4. Qual é a pessoa em quem você está pensando?
5. Você conhece a moça para quem estou olhando?
6. Tivemos um bom jantar, depois do que fomos para casa.
7. Vi vários amigos na livraria, entre os quais o Jorge.
8. O meu professor de primeiro ano, de quem não me lembro mais, foi morar noutra cidade.
9. A pessoa de quem recebi esta carta está na Europa.
10. Esta é a escola à qual eu vou.

Exercise E. Fill each blank with the correct form of the verb in parentheses:

1. (saber) Não há ninguém que não ＿＿＿＿＿isto.
2. (poder) Há alguém que＿＿＿＿＿ dirigir este carro?
3. (assar) Estou procurando a Maria, que＿＿＿＿＿ a carne bem.
4. (comer) Nunca vi um rapaz que ＿＿＿＿＿ tanto.
5. (parecer) Lá conheci uma moça que＿＿＿＿＿ com você.
6. (querer) Todo o homem que ＿＿＿＿＿jantar deve escrever o nome aqui.
7. (nadar) Quem ＿＿＿＿＿nesta piscina tem que usar calção.
8. (ouvir) Ele falou tão baixo que não houve quem ＿＿＿＿＿ .
9. (cair) Quebrou-se o copo que＿＿＿＿＿ de lá.
10. (vir) Ele estava preparado para o que＿＿＿＿＿ .

Exercise F. Say in Portuguese:
1. He hates (the) dogs.
2. Comb your hair and put on your shoes.
3. The pool is [over] beyond the hill.

4. The square in front of the fountain was crowded with people.

5. He climbs like a cat.

6. They scattered bread on the ground.

7. He drives like a professional.

8. We ate lunch on the sand of the beach.

9. Do you take a towel when you go bathing?

10. I don't have any luck today.

11. I have never seen such children.

12. He is a former colleague of mine.

Exercise G. Say in Portuguese:

1. This is the uncle I told you about.

2. What you need is a new maid.

3. I wonder what he took with him.

4. Whoever does a thing like that will be caught.

5. You are the one that has to do the work.

6. If you are caught in the rain, call at the door you are in front of.

7. We went bicycle riding with the fellow you have heard about.

8. I will do whatever you say.

9. He wants to buy a house that has large windows.

10. I'm looking for a restaurant that has (= gives) scrambled eggs for breakfast.

11. There is not a room in this hotel that doesn't have two windows.

12. I want a shoemaker that can fix my shoes.

13. I don't want a milkman that comes early.

14. According to John, the boys are to wear bathing trunks.

15. Even John swims like a fish (= *peixe*).

Lesson XXIX

140. The subjunctive with relative adverbs. Each of the relative adverbs *como, quando, onde, quanto* is given an indefinite meaning referring to any manner, time, place or quantity, when the subjunctive follows. The subjunctive is nearly always future (or imperfect). In some instances in which the reference is to one situation which will fulfill stated conditions, the present is used.

Você fará isso como quiser.	You will do that as you wish.
Vem a minha casa quando puder.	Come to my house when (ever) you can.
Compraremos balas onde acharmos.	We'll buy candy wherever we find it.
O sr. pode cantar quanto quiser.	You may sing all you wish.
Quero um hotel onde possa ir à ̀praia.	I want a hotel where I can go to the beach.

141. The subjunctive with *talvez* and similar words. Any verb modified by *talvez* or synonymous words or expressions which *precede* it, is in the subjunctive. If such words follow, the verb is in the indicative. The future subjunctive is not used.

Talvez o João jante conosco.	Perhaps John will have dinner with us.
Quiçá queira assistir à reunião.	Perhaps he wants to attend the meeting.
Pode ser que chova amanhã.	Maybe it'll rain tomorrow.
João está em casa, talvez.	John is at home, perhaps.

142. Subjunctive in indirect commands, suggestions to third persons, etc. The subjunctive is used when one suggests or orders that a third-person subject perform an act. The English equivalent is *let*.

Se ele quiser ir embora, que chame um taxi.	If he wants to go away, let him call a cab.
Se os meninos estão com fome, que venham comer.	If the boys are hungry, let them come to eat.

143. Such expressions as "Let it be as it may." In these expressions the present subjunctive is used in the first part, followed by the future. Both forms are put in the imperfect to express past time.

Seja como for, não gosto da situação.	Let that be as it may, I don't like the situation.
Chame quem chamar, não atendo.	Let anybody (who will) call, I won't answer.
Corra quanto correr, não vai pegar o cachorro.	Let him run as much as he will, he won't catch the dog.
Fosse como fosse.	Let that be as it might.

144. Diminutives and augmentatives. BF uses very many diminutives and quite a lot of augmentatives. Many of these must be learned with care, since the connotations, the choice of suffix in each case, and the form of the suffix may vary.

The most frequently used of the suffixes forming a diminutive is *-(z) inho*. It is applied freely to almost any noun or adjective, and sometimes to other words. A final unaccented vowel is dropped before *-inho*. The form *-zinho* is added to the entire word in the following cases:

a. After words ending in a diphthong, oral or nasal.

mãe	mother	mãezinha	little mother, dear mother
boi	ox	boizinho	little ox.

b. After a final accented vowel, oral or nasal.

irmã	sister	irmãzinha	little sister
pá	spade	pazinha	little spade

c. After final *-l*.

animal	animal	animalzinho	little animal

d. After final *-r*. In the pronunciation of most Brazilians, the final *-r* is silent, leaving a final stressed vowel.

dor	pain	dorzinha	little pain
par	pair	parzinho	little pair

But: devagar   devagarinho *or* devagarzinho

The plurals of diminutives are formed from the plurals of the nouns and adjectives, and have all the changes found in those plurals.

cão	cãezinhos	animal	animaizinhos
lição	liçõezinhas	pires	pirezinhos

All diminutives which are formed freely on the base words and which are felt as diminutives
also retain the quality of the vowel which was stressed in the base word, even though certain
vowels are not normally heard in unstressed syllables.

copo /ó/	glass	copinho /ó/	little glass
pé	foot	pezinho /é/	little foot

The most frequently used augmentative suffix is *-ão*, sometimes preceded by any one of several syllables to give it reinforced vigor. The feminine form is *-ona*, but many feminine nouns
that do not denote persons take masculine augmentative endings.

a mesa	table	o mesão	large table
grande	large	grandalhão, f. grandalhona	huge
a casa	house	o casarão	mansion
carro	car	carrão	big car
bonito	pretty	bonitão, bonitona	very handsome

Vocabulary

Nouns

as balas	candy
a reunião	meeting
o táxi /ks/	taxi
a situação	situation
o boi	ox
a pá	spade
a dor /ô/	pain
o par	pair; partner (dancing)
o Carnaval	Carnival
o desfile	parade
a sede /é/	seat, base
a fantasia	costume
o passo	step
povo /ô/ pl. /ó/	people
sócio	member
a dança	dance

Adverbs

talvez /ê/	perhaps
quiçá (literary)	perhaps

Adjective

popular	popular, of the people
oficial	official

Nouns

a Quaresma /é/	Lent
a Páscoa	Easter
o compositor	composer
o samba	samba
a marcha	march (music)
a canção	song
a organização	organization
o, a habitante	inhabitant
a atividade	activity

Verbs

reunir-se	meet, gather
atender	take care of, answer
preceder	precede
compor	compose
lançar	launch, throw
aceitar	accept
p.p. aceito, aceitado	
promover	promote
desfilar	parade
dançar	dance
planejar	plan
assistir a	be present at, attend (once)
concorrer	compete

Expressions

Pode ser que ele venha.	Maybe he'll come.
Ele atende os fregueses.	He takes care of customers.

Leitura

Para o carioca o grande feriado e a grande festa do ano é o Carnaval. O povo se prepara durante meses para os três dias oficiais (precedidos de vários dias não oficiais) desta festa tradicional. Vem logo antes da Quaresma uns quarenta dias antes da Pascoa. Nos morros o povo compõe sambas e marchas que tenta lançar para ver se são aceitos pelo público como as canções mais populares do Carnaval.

Em vários morros do Rio existem "Escolas de Samba," que são organizações dos habitantes do morro para promover as atividades do desfile de Carnaval. Cada escola tem uma sede onde os sócios se reúnem para preparar-se para desfilar, cantando e dançando, durante os dias oficiais. Planejam e fazem as fantasias que vão usar. Tocam as músicas que preferem, practicam os passos das danças e se preparam para concorrer aos prêmios dos desfiles.

Exercise A. Fill each blank with a correct form of the verb in parentheses:

1. (existir) Não creio que tal coisa _____ .
2. (promover) Vão escolher o homem que o patrão _____ .
3. (lançar) Não há ninguém que _____ este livro.
4. (aceitar) Talvez você _____ este presente.
5. (ir) Eu sigo você a toda parte onde _____ .
6. (compor) Estas pessoas talvez _____ a classe.
7. (desfilar) Esteja na praça amanhã quando a escola de samba _____ .
8. (vir) Tira a água daí e _____ uma cerveja.
9. (ser) Seja como _____ , perdemos o nosso tempo.
10. (reunir-se) Vou falar com ele sobre isto quando nós _____ .

Exercise B. Say in Portuguese, using the subjunctive or the infinitive, or both when possible:

1. George told them to dance.
2. It was impossible for us to stay in town.
3. I don't think I'll go to the movies tonight.
4. He ordered us to parade in front of him.
5. He sat down so that he could rest.
6. We sucked oranges until we lost our thirst.
7. I wish I had a piece of sugar cane.
8. Let's not leave before the game ends.
9. Read you lesson in [such a] way [as] to learn it.
10. They will come after they eat breakfast.

Exercise C. Say in Portuguese:

1. He has been living here six months.
2. I have never seen you till now.
3. They have paid what they owed.
4. It has been very cold these last [few] weeks.
5. You should have this dress washed.
6. He will have to help me.
7. We will tell you about him when we get back, if we have seen him.
8. If I had done that, I would have told you.
9. I can't talk to him unless he will see me.
10. If you were to call him, you might be able to see him.
11. Maybe he will stay at home tomorrow.
12. He doesn't like horses, although he lives on a farm.
13. I would have introduced him if I had remembered his name.
14. Every time we have seen John lately, he has been watching TV.
15. Had I known that I wouldn't have gone.

Exercise D. Say in Portuguese:

1. There is not a man here who can do it.
2. Do you have a friend who speaks Portuguese?
3. The one who opens the door will be surprised.
4. That river fills [up] when it rains.
5. Anyone who wishes [to] may go.
6. We will find the dog wherever it may be.
7. Whoever intends to go with us had better get ready.
8. What you will see is a little house.
9. To whom did you give the hammock?
10. Here's the fellow I lent the bicycle to.

Exercise E. Give a diminutive form of each of the following words:

1. Cadeira	6. Flor	11. Preto
2. Homem	7. Carro	12. Baixo
3. Inglês	8. Ruim	13. Velho
4. Manhã	9. Bom	14. Nova
5. Café	10. Boa (boazinha)	15. Papel

Exercise F. Give an augmentative form of each of the following words:

1. Sapato	6. Pé
2. Festa	7. Escada
3. Tempo	8. Gorda
4. Sala	9. Solteira
5. Dinheiro	10. Casa

Exercise G. Read each word aloud and give the corresponding third-person form:

1. Construo	11. Subo	21. Caio
2. Devo	12. Encho	22. Hei
3. Visto	13. Vôo	23. Caibo
4. Peço	14. Chego	24. Instruo
5. Morro	15. Ouço	25. Cubro
6. Pego	16. Valho	26. Trago
7. Perco	17. Sumo	27. Digo
8. Introduzo	18. Mexo	28. Faço
9. Passeio	19. Fecho	29. Sigo
10. Durmo	20. Despeço	30. Sei

Appendix

§145.   Conjugation of regular verbs. The following verbs are given in the traditional six forms in each tense, including the old second person forms used with *tu* and *vós*.

Impersonal infinitive.

falar	comer	abrir

Personal infinitive

eu	falar	comer	abrir
tu	falares	comeres	abrires
ele	falar	comer	abrir
nós	falarmos	comermos	abrirmos
vós	falardes	comerdes	abrirdes
eles	falarem	comerem	abrirem

Present participle

falando	comendo	abrindo

Past participle

falado	comido	aberto (irregular)

Present indicative

eu	falo	como	abro
tu	falas	comes	abres
ele	fala	come	abre
nós	falamos	comemos	abrimos
vós	falais	comeis	abris
eles	falam	comem	abrem

Preterit indicative

eu	falei	comi	abri
tu	falaste	comeste	abriste
ele	falou	comeu	abriu
nós	falamos	comemos	abrimos
vós	falastes	comestes	abristes
eles	falaram	comeram	abriram

Imperfect indicative

eu	falava	comia	abria
tu	falavas	comias	abrias
ele	falava	comia	abria
nós	falávamos	comíamos	abríamos
vós	faláveis	comíeis	abíeis
eles	falavam	comiam	abriam

Future indicative

eu	falarei	comerei	abrirei
tu	falarás	comerás	abrirás
ele	falará	comerá	abrirá
nós	falaremos	comeremos	abriremos
vós	falareis	comereis	abrireis
eles	falarão	comerão	abrirão

Conditional

eu	falaria	comeria	abriria
tu	falarias	comerias	abririas
ele	falaria	comeria	abriria
noś	falaríamos	comeríamos	abriríamos
vós	falaríeis	comeríeis	abriríeis
eles	falariam	comeriam	abririam

Simple pluperfect

eu	falara	comera	abrira
tu	falaras	comeras	abriras
ele	falara	comera	abrira
nós	faláramos	comêramos	abríramos
vós	faláreis	comêreis	abríreis
eles	falaram	comeram	abriram

Imperative mood

fala (tu)	come (tu)	abre (tu)
falai (vós)	comei (vós)	abri (vós)

Present subjunctive

que eu	fale	coma	abra
que tu	fales	comas	abras
que ele	fale	coma	abra
que nós	falemos	comamos	abramos
que vós	faleis	comais	abrais
que eles	falem	comam	abram

Imperfect subjunctive

eu	falasse	comesse	abrisse
tu	falasses	comesses	abrisses
ele	falasse	comesse	abrisse
nós	falássemos	comêssemos	abríssemos
vós	falásseis	comêsseis	abrísseis
eles	falassem	comessem	abrissem

Future subjunctive

eu	falar	comer	abrir
tu	falares	comeres	abrires
ele	falar	comer	abrir
nós	falarmos	comermos	abrirmos
vós	falardes	comerdes	abrirdes
eles	falarem	comerem	abrirem

146. Forms of the auxiliary *ter,* used in the perfect tenses. The preterit indicative is not used as an auxiliary.

Impersonal infinitive		*Personal infinitive*	
ter		(eu) ter	(nós) termos
		(tu) teres	(vós) terdes
		(ele) ter	(eles) terem

Present indicative		*Imperfect indicative*	
tenho	temos	tinha	tínhamos
tens	tendes	tinhas	tínheis
tem	têm	tinha	tinham

Future indicative		*Conditional*	
terei	teremos	teria	teríamos
terás	tereis	terias	teríeis
terá	terão	teria	teriam

Present subjunctive		*Imperfect subjunctive*	
tenha	tenhamos	tivesse	tivéssemos
tenhas	tenhais	tivesses	tivésseis
tenha	tenham	tivesse	tivessem

Future subjunctive	
tiver	tivermos
tiveres	tiverdes
tiver	tiverem

147. Forms of *haver* used as auxiliaries of perfect tenses in literary writing.

Impersonal infinitive		*Personal infinitive*	
haver		haver	havermos
		haveres	haverdes
		haver	haverem

Imperfect indicative		*Imperfect subjunctive*	
havia	havíamos	houvesse	houvéssemos
havias	havíeis	houvesses	houvésseis
havia	haviam	houvesse	houvessem

148. Radical-changing verbs.
First conjugation, vowel *e: levar*

Present indicative		*Present subjunctive*	
levo /é/	levamos	leve /é/	levemos
levas /é/	levais	leves /é/	leveis
leva /é/	levam /é/	leve /é/	levem /é/

Imperative singular: leva /é/

Verbs which do not change:

a. Verbs in which *e* is followed by *m* or *n*. E.g., *remar, sentar.*

b. Verbs in *-ejar* except. *invejar.* E.g., *desejar.*

c. *Aconselhar, chegar.*

d. *Fechar* varies with the region.

e. Verbs in *ear.* See §149, below.

First conjugation, vowel *o: notar*

Present indicative.

noto /ó/	notamos
notas /ó/	notais
nota /ó/	notam /ó/

Imperative singular: nota /ó/

Present subjunctive

note /ó/	notemos
notes /ó/	noteis
note /ó/	notem /ó/

Verbs which do not change:

a. Verbs in which *o* is followed by *m* or *n*. E.g., *tomar, contar.*

b. Verbs in *-oar.* E.g., *voar.*

Second conjugation, vowel *e: dever*

Present indicative

devo /ê/	devemos
deves /é/	deveis
deve /é/	devem /é/

Imperative singular: deve /é/

Present subjunctive

deva /ê/	devamos
devas /ê/	devais
deva /ê/	devam /ê/

Verbs in which *e* is followed by *m* or *n* do not change. E.g., *temer,*

Second conjugation, vowel *o: mover*

Present indicative

movo /ô/	movemos
moves /ó/	moveis
move /ó/	movem /ó/

Imperative singular: move /ó/

Present subjunctive

mova /ô/	movamos
movas /ô/	movais
mova /ô/	movam /ô/

Verbs in which *o* is followed by *m* or *n* do not change. E.g., *comer.*

Third conjugation, vowel *e: vestir*

Presdent indicative

visto	vestimos /vi/
vestes /é/	vestis /vi/
veste /é/	vestem /é/

Present subjunctive

vista	vistamos
vistas	vistais
vista	vistam

Note: Verbs in which *e* is followed by *m* or *n* change only the first person singular. E.g., *sentir.* All present subjunctives change.

Not all verbs of the third conjugation with the vowel *e* have this change; some have others.

Third conjugation, vowel *o: engolir* /u/

Present indicative		Present subjunctive	
engulo	engolimos /u/	engula	engulamos
engoles /ó/	engolis /u/	engulas	engulais
engole /ó/	engolem /ó/	engula	engulam

Imperative singular: engole /ó/

Note: Verbs in which *o* is followed by *m* or *n* change only the first person singular of the present indicative and all the present subjunctive.

Third conjugation, vowel *u: subir*

Present indicative				*Present subjunctive*	
eu	subo	nós	subimos	suba	subamos
tu	sobes /ó/	vós	subis	subas	subais
ele	sobe /ó/	eles	sobem /ó/	suba	subam

Note: Verbs in which *u* is followed by *m* or *n* change this vowel to *o* in the three forms of the indicative, but it is closed /õ/. E.g., *sumir*.

149. Special types of verbs.

Verbs in -*ear. passear*

Present indicative		*passear*		*Present subjunctive*	
eu	passeio	nós	passeamos	passeie	passeemos
tu	passeias	vós	passeais	passeies	passeeis
ele	passeia	eles	passeiam	passeie	passeiem

Note: The verb *odiar* similarly changes *i* to *ei* in the stressed forms.

Verbs in -*uir* and -*oer. instruir, roer*

Present indicative				*Present indicative*	
eu	instruo	nós	instruimos	rôo	roemos
tu	instruis	vós	instruís	róis	roeis
ele	instrui	eles	instruem	rói	roem /ó/

Note: All verb forms in the indicative in which the personal ending -*e* would follow a stressed vowel change this ending to -*i*, to indicate the fact that the two vowels form a diphthong:

Verbs in -*iar* and -*uar. principiar, continuar.*

Present indicative				*Present indicative*	
eu	principio	nós	principiamos	continuo	continuamos
tu	principias	vós	principiais	continuas	continuais
ele	principia	eles	principiam	continua	continuam

Note: Verbs in -*iar* (except *odiar,* see above), and verbs in -*uar*, are stressed on the next-to-last vowel regularly.

Verbs in -*air*. These verbs, of which there are about fifteen, have certain irregularities in common. *cair*

eu	caio	nós	caímos
tu	cais	vós	caís
ele	cai	eles	caem

Preterit indicative

eu	caí	nós	caímos
tu	caíste	vós	caístes
ele	caiu	eles	caíram

Present subjunctive: caia, etc.
Imperfect indicative: caía, etc.
Pluperfect indicative: caíra, etc.
Imperfect subjunctive: caísse, etc.
Future subjunctive and personal infinitive: cair, caíres, cair, cairmos, cairdes, caírem.
Imperative: cai, caí.

150. Irregular verbs. The conjugation of most irregular verbs can be easily derived from four forms: the infinitive, which gives those forms that are regular; the first person singular present indicative, which gives the present subjunctive; the third person plural preterit, which gives the imperfect and future subjunctive and the simple pluperfect; and the past participle, which gives all the compound perfect tenses. All forms which cannot be derived from these are given in full.

151. Caber   caibo   couberam /é/   cabido

Preterit

coube
coubeste /kubésti/
coube
coubemos /ku/
coubestes /kubéstis/
couberam /kubérõ/

152. Crer   creio   creram /ê/   crido

Present indicative

creio	cremos
crês	credes /ê/
crê	crêem

Imperative

crê (tu)
crede (vós)

153. Dar   dou   deram /é/   dado

Present indicative

dou	damos
dás	dais
dá	dão

Preterit

dei	demos
deste /é/	destes /é/
deu	deram /é/

Present subjunctive

dê	demos
dês	deis
dê	dêem

154. Dizer digo disseram /é/ dito

Present indicative

		Preterit	
digo	dizemos	disse	dissemos
dizes	dizeis	disseste /é/	dissestes /é/
diz	dizem	disse	disseram /é/

Future indicative

		Conditional	
direi	diremos	diria	diríamos
dirás	direis	dirias	diríeis
dirá	dirão	diria	diriam

Imperative

diz (tu)
dizei (vós)

155. Estar estou estiveram /é/ estado

Present indicative

		Preterit	
estou	estamos	estive	estivemos
estás	estais	estiveste /é/	estivestes /é/
está	estão	esteve /ê/	estiveram /é/

Present subjunctive

		Imperative
esteja /ê/	estejamos	está (tu)
estejas /ê/	estejais	estai (vós)
esteja /ê/	estejam /ê/	

156. Fazer faço fizeram /é/ feito

Present indicative

		Preterit	
faço	fazemos	fiz	fizemos
fazes	fazeis	fizeste /é/	fizestes /é/
faz	fazem	fêz	fizeram /é/

Future indicative

		Conditional	
farei	faremos	faria	faríamos
farás	fareis	farias	faríeis
fará	farão	faria	fariam

Imperative

faz (tu)
fazei (vós)

157. Haver hei houveram /é/ havido

Present indicative

		Preterit	
hei	havemos	houve	houvemos
hás	haveis	houveste /é/	houvestes /é/
há	hão	houve	houveram /é/

158.   Ir   vou   foram /ô/   ido

Present indicative   *Preterit*

vou   vamos   fui   fomos
vais   ides   foste /ô/   fostes /ô/
vai   vão   foi   foram /ô/

Present subjunctive   *Imperative*

vá   vamos   vai (tu)
vás   vades   ide (vós)
vá   vão

159.   Ler   leio   leram /ê/   lido

Present indicative   *Imperative*

leio   lemos   lê (tu)
lês   ledes /ê/   lede (vós)
lê   lêem

160.   Ouvir   ouço   ouviram   ouvido

Present indicative

ouço   ouvimos
ouves   ouvis
ouve   ouvem

161.   Pedir   peço /é/   pediram   pedido

Present indicative

peço /é/   pedimos
pedes /é/   pedis
pede /é/   pedem /é/

162.   Poder   posso /ó/   puderam /é/   podido

Present indicative   *Preterit*

posso /ó/   podemos /pu/   pude   pudemos
podes /ó/   podeis /pu/   pudeste /é/   pudestes /é/
pode /ó/   podem /ó/   pôde   puderam /é/

163.   Pôr   ponho   puseram /é/   posto

Present indicative   *Preterit*

ponho   pomos   pus   pusemos
pões   pondes   puseste /é/   pusestes /é/
põe   põem   pôs   puseram /é/

Imperfect indicative   *Imperative*

punha   púnhamos   põe (tu)
punhas   púnheis   ponde (vós)
punha   punham

146

164. Querer   quero /é/   quiseram /é/   querido

Present indicative

quero /é/	queremos		
queres /é/	quereis		
quer /é/	querem /é/		

Preterit

quis	quisemos
quiseste /é/	quisestes /é/
quis	quiseram /é/

Present subjunctive

queira	queiramos
queiras	queirais
queira	queiram

Imperative

quer (tu)
querei (vós)

165. Rir   rio   riram   rido

Present indicative

rio	rimos
ris	rides
ri	riem

Imperative

ri (tu)
ride (vós)

166. Saber   sei   souberam /é/   sabido

Present indicative

sei	sabemos
sabes	sabeis
sabe	sabem

Preterit

soube	soubemos
soubeste /é/	soubestes /é/
soube	souberam /é/

Present subjunctive

saiba	saibamos
saibas	saibais
saiba	saibam

167. Ser   sou   foram /ô/   sido

Present indicative

sou	somos
es /é/	sois
é	são

Preterit

fui	fomos
foste /ô/	fostes /ô/
foi	foram /ô/

Imperfect indicative

era /é/	éramos
eras /é/	éreis
era /é/	eram /é/

Present subjunctive

seja /ê/	sejamos
sejas /ê/	sejais
seja /ê/	sejam /ê/

Imperative

sê (tu)
sêde (vós)

168. Ter   tenho   tiveram /é/   tido

Present indicative

		Preterit	
tenho	temos	tive	tivemos
tens	tendes	tiveste /é/	tivestes /é/
tem	têm	teve /ê/	tiveram /é/

Imperfect indicative

		Imperative
tinha	tínhamos	tem (tu)
tinhas	tínheis	tende (vós)
tinha	tinham	

169. Trazer   trago   trouxeram /é/   trazido

Present indicative

		Preterit	
trago	trazemos	trouxe /ôs/	trouxemos /usẽ/
trazes	trazeis	trouxeste /usé/	trouxestes /usé/
traz	trazem	trouxe /ôs/	trouseram /usé/

Future indicative

		Conditional	
trarei	traremos	traria	traríamos
trarás	trareis	trarias	traríeis
trará	trarão	traria	trariam

170. Valer   valho   valeram /ê/   valido

Present indicative

valho	valemos
vales	valeis
vale	valem

171. Ver   vejo /ê/   viram   visto

Present indicative

		Preterit	
vejo /ê/	vemos	vi	vimos
vês	vedes /ê/	viste	vistes
vê	vêem	viu	viram

Imperative

vê (tu)
vede (vós)

172. Vir   venho   vieram /é/   vindo

Present indicative

		Preterit	
venho	vimos	vim	viemos
vens	vindes	vieste /é/	viestes /é/
vem	vêm	veio	vieram /é/

Imperfect indicative		Imperative
vinha	vínhamos	vem (tu)
vinhas	vínheis	vinde (vós)
vinha	vinham	

173. Irregular past participles. The following verbs given in this text have irregular past participles:

abrir	aberto /é/	ganhar	ganho
aceitar	aceitado, aceito		
cobrir	coberto /é/	gastar	gasto
descobrir	descoberto /é/	morrer	morrido (with *ter*)
dizer	dito		morto (elsewhere)
entregar	entregue /é/	pagar	pago
escrever	escrito	pôr	posto
fazer	feito	ver	visto
		vir	vindo

174. Object pronouns of the third person. The following object pronouns are almost completely unused in BF, and are increasingly rare in the literary language.

o	him, it	os	them
a	her, it	as	them

When these forms follow a verb form ending in -r, -s, or -z, this letter drops, and the object pronoun takes an initial-*l*, thus:

ver:	vê-lo	olhar:	olhá-lo	sentir:	senti-lo
ves¨	vê-lo	olhas:	olha-lo	sentes:	sente-lo
vemos:	vemo-lo	olhamos:	olhamo-lo	sentimos:	sentimo-lo
faz:	fá-lo	fiz:	fi-lo	fez:	fe-lo

When these forms follow a verb form which ends in a nasal sound, they take an intial *n*-, thus:

dão:	dão-no	falam:	falam-no

When these direct objects are combined with indirect object pronouns they produce the following forms:

me + o = mo	te + o = to, etc.
me + a = ma	lhe *or* lhes + o = lho, etc.
me + os = mos	
me + as = mas	
nos + o = no-lo	vos + o = vo-lo
nos + a = no-la	vos + a = vo-la
nos + os = no-los	vos + os = vo-los
nos + as = no-las	vos + as = vo-las

These pronouns or combinations may be placed between the infinitive and the endings of forms of the future and conditional. Thus:

Dar-mo-á	He will give it to me.
Falar-lho-ei.	I shall speak it to him.
Contar-vo-lo-íamos.	We should tell it to you.
conhecê-lo-á.	He will recognize you.

175. Forms of pronouns of the old second person.

tu	you (thou)	vós	you (ye)
te	you (thee, to thee)	vos /u/	you, to you
a ti	to you (to thee)	a vós	to you
teu, fem. tua	your (thy)	vosso, -a /ó/	your

Vocabularies

Abbreviations used in the vocabularies

adj.	adjective	num.	number
adv.	adverb	obj.	object
art.	article	pl.	plural
conj.	conjunction	p.p.	past participle
contr.	contraction	prep.	preposition
def.	definite	pres.	present tense
f.	feminine noun	pron.	pronoun
fem.	feminine	reflex.	reflexive
indef.	indefinite	rel.	relative
interrog.	interrogative	s.	singular
m.	masculine noun	subj.	subjunctive
n.	noun	superl.	superlative
neut.	neuter	v.	verb

English-Portuguese

a, indef. art. um, uma
abandon, v, deixar, abandonar
able, adj. capaz; *be able,* poder.
about, prep. *about ten o'clock* lá pelas
    dez horas.
absent, adj. ausente.
    be——, faltar.
accent, n. (foreign) sotaque, m. (written),
    acento, m.
accept, v. aceitar.
according to, prep. segundo.
acquainted: be —— *with,* conhecer.
activity, n. atividade, f.
advisable, adj. aconselhável.
advise, v. aconselhar.
afraid, adj. com medo, medroso.
    be ——, ter medo, estar com medo.
after, adv. depois.
    prep. depois de
    conj. depois que.
afternoon, n. tarde, f.
afterwards, adv. depois, mais tarde.

ago, há, atrás
    a year ago, há um ano, faz um ano, um
    ano atrás.
agreeable, adj. agradável, simpático.
ahead, adv. adiante.
    ahead of the car, na frente do carro.
air, n. ar, m.
airplane, n. avião, m.
all, adj. todo, inteiro. pron. todo
    neut. pron. tudo
allow, v. deixar, permitir.
almost, adv. quase.
alone, adj. só, sozinho.
along, prep. ao longo de.
aloud, adv. alto.
already, adv. já.
also, adv. também.
although, conj. embora, ainda que, posto
    que.
always, adv. sempre.
a.m., da manhã.
American, n., adj. americano.

among, prep. entre.

amuse, v. divertir (divirto).

an, indef. art. um, uma.

ancient, adj. antigo.

and, conj. e.

anger, n. raiva, f.

angry, adj. com raiva.

   be —, ter raiva, estar
   com raiva.

animal, n. animal, m.; bicho, m.

anniversary, n. aniversário, m.

another, adj., pron. outro, um outro.

answer, v. responder.

   — telephone, atender o telefone.

appear, v. (*seem*) parecer; (*become visible*)
   aparecer.

apple, n maçã, f.

April, n. abril, m.

architect, n. arquiteto, m.

architecture, n. arquitetura, f.

around, prep.

   around here, por aqui.

arrange, v. (*fix up*) arranjar.

arrive, v. chegar.

as, conj. como.

   do it as he does, faz como ele.

   read as you wait, lê enquanto esperar.

   as cold as, tão frio como.

   as far as, prep. até.

   as soon as, conj. logo que, assim que.

ashamed, adj. com vergonha.

   be —, estar com vergonha.

ask, v. (*question*) perguntar.

   — for, pedir

   — to, pedir para.

   ask a question, fazer uma pergunta.

at, prep. (*time*) a.

   (*place*) em.

   — once, já.

attend, v. (regularly) freqüentar.

   (once) assistir a.

attention, n. atenção, f.

   pay —, prestar atenção.

attract, v. atrair.

August, n. agosto, m.

aunt, n. tia, f.

   Aunty, Titia.

autumn, n. outono, m.

avenue, n. avenida, f.

away, adv. embora.

   he is —, está fora.

bad, adj. mau, ruim.

badly, adv. mal.

baker, n. padeiro.

ball, n. bola, f.

bashful, adj. com vergonha.

   be —, estar com vergonha.

bashfulness, n. vergonha, f.

bath, n. banho, m.

   take a bath, tomar banho.

bathing suit, n. roupa de banho.

   woman's —, maiô, m.

   men's —, calção de banho, m

bathing trunks, n. calção de banho, m.

be, v. ser; estar, ficar,

   — located, achar-se.

   — able, poder.

   be cold, hot, etc. ter frio, calor,

beach, n. praia, f.

beans, n. feijão, m. sing.

beard, n. barba, f.

beat, v. dar em.

   be beaten, apanhar.

beautiful, adj, lindo.

because, conj. porque.

   — of, prep. por causa de.

bed, n. cama, f.

   to to —, deitar-se; ir para a cama.

bedroom, n. quarto, m.

beef, n. carne, f. de vaca.

beefsteak, n. bife, m.

before, adv. antes.

   prep. antes de.

   conj. antes que.

beg, v. pedir.

begin, v. começar (a).

behind, adv. atrás.

   prep. atrás de.

believe, v (*in*), crer, acreditar, (em).

belong, v. (*to*), pertencer (a).

below, adv. em baixo.

   prep., em baixo de.

beside, prep. ao lado de.

besides, adv. além disso.

   prep. além de.

best, superl. of *good,* melhor.

better, adj., adv. melhor.

between, prep. entre

beyond, prep. para lá de.

bicycle, n. bicicleta, f.

big, adj. grande.

bigger, biggest, adj. maior.

bird, n. pássaro, m.
birthday, n. aniversário, m.
   have a —, fazer anos.
black, adj. preto.
blackboard, n. quadro-negro, pedra.
blond, adj. louro.
bloom, n. flor, f.
   in —, em flor.
blossom, n. flor, f.
blow, v. ventar.
blue, adj. azul.
boiled, adj. cozido.
book, n. livro, m.
bookseller, n. livreiro, m.
bookstore, n. livraria, f.
born, adj. nascido.
   be —, nascer.
boss, n. patrão, m., patroa, f.
boy, n. menino, m., garoto, m. (*older*)
   rapaz, m.
boy-friend, n. namorado, m.
Brazil, n. o Brasil.
Brazilian, n., adj. brasileiro.
bread, n. pão, m.
break, v. quebrar.
breakfast, n. café, (m.) da manhã.
   eat —, tomar o café da manhã.
   for —, com o café da manhã.
breeze, n. brisa, f.
bride, n. noiva, f.
bright, adj. brilhante.
bring, v. trazer.
brother, n. irmão, m.
brown, adj. (*eyes, hair*) castanho;
   (*clothes,* etc.) marrom.
brush, n. (*bushes*) mato, m.
building, n. edificio, m.
bundle, n. embrulho, m.
burn, v. queimar.
bus, n. ônibus, m.
bush, n. (*low growth*) mato, m.
but, conj. mas.
butter, n. manteiga, f.
buy, n. compra, f.
   v. comprar.
by, prep. por
   — *Thursday*, até quinta-feira.
   — *sea*, por mar.
   — *bus*, de ônibus.

café, n. café, m.
call, v. chamar.
   be called, chamar-se.
can, v. poder.
candy, n. balas, f. pl.
cane, n. cana, f.
capital, n. (city) capital, f.
car, n. carro, m.
Carnival, n. Carnaval, m.
carry, v. levar.
case, n. caso, m.
   in case, conj. caso.
castle, n., castelo, m.
catch, v. pegar, apanhar.
   — *sight of*, enxergar.
center, n. centro, m.
certain, adj. certo, seguro.
city, n. cidade, f.
chair, n. cadeira, f.
chalk, n. giz., m.
change, v. mudar.
chat, v. conversar.
child, n. criança, f.
   children, crianças, filhos, meninos.
choose, v. escolher.
church, n. igreja, f.
class, n. aula, f.
   (*group of students*) turma, f.
classmate, n. colega, m. or f.
classroom, n. (sala de) aula, f.
clean, adj. limpo.
clear off, v. (*table*) tirar.
clock, n. relógio, m.
close, v. fechar.
clothes, n. roupa, f.
cloudy, adj. nublado.
coast, n. costa, f.
coat, n. (*suit*) paletó, m.
   (*topcoat*) casaco, m.
coffee, n. café, m.
coffee pot, n. cafeteira, f.
cold, adj. frio.
   n. frio, m.
   I am —, estou com frio.
   It is —, está fazendo frio.
colleague, n. colega, m. or f.
college, n. faculdade, f.
color, n. cor, f.
comb, n. pente, m.
   v. pentear,

come, v. vir, (*arrive*) chegar.
— *back,* voltar.
— *down,* descer.
— *in,* entrar.
— *out,* sair.
— *up,* subir, (sun) nascer.
comma, n. vírgula, f.
common, adj. comum.
company, n. companhia, f.
compete, v. concorrer.
compose, v. compor.
composer, n. compositor, m.
conduct, v. conduzir.
consult, v. consultar.
contain, v. conter.
be — ed in, caber.
continue, v. seguir, continuar.
contract, n. contrato, m.
conversation, n. conversa, f.
cool, adj. fresco.
corn, n. milho, m.
corner, n. esquina, f.
correct, adj. correto, certo.
cost, v. custar.
costume, n. fantasia, f.
count, v. contar.
country, n. (*nation*) país, m.
(*rural*) campo, m., roça, f.
course, n. curso, m.
cousin, n. primo, m. prima, f.
cover, v. cobrir.
covered, adj. coberto.
cow, n. vaca, f.
cross, v. atravessar.
crowded, adj. (*with*), apinhado (de).
cuisine, n. cozinha, f.
cultivated, adj. cultivado.
— *field,* n. roça, f.
cup, n. xícara, f. xicrinha, f.
cut, v. cortar.

Daddy, n. Papai, m.
dance, n. dança, f.
v. dançar.
dark, adj. escuro.
(*complexion*) moreno.
date, n. (*month*) data, f.
v. — *a girl,* namorar.
daughter, n. filha, f.

day, n. dia, m.
good —, bom dia.
in the — time, de dia.
December., n. dezembro, m.
delay, v. tr. atrasar.
v. intr. atrasar-se, demorar.
deliver, v. entregar.
demi-tasse, n. xicrinha, f.
depart, v. partir.
desirable, adj. desejável.
desire, v. desejar.
desk, n. mesa, f.
difference, n. diferença, f.
difficult, adj. difícil.
difficulty, n. dificuldade, f.
(*trouble*), encrenca, f.
dine, v. jantar.
dinner, n. jantar, m.
eat —, jantar.
direct, v. dirigir.
dirty, adj. sujo.
disappear, v. sumir.
dish, n. prato, m.
dispose, v. dispor.
district, n. (*city*) bairro, m.
Federal —, Distrito Federal, m.
divided, adj. dividido.
do, v. fazer.
I do read, eu sim leio.
doctor, n. (MD) médico, m.
dog, n. cão, m. cachorro, m.
door, n. porta, f.
doubt, n. dúvida, f.
v. duvidar.
down, adv. (*place*) em baixo.
(*direction*) para baixo.
lie —, deitar.
downtown, n. a cidade, f.
dream, n. sonho, m.
v. sonhar.
dress, n. vestido, m.
v. vestir (-se).
drink, v. beber, tomar.
drive, n. passeio, m.
v. passear (de carro)
— *a car,* dirigir carro.
duck, n. pato, m.
during, prep. durante, por.

each, adj. cada.

    pron. cada um.

    — *other,* um ao outro.

early, adv. cedo.

earn, v. ganhar.

earth, n. terra, f.

east, n. leste.

    — *of,* a leste de.

Easter, n. Pascoa, f.

eat, v. comer.

    — *breakfast,* tomar o café da manhã.

    — *lunch,* almoçar.

    — *dinner,* jantar.

    — *ice cream,* tomar sorvete.

egg, n. ovo, m.

eh? adv. hein?

eight, num. oito.

    — *hundred,* oitocentos.

eighth, adj. oitavo.

eighty, num. oitenta.

either, conj.

    — . . . *or,* ou . . . ou.

    not —, também não.

employee, n. empregado, m. empregada, f.

employer, n patrão, m. patroa, f.

empty, adj. vazio.

end, v. acabar.

endure, v. agüentar.

Englishman, n. inglês.

English, adj. inglês.

enough, adv., adj. bastante.

enter, v. entrar (em).

entire, adj. inteiro.

even, adv. até.

even if, conj. embora, ainda que, posto que.

every, adj. todo, todos os.

everybody, pron. todo mundo.

everything. tudo.

everywhere, adv. (em) toda parte.

evil, adj. mau.

exist, v. existir.

explain, v. explicar.

extend, v. estender-se.

eye, n. olho, m.

fact, n. fato, m.

fall, n. (*season*) outono, m.

    v. cair.

    — *asleep,* cair no sono.

family, n. família, f.

famous, adj. famoso. f.

far, adv. longe

    — *from,* prep. longe de.

farm, n. fazenda, f.

farmer, n. fazendeiro, m.

fast, adv. depressa.

father, n. pai, m.

fear, n. medo, m.

    v. temer.

February, n. fevereiro, m.

federal, adj. federal.

feel, v. sentir.

    — *like,* ter vontade de.

fellow, n. rapaz, m.

few, adj., pron. poucos.

fewer, adj. menos.

fiancé, n. noivo, m.

fiancée, n. noiva, f.

field, n. campo, m. roça, f.

fifth, adj. quinto.

fifty, num. cinqüenta.

fill, v. encher.

finally, adv. em fim.

find, v. achar, encontrar.

    — — *out,* saber.

finger, n. dedo (m.) da mão.

finish, v. acabar.

fire, n. fogo, m.

    v. despedir.

firm, adj. adv. firme.

first, adj., adv. primeiro.

fit into, v. caber.

five, num. cinco.

five hundred, num. quinhentos.

fix, v. (*mend*) consertar.

    — *up with,* arranjar (para)

floor, n. chão, m.

flower, n. flor, f.

follow, v. seguir.

following, adj. seguinte.

food, n. comida, f.

foot, n. pé, m.

football, n. (*soccer*) futebol, m.

for, prep. para, por.

forbid, v. proibir.

forest, n. mata, f.

forget, v. esquecer.

    — *to,* esquecer-se de.

fork, n. garfo, m.

form, v. formar.

former, adj. antigo.

formerly, adv. antigamente.
forty, num. quarenta.
fountain, n. chafariz, m.
four, num. quatro.
four hundred, num. quatrocentos.
fourth, adj., n. quarto, m.
French, adj., n. francês.
Frenchman, n. francês, m.
fresh, adj. fresco.
Friday, n. sexta-feira, f.
fried, adj. frito.
friend, n. amigo, m., amiga, f.
from, prep. de.
front, n. frente, f.
   in — of, prep. em frente de,
   diante de.
fruit, n. fruta, f.
fry, v. fritar.
full, adj. cheio.
fuss, n. escândalo, m.

game, n. jogo, m.
"gang," n. (the gang) turma, f.
garden, n. (flower) jardim.
   (vegetable) horta, f.
gather, v. reunir-se.
general, adj. geral.
generally, adv. geralmente.
geography, n. geografia, f.
German, n., adj. alemão.
get, v. (receive) receber.
   (become) ficar.
   (get for one) arranjar.
   — behind, atrasar-se.
   — in, entrar.
   — married, casar (-se).
   — off, saltar.
   — ready, preparar-se.
   — a present, ganhar um presente.
   — up, levantar (-se)
   — well, repor-se.
gift, n. presente, m.
girl, n. (small) menina, garota.
   (older) moça, f.
girl friend, n. namorada, f.
give, v. dar.
glad, adj. contente.
glass, n. (water) copo, m.
go, v. ir, andar.
   — away, partir, ir (-se) embora.
   — back, voltar.
   — down, descer.

   — driving, passear (de carro).
   — in, entrar.
   — on, seguir.
   — out, sair.
   — up, subir.
   — to bed, deitar (-se).
   — to sleep, dormir.
goat, n. cabra, f.
good, adj. bom.
   — morning, bom dia.
   — evening, boa tarde, boa noite.
   — night, boa noite.
good-bye, até logo.
   say —, despedir-se.
graduate, v. (college) formar-se.
grandfather, n. avô, m.
grandmother, n. avó, f.
great, adj. grande.
greater, greatest, adj. maior.
green, adj. verde.
grief, n. dor, f.
groom, n. noivo, m.
ground, n chão, m.
group, n. grupo, m.
grow, v. crescer.

hair, n. cabelo, m.
half, adj. meio.
ham, n. presunto, m.
hammock, n. rede, f.
hand, n mão, f.
   v. entregar.
happy, adj. feliz, contente.
hard, adj. (difficult) difícil.
haste, n. pressa, f.
hasten, v. correr.
hat, n. chapéu, m.
hate, v. odiar.
have, v. ter, estar com.

   — dinner, jantar.
   — a picnic, fazer um piquenique.
   — lunch, almoçar.
   — supper, cear.
   — something done, mandar fazer uma
   coisa.
he, pron. ele.
health, n. saúde, f.
heart, n. coração, m.
hear, v. ouvir.
   — that, ouvir dizer que.
heat, n. calor, m.

heaven, n. céu, m.
heavy, adj. pesado.
help, v. ajudar.
hen, n. galinha, f.
her, pron. ela.
    poss. pron. dela.
here, adv. aqui, cá.
high, adj. alto.
highway, n. estrada, f.
him, pron. ele
history, n. história, f.
hit, v, dar em.
hold, v. segurar.
    — firm, agüentar.
holiday, n. (dia) feriado, m.
home, n. casa, f.
    at —, em casa.
hope, v. esperar.
    I hope that, tomara que.
horse, n. cavalo, m.
    ride a —, montar a cavalo.
horseback, adv. a cavalo.
hot, adj. quente.
hour, n. hora, f.
house, n. casa, f.
how, adv. como.
    — much, quanto.
    — many, quantos.
hundred, num. cem, cento.
hunger, n. fome, f.
hungry, adj. com fome.
    be —, estar com fome.
hunh? , adv. hein?
hurriedly, adv. com pressa.
hurry, n. pressa, f.
    be in a —, ter pressa.
    v. correr.

ice cream, n. sorvete, m.
if, conj. se.
ill, adj. doente.
    adv. mal.
important, adj. importante.
impossible, adj. impossível.
improbable, adj. improvável.
in, prep. em
    — front of, prep. em frente de.
    — order to, prep. para
    — order that, conj. para que.
    — short, adv. enfim.
    — spite of, prep. apesar de.

incorrect, adj. errado.
incredible, adj. incrível.
induce. v. induzir.
inevitable, adj. inevitável.
inhabitant, n. habitante, m. or f.
inside, adv. dentro.
    — of, prep. dentro de.
interior, n., adj. interior.
into, prep. em.
introduce, v, (lead into) introduzir.
    (person) apresentar.
invite, v. convidar.
it, pron. ele, ela. Neut. isso.
jack fruit, n. jaca, f.
January, n. janeiro.
Japanese, n., adj. japonês.
John, n. João.
jolly, adj. alegre.
Joseph, n. José.
July, n. julho, m.
jump, v. saltar.
June, n. junho, m.
jungle, n. selva, f.
just, adj. justo.
    adv. só.

kale, n. couve, f.
keep, v. guardar
    — on, seguir.
key, n. chave, f.
kid, n. (child) menino.
    v. brincar.
kind, n. espécie, f.
king, n. rei, m.
kitchen, n. cozinha, f.
knife, n. faca, f.
know, v. (fact) saber.
    — how, saber.
    — (person) conhecer.

lack, n. falta, f.
    v. faltar.
    be lacking, faltar.
ladder, n. escada, f.
lady, n. moça, f.
lag behind, v. ficar atrás.
lake, n. lago, m.
land, n. terra, f.
language, n. língua, f.
large, adj. grande.
larger, largest, adj. maior.

last, adj. (*recent*) passado.
  (*of series*) último.
late, adv. tarde.
lately, adv. ultimamente.
lateral, adj. lateral.
laugh, v. rir.
launch, v. lançar.
lawn, n. jardim, m.
lay (down), v. deitar.
lead, v. conduzir, levar.
  — *into*, introduzir.
learn, v. aprender
least, adj. menor.
  adv. menos.
leave, v. (*go away*) partir, sair.
  (*abandon*) deixar.
leg, n. perna, f.
lend, v. emprestar.
  (*fig. sense*) prestar.
Lent, n. Quaresma, f.
less, adj., adv. menos.
lesson, n. lição, f.
let, v. deixar, permitir
  let's, vamos.
  — *him do it*, que ele faça.
letter, n. (*epistle*) carta, f.
lie (down) v. deitar (-se)
light, n. luz, f.
  adj. (*weight*) leve.
  adj. (*color*) claro.
  v. acender.
lightly, adv. de leve, levemente.
like, v. gostar de
  — *better*, preferir.
  prep. como, feito.
likely, adj. fácil, provável.
listen, v. escutar.
  — (*to the radio*), ouvir.
little, adj. (*quantity*) pouco.
  a —, um pouco.
  (*size*) pequeno.
live, v. (*be alive*) viver.
  (*reside*) morar.
loaf, n. (*bread*) pão, m.
long, adj. (*space*) comprido.
  (*time*) longo.
  be —, demorar.
look, v. (*at*) olhar (para).
  — *for*, procurar.
  — *like*, parecer (-se) com.
lose, v. perder.

lot, n.
  a — *of*, muito.
  lots of, muito.
loud, adj., adv. alto.
love, v. gostar de.
low, adj. baixo.
luck, n. (*good*) sorte, f.
  (*bad*) azar, m.
lucky, adj. com sorte.
  be —, ter sorte.
lunch, n. almoço, m.
  v. almoçar.

ma'am, n. senhora.
machine, n. máquina, f.
maid, n. empregada, f.
mail, n. correio, m.
  v. pôr no correio.
make, v. fazer.
  — *fun of*, caçoar de.
man, n. homem, m.
mango, n. (*fruit*) manga, f.
mango tree, n. mangueira, f.
manner, n. maneira, f., modo, m. jeito, m.
many, adj. muitos.
March, n. março.
march, n. (*music*) marcha, f.
maroon, adj. marrom.
marry, v. casar-se (com).
Mary, n. Maria.
mass, n. (*church*) missa, f.
matter, n.
  what's the —? O que você tem?
May, n. maio, m.
may, v. poder.
maybe, adv. talvez.
me, pron. me.
meal, n. (e.g., *dinner*) refeição, f.
meat, n. carne, f.
meet, v. (be introduced) conhecer.
  (run into) encontrar.
  (gather) reunir-se.
meeting, n. reunião, f.
member, n. sócio, m.
mend, v. consertar.
mess, n. (*trouble*) encrenca, f.
midnight, n. meia-noite, f.
milk, n. leite, m.
milkman, n. leiteiro, m.
million, n. milhão, m.
mine, poss. pron. (o) meu.

minute, n. minuto, m.
miss, n. (title) senhorita, f.
miss, v.
    — *a train*, perder um trem.
    — *(a person)* ter saudade de.
    — *class*, faltar à aula.
missing, adj. em falta.
mister, n. (title) senhor.
mix, v. mexer.
Mommy, n. Mamãe.
Monday, n. segunda-feira, f.
money, n. dinheiro, m.
month, n. mês, m.
moon, n. lua, f.
more, adj., adv. mais.
morning, *n.* manhã.
    in the —, de manhã.
    good —. bom dia
most, adj., adv. (o) mais.
motel, n. motel, m.
mother, n., mãe, f.
mountain, n. montanha, f.
move v. mudar, mover, mexer.
movie, n. cinema, m.
Mr. (title) senhor.
Mrs. (title) senhora.
much, adj., adv. muito.
    not —, nem muito.
    how much, quanto.
music, n. música, f.
must, v.
    I — *go*, tenho que ir.
    it must be late, deve ser tarde.

name, n. nome, m.
    my — *is*, Chamo-me.
narrow, adj. estreito.
natural, adj. natural.
near, adv. perto.
    prep. perto de.
nearby, adv. perto.
nearly, adv. quase.
necessary, adj. preciso, necessário.
need, n. falta, f.
    v. precisar de.
neither, conj. nem
net, n. rede, f.
network, n. rede, f.
never, adv. nunca.
new, adj. novo.
newspaper, n. jornal.

next, adj. (following) seguinte.
    (*nearest*) próximo.
nice, adj. simpático.
night, n. noite, f.
    at —, de noite
    good —, boa noite.
    last —, ontem à noite.
nine, num. nove.
nine hundred, num. novecentos.
nineteen, num. dezenove.
ninety, num. noventa.
ninth, adj. nono.
no, adv. não
    adj. nenhum.
    no one, pron. ninguém
noise, n. barulho.
none, pron. nenhum.
noon, n. meio-dia, m.
nor, conj. nem.
    neither, . . —,
    nem . . . nem.
north, n. norte, m.
    — *of*, ao norte de.
not, adv. não.
    — *much*, nem muito.
    — *always*, nem sempre.
    — *all*, nem todos.
notebook, n. caderno, m.
nothing, pron. nada.
November, n. novembro, m.
number, n. número, m.

October, n. outubro, m.
o'clock, adv. hora, f.
odor, n. cheiro, m.
of, prep. de
office, n. (*doctor's*) consultório, m.
O.K., adv. está bem.
okra, n. quiabo, m.
old, adj. velho.
on, prep. em, sobre.
    on top of, prep. sobre.
once, adv. uma vez.
one, num. um.
only, adv. só, apenas.
onto, prep. em.
open, adj. aberto.
    v. abrir.
oppose, v. opor-se a.
or, conj. ou
    either . . . —, ou . . . ou.

orange, n. laranja, f.
orange tree, n. laranjeira, f.
orchard, n. pomar, m.
order, n. ordem, f.
    v. mandar.
    in — *to*, para.
    in order that, conj. para que.
organization, n. organização, f.
orphan, n. órfão, m. órfã, f.
other, adj., pron. outro.
ought, v. deve, devia.
our, ours, pron. (o) nosso.
out, adv. fora
    — *of stock,* em falta.
    — *there,* lá fora.
    — *here,* cá fora.
outside, adv. fora.
    prep. fora de.
over, adv. sobre, em cima de.
owe, v. dever.
ox, n. boi, m.

pack (v,) *bags,* fazer as malas.
package, n. embrulho, m.
pain, n. dor, f.
pair, n. par, m.
paper, n. papel, m.
    news —, jornal, m.
parade, n. desfile, m.
    v. desfilar.
parents, n. pais, m. pl.
park, n. parque, m.
part, n. parte, f.
partner, n. (*dancing*) par, m.
party, n. festa, f.
pass, v. passar.
past, adj. passado.
pay, v. pagar.
    — *attention,* prestar atenção.
peach, n. pêssego.
pen, n. caneta, f.
    — *point*, pena, f.
pencil, n. lápis, m.
people, n. (*nation*) povo, m.
    (*persons*) pessoas, f. pl.
    (*in general*) a gente.
per, prep. por.
perhaps, adv. talvez, quiçá.
permit, v. permitir, deixar.
person, n. pessoa, f.

pick, v. *pick out*, escolher.
    — *up*, apanhar.
picture, n. quadro, m.
    (*photo*) foto (grafia), f.
piece, n. pedaço, m.
pineapple, n. abacaxi, m.
pity, n. pena, f.
photograph, n. foto (grafia), f.
place, n. lugar, m.
plain, n. planície, f.
plan, v. planejar.
plane, avião, m.
    by —, de avião. (*person*)
    by —, por avião. (*letter*)
plant, n. planta, f.
    v. plantar.
plate, n. prato, m
play, v. brincar, (*games*) jogar,
    (music) tocar.
pleased, adj. contente.
pleasure, n. prazer. m.
plus, mais.
p.m., da tarde, da noite.
pool, n. *(swimming)* piscina, f.
poor, adj. pobre,
    — *fellow*, coitado.
poorly, adv. mal.
popular, adj. popular.
pork, n. (carne de) porco.
Portuguese, n., adj. português.
possible, adj. possível.
post office, n. (casa de) correio.
potato, n. batata, f.
    Irish —, batata inglesa.
    sweet —, batata doce.
pour, v. pôr
precede, v. preceder.
prefer, v. preferir.
present, n. presente.
    adj. presente
present, v. apresentar.
pretty, adj. bonito.
price, n. preço, m.
prize, n. prêmio, m.
probable, adj. provável.
produce, v. produzir.
profession, n. profissão, f.
professional, adj. profissional.
professor, n. professor, m.
    professora, f.

prohibit, v. proibir.
promote, v. promover.
proof, n prova, f.
propose, v. propor.
purchase, n. compra, f.
   v. comprar.
put, v. pôr, botar.
   — away, guardar.
   — back, repor, devolver.
   — on (clothes) pôr.
   — on (shoes) calçar.
   — out (side)pôr fora.
   — out (light) apagar.

quarrel, v. escândalo, m.
quarter, n. (fourth) quarto, m.
question, n. pergunta, f.
   ask a —, fazer uma pergunta.
quick (ly), adv. depressa.
quite, adv. bastante.
   — a bit of, (adj) bastante

radio, n. rádio, m.
   — station, rádio, f.
rage, n. raiva, f.
rain, n. chuva, f.
   v. chover.
rainy, adj. chuvoso.
raise, v. (elevate) levantar.
   (animals) criar.
ranch, n. fazenda, f.
range, n. (mountain) serra, f.
rare, adj. raro.
   — (meat), mal passado.
rather, adv. bastante.
   I'd —, prefiro.
   or —, aliás.
read, v. ler.
reading, n. leitura, f.
reason, n. razão, f.
receive, v. receber.
recite, v. dar a aula.
recognize, v. conhecer.
recover, v. repor-se.
reduce, v. reduzir.
regret, v. sentir.
relative, n. parente, m. or f.
remain, v. ficar.
remember, v. lembrar (-se) (de).
remind, v. lembrar a.
repair, v. consertar.

resemble, v. parecer-se com.
restaurant, n. restaurante, m.
return, v. voltar, devolver.
reunion, n. reunião, f.
rice, n. arroz, m.
rich, adj. rico.
ride, n. passeio (de carro, a cavalo)
   v. passear de carro, a cavalo.
right, adj. certo, correto.
   be —, ter razão.
   — there, ali mesmo.
   — here, aqui mesmo.
ring, v. tocar.
ripped, adj. rasgado.
rise, v. (person) levantar (-se)
   (sun) nascer.
river, n. rio, m.
road, n. estrada, f.
roast, v. assar.
rock, n. pedra, f.
room, n. sala, f.
   bed —, quarto, m.
run, v. correr.

sack, n. saco, m.
salt, n. sal. m.
samba, n. samba, m.
same, adj., pron. mesmo.
sand, n. areia, f.
sandwich, n. sanduíche, m.
Saturday, n. sábado, m.
say, v. dizer.
   — good bye, despedir-se.
scatter, v. espalhar,
school, n. escola, f.
   — (of university), faculdade, f.
scold, descompor, xingar.
scramble, v. mexer.
sea, n. mar, m.
season, n. estação, f.
seat, n. (of organization) sede, f.
second, n., adj. segundo, m.
see, v. ver.
   —(with difficulty) enxergar.
seem, v. parecer.
select, v. escolher.
self, int. pron. mesmo.
sell, v. vender.
September, n. setembro, m.

set, v. pôr, botar.
   (*sun*) pôr-se.
   — *down*, deitar.
   — *up*, armar.
   — *table*, pôr a mesa.
seven, num. sete.
seven hundred, num. setecentos.
seventeen, num. dezessete.
seventh, adj. sétimo.
seventy, num. setenta.
several, adj. vários.
shame, n. vergonha, f.
shave, v. fazer a barba.
she, pron. ela.
shine, v. brilhar.
shining, adj. brilhante.
shirt, n. camisa, f.
shoe, n. sapato, m.
shoemaker, n. sapateiro, m.
shop, n. loja, f.
   v. fazer compras.
short, adj. (*length*) curto.
   (*stature*) baixo.
   (*time*) breve.
   in —, enfim.
shortage, n. falta, f.
shorts, n. (*men's*) short, m.
   bathing —, calção, m.
should, v. deve, devia.
shut, v. fechar.
sick, adj. doente.
side, n. lado, m.
   on this — *of*, para cá de.
   on that — *of*, para lá de.
   on the other side of, do outro lado de.
sidewalk, n. calçada, f.
simple, adj. simples.
sing, v. cantar.
sir, senhor.
sister, n. irmã.
sit (down) v. sentar (-se)
situation, n. situação, f.
six, num. seis.
six hundred, num. seiscentos.
sixteen, num. dezesseis.
sixth, adj. sexto.
sixty, num. sessenta.
sky, n. céu, m.
sleep, n. sono, m.
   v. dormir,
   go to —, dormir.

sleepiness, n. sono.
sleepy, adj. com cono.
   be —, ter sono.
slow (ly), adv. devagar.
small, adj. pequeno.
smaller, smallest, adj. menor.
smell, n. cheiro, m.
   v. sentir um cheiro.
smile, v. sorrir.
snow, n. neve, f.
   v. nevar.
so, adv. tão, assim
   — *much*, tanto.
   — *many*, tantos.
   conj. de modo que, de jeito que
   conj. (*purpose*) para que.
soccer, n. futebol, m.
soldier, n. soldado, m.
some, adj., pron. algum.
sometime, alguma vez.
sometimes, às vezes.
somewhat, um pouco.
somewhere, nalguma parte.
son, n. filho, m.
song,, n. canção, f.
soon, adv. (*early*) cedo.
   (*immediately*) já, logo.
   as — *as*, conj. logo que,
sorry, adj. com pena.
   be —, sentir
   be — *for*, ter pena de.
south, n. sul, m.
   — *of*, ao sul de.
spade, n. pá, f.
Spaniard, n espanhol, m.
Spanish, adj. espanhol.
speak, v. falar.
spend, v. (*money*) gastar.
   (*time*) passar.
spite, n.
   in — *of*, prep. apesar de.
spoon, n. colher, f.
sport, n. esporte, m.
spread, v. espalhar.
spring, n. (*season*) primavera, f.
square, n. (*city*) praça, f.,
   largo, m.
stair, n. escada, f.
stand, v. ficar em pé.
   — *up*, pôr-se em pé.
   (*endure*) agüentar.

start, v. começar.
state, n. estado.
station, n. estação, f.
stay, v. ficar.
steady, adj. firme.
steak, n. bife, m.
step, n. passo, m.
stewed, adj. cozido.
still, adv. ainda
stir, v. mexer.
stone, n. pedra, f.
stop, v. intr. parar.
   v. tr. deter.
   — *doing it*, deixa de fazer
   — *it!* deixa!
store, n loja, f.
story, n. história, f.
strawberry, n. morango, m.
street, n. rua, f.
strike, v. dar.
stroll, n. volta, f. passeio, m. v. dar uma
   volta.
strong, adj. forte.
student, n estudante, m. or f.
study, v. estudar.
such, adj. tal.
suck, v. chupar.
sugar, n açúcar, m.
suggest, v. propor.
sultry, adj. abafado.
summer, n. verão, m.
sun, n. sol, m.
Sunday, n. domingo, m.
sunny, adj. de sol.
supper, n. ceia, f.
   eat —, cear.
suppose, v. supor.
sure, adj. seguro, certo.
surprise, v. surpreender.
swallow, v. engolir.
sweet, adj. doce.
swim, v. nadar.
swimming pool, n. piscina, f.

table, n. mesa, f.
tablecloth, n. toalha (f) de mesa.
take, v. (*possession of*) tomar.
   (drink) tomar.
   (conduct) levar, conduzir.
   — *care of*, atender.
   — *leave*, despedir-se.

   — *a look*, dar uma olhada.
   — *off*, tirar, despir.
   — *out*, tirar.
   — *a picture*, tirar uma foto.
   — *a trip*, fazer uma viagem.
   — *time*, levar tempo.
   — *a walk*, passear em pé.
talk, n. conversa, f.
   v. falar, conversar.
tall, adj. alto.
taste, n. gosto, m.
   v. (*try out*) provar.
   (*have a taste*) ter gosto.
taxi, n. táxi, m.
tea, n. chá, m.
teach, v. ensinar.
teacher, n. professor, m.
   professora, f.
team, n. time, m.
telephone, n. telefone, m.
television, n. televisão, f.
tell, v. (*say*) dizer.
   (*order*) dizer.
   (*story*) contar.
ten, num. dez
tenth, adj. décimo.
territory, n território, m.
test, n. prova, f.
   v. provar.
than, conj. que, do que.
   more — *two*, mais de dois.
thanks, *thank you*, obrigado.
that, demon. pron. esse, aquele
   rel. pron. que.
   conj. que.
   — *way*, por ali.
   that which, o que.
theater, n. teatro, m.
their, *theirs*, poss. pron. deles, delas
then, adv. então.
thence, adv. daí, dali.
there, adv. *(near you)* aí.
   (distant) lá.
   right over —, ali.
   (to that place) para lá.
they, pron. eles, elas.
thick, adj. grosso.
thing, n. coisa, f.
   something, alguma coisa.
   anything, alguma coisa.
   nothing, nada.

think, v. pensar.

   (have an opinion) achar.

third, adj. terceiro.

thirst, n. sede, f.

thirsty, adj. com sede.

   be — ter sede.

thirty, num. trinta.

this, dem. pron. este.

   this way, por aqui.

thousand, num. mil.

   n. milhar, m.

three, num. três.

three hundred, num. trezentos.

through, prep. por.

throw, v. jogar.

Thursday, n. quinta-feira, f.

thus, adv. assim.

till, prep. até.

time, n. tempo, m.

   (occasion) vez, f.

   three times, três vezes.

   two times two, duas vezes dois.

   what time is it? Que horas são?

   this time, desta vez.

   have a good time, divertir-se.

tire, v. cansar.

   get tired, cansar-se.

to, prep. a, para.

today, adv. hoje.

toe, n dedo (do pé) m.

together, adj. juntos.

tomorrow, adv. amanhã.

tongue, n. língua, f.

tonight, adv. hoje (à noite).

too, adv. *(also)* também.

   (excessively) muito.

tooth, n. dente, m.

topcoat, n. casaco, m.

torn, adj. rasgado.

touch, v. tocar.

toward, prep. para.

towel, n. toalha, f.

town, n. cidade, f.

toy, n. brinquedo, m.

train, n. trem, m.

trash, n. lixo, m.

travel, v. viajar.

treat, v. tratar.

tree, n árvore, f.

trip, n. viagem, f.

trouble, n. pena, f.

   (difficulty) encrenca, f.

   it's no —, não dá trabalho.

true, adj. verdadeiro.

   it's —, é verdade.

truth, n. verdade, f.

try, v. tentar, procurar.

Tuesday, n. terça-feira, f.

turn on (light) acender.

turn, n. volta, f.

twenty, num. vinte.

twice, adv. duas vezes.

two, num. dois.

two hundred, num. duzentos.

ugly, adj. feio.

uncle, n. tio, m.

   Uncle, Titio.

understand, v. compreender, entender.

undesirable, adj. indesejável.

undress, v. despir (-se).

unfortunate, adj. infeliz, lastimável.

   it is —, é pena.

United States, n. Estados Unidos, m. pl.

university, n. universidade, f.

unjust, adj. injusto.

unless, conj. se . . . não.

unlikely, adj. difícil, improvável.

unlucky, adj. sem sorte, com azar.

   be —, não ter sorte, ter azar.

until, prep. até.

   conj. até que, enquanto . . não.

up, adv. *(place)* em cima, lá em cima.

   (direction) lá para cima.

   go —, subir.

   come —, subir.

upstairs, adv. lá em cima.

urgent, adj. urgente.

us, pron. nos.

use, v. usar.

useful, adj. útil.

useless, adj. inútil.

vacation, n. férias, f. pl.

variety stores. Lojas Brasileiras, f. pl.

vary, v. variar.

veal, n. vitela, f.

very, adv. muito.

visit, n. visita, f.

   v. visitar.

   pay a —, fazer uma visita.

   on a —, de visita.

visitor, n. visita, f.
voice, n. voz, f.

wait, v. esperar.
waiter, n. garçom m.
waitress, n. garçonete, f.
wake up, v. acordar.
walk, n passeio, m.
   v. ir a pé, andar.
   (for pleasure) passear a pé.
   (side) walk, n. calçada, f.
war, n. guerra, f.
warm, adj. quente.
   I'm —, estou com calor.
   it's warm, está fazendo calor.
wash, v. lavar (-se)
watch, n. relógio, m.
   v. olhar.
   —TV, ver televisão
water, n. água, f.
way, n *(manner)* maneira, f. modo, m,
   jeito, m.
   do it this way, faz assim.
   go that way, vai por ali.
we, pron. nós
weak, adj. fraco.
wear, v. usar, vestir.
weather, n. tempo. m.
Wednesday, n. quarta-feira, f.
week, n. semana, f.
well, adv. bem.
   — done (food) bem passado.
west, n. oeste, m.
   — of, a oeste de.
what, interrog. pron. que, o que.
   rel. pron. o que.
   interrog. adj. que
when, adv. quando.
where, adv. onde.
   (direction) aonde, para onde.
   where is, cadê.
whether, conj. se.
which, rel. pron. que.
   interrog. pron. qual.
while, conj. enquanto.
white, adj. branco.
who, interrog. pron. quem.
   rel. pron. que, quem.

whole, adj. inteiro.
wide, adj. largo.
wife, n. mulher, f. esposa, f.
will, n. vontade, f.
   v. haver de.
   — you? você quer?
win, v. ganhar.
wind, n. vento, m.
window, n. janela, f.
windy, adj.
   be —, ventar.
winter, n. inverno, m.
wish, n. vontade, f.
   v. querer, desejar.
   I wish that, tomara que
with, prep. com,
within, adv. dentro.
   prep. dentro de.
without, prep. sem.
woman, n. mulher, f.
wonder, v. querer saber
word, n. palavra, f.
work, n. trabalho, m.
   v. trabalhar.
worker, n. trabalhador, m.
world, n. mundo, m.
worse, worst, adj. pior.
worth, adj.
   be —, valer.
   be — while, valer a pena.
would, v.
   — that, tomara que.
write, v. escrever.
wrong, adj. errado.
   be —, não ter razão.

yard, n. *(of house)* jardim, m.
year, n. ano, m.
yellow, adj. amarelo.
yes, adv. (use verb repetition)
yesterday, adv, ontem.
yet, adv. *(still)* ainda.
   not —, ainda não.
you, pron. você, pl. vocês.
young, adv. novo, moço.
your, poss. adj. seu, f. sua.

a, prep. to, at.

a, obj. pron. her, it.

a, as, article, the.

à, às, contr. to the.

abacaxi, m. pineapple.

abafado, adj. sultry.

abaixo, adv. down (ward).

aberto /é/, adj. open, opened.

abril, m. April

acabar, to finish, to end.

ação, f. action.

aceitar, to accept.

    p.p. aceito & aceitado.

acender, to light (lamp, fire)

    to turn on (lights)

achar, to find.

    eu acho, I think so.

    acho que sim, I think so

    eu não acho, I think not.

    achar-se, to be (located).

aconselhar (a), to advise (to).

aconselhável, adj. advisable.

acordar, to wake, to wake up.

acreditar (em), to believe (in).

açúcar, m. sugar.

agosto, /ô/, m. August.

água, f. water.

agüentar, to stand, to endure (pain), to

    hold firm.

aí, adv. there (near you).

ainda, adv. still, yet.

    — não, not yet.

    — que, although, even though

ajudar, to help.

alegre adj. /é/, jolly, happy.

além de, prep. besides.

    além disso, besides.

alemão, adj.; f. alemã, German.

algum, f. alguma, adj. & pron. some, any.

    alguma coisa, something.

    alguma parte, somewhere.

    algumas vezes, sometimes.

ali, adv. there, right there.

aliás, adv. besides, or rather.

almoçar, to eat lunch.

alto, adj., high, tall, loud (voice)

    adv. aloud.

amanhã, adv. tomorrow.

amarelo, adj /é/, yellow.

americano, adj American

amiga, f. friend.

amigo, m., friend.

andar, to walk, to go.

    a máquina anda, the machine runs.

animal, m. animal.

aniversário, m. birthday, anniversary.

ano, m. year.

    fazer anos, have a birthday.

antes, adv. before.

    antes de, prep. before.

    antes que, conj. before.

antigamente, adv. formerly.

antigo, adj. ancient, former

anzol, m. /ó/ fishhook.

ao, aos, contr. to the.

apagar, to put out (fire).

apanhar, to pick up. to catch, to be

    beaten.

aparecer, to appear (become visible).

apesar de, prep. in spite of.

apinhado (de) adj. crowded (with).

aprender (a), to learn (to).

apresentar, to present (play),

    introduce (person).

aquele /ê/, pron., adj. that.

àquele /ê/, contr. to that.

aqui, adv. here.

aquilo, neut. pron. that.

ar, m. air.

areia, f. sand.

armar, to set up, put up.

arquiteto /é/, m. architect.

arquitetura, f. architecture.

arranjar, to get (for one), to arrange,

    to fix (one) up with

arroz /ô/, m. rice.

árvore, f. tree.

assar, to roast.

assim, adv. thus, so.

    assim que, conj. as soon as.

assistir a, to attend (once).

até, prep. until, as far as.

    até logo, see you soon.

    até amanhã, see you tomorrow,

    adv. even.

    até que, conj. until.

atender, to take care of, to answer
  (door, phone, etc.)
atividade, f. activity.
atrair, to attract.
atrás, adv. back, behind.
  atrás de, prep. behind.
atrasar (-se), to delay, to get behind,
  (clock) to lose time.
atravessar, to cross.
audaz, adj. bold.
aula, f. class, classroom.
  sala de aula, classroom.
ausente, adj. absent.
avenida, f. avenue.
avião, m. airplane.
avô, m. grandfather.
avó, f. grandmother.
azar, m. bad luck.
azul, adj. blue.

bairro,, m. district (of city).
baixo, adj. low, short (stature).
  em baixo, adv. below, underneath.
  em baixo de, prep. under.
bala, f. piece of candy.
banheiro, m. bathroom.
banho, m. bath.
  roupa de banho, bathing suit.
  calção de banho, bathing trunks.
  tomar banho de mar, go swimming.
barba, f. beard.
  fazer a barba, to shave.
barril, m. barrel.
barulho, m. noise.
bastante, adj. enough, quite a bit of adv.
  rather, quite.
batata, f. potato.
  batata inglês, Irish potato.
  batata doce, sweet potato.
beber, to drink.
bem, adv. well.
  está bem, O. K.
  bem passado, well done.
bênção, f. blessing.
bicho, m. animal (any living thing, from
  germ to whale).
bicicleta /é/, f. bicycle.
bife, m. steak.
boa, /ô/ f. of bom, good.
boi, m. ox.
bola, /ó/ f. ball

bolso, m. /ô/ pocket.
bom, adj. good.
  bom dia, good morning.
  boa tarde, good evening.
  boa noite, good evening, good night.
bonito /bu/, adj. pretty, handsome
botar, to put.
branco, adj. white.
Brasil, m. Brazil
brasileiro, m. Brazilian.
breve /é/, adj. short, brief.
  em breve, soon.
brilhante, adj. brilliant, bright.
brilhar, to shine.
brincar, to play, to "kid"
brinquedo /ê/, m. toy.
brisa, f. breese.

cá, adv. here.
  para cá, (to) here.
  por cá, hereabouts.
cabelo /ê/, m. hair
caber, to fit into, to be contained in.
  Não cabe dúvida, there's no doubt.
cabra, f. goat.
cachorro, /ô/ m. dog.
caçoar (de), to make fun of.
cada, adj. each.
  cada um, pron. each.
cadê, adv. where is (are)
cadeira, f. chair.
caderno, /é/ m. notebook.
café, m. coffee, café
  café da manhã, breakfast.
cafeteira, f. coffee pot.
cair, to fall
  cair na água, to go in swimming.
calçada, f. sidewalk.
calção, m. athletic shorts.
  calção de banho, swimming trunks.
calçar, to put on (shoes).
calor, /ô/ m. heat.
  tenho calor, I'm hot.
  estou com calor, I'm hot.
  faz calor, it's hot (weather)
cama, f. bed.
camisa, f. shirt.
campo, m. field; the country.
cana, f. (sugar) cane.
canção, f. song.
caneta /ê/, f. pen.

cansar (-se) to tire, get tired.

cantar, to sing.

cão, m. pl. cães, dog.

capital, f. capital (city).

carioca, /ó/ adj, m. & f. native of Rio.

Carnaval, m. Carnival.

carne, f. meat, esp. beef.

    carne de porco, pork.

carro, m. car.

    de carro, by car.

carta, f. letter, (playing) card.

casa, f. house, home.

    em casa, at home.

    na casa, in the house.

casaco, m. topcoat; ladies' coat.

casar (-se) (com) to marry, get married (to)

caso, m. case.

    conj. in case.

castanho, adj. brown.

castelo /é/, m. castle.

cavalo, m. horse.

cear, to eat supper.

cedo /ê/, adv. early, soon.

cego /é/, adj. blind.

ceia, f. supper.

cem, num. one hundred.

cento, m. one hundred.

centro, m. center.

certo, /é/ adj. certain, correct, right, true.

cerveja, /ê/ f. beer.

céu, m. sky, heaven.

chá, m. tea.

chafariz, m. fountain.

chamar, to call.

    chamar-se, to be named.

chão, m. ground, floor.

chapéu, m. hat.

chave, f. key.

chegar, to arrive, come.

    chegar em, arrive in.

    chegar a, to amount to.

    chegar para, to be enough for.

    chega para cá, some closer.

cheio, adj. full.

cheiro, m. smell, odor.

chover, to rain.

chupar, to suck.

chuva, f. rain.

chuvoso, /ô/ adj. rainy.

cidade, f. city, town, downtown.

cima, adv.

    em cima, above, upstairs.

    em cima de, prep. above,

cinema, m. movie

cinco, num. five

cinqüenta, num. fifty.

coberto, /é/ adj. & p. p., covered.

cobrir, to cover.

coisa, f. thing.

    alguma coisa, something.

    outra coisa, something else.

coitado, m. poor fellow

colega, /é/, m., f. classmate; colleague

colher /é/, f. spoon

com, prep. with.

começar, to begin.

comer, to eat.

comida, f. food.

comigo, pron. with me.

como, adv. & conj. how, as, like.

companhia, f. company.

compor, to compose, make up.

compositor, m. composer.

compra, f. purchase, buy.

comprar, to buy, purchase.

compreender, to understand.

comprido, adj. long (in space)

comum, adj. common.

concorrer, to compete.

conduzir, to conduct, to lead.

conhecer, to know, to meet, to recognize

conosco /ô/, pron. with us.

consertar, to fix, mend, repair.

consigo, pron. with him (self) your (self)

    themselves, yourselves, etc.

consulta, f. consultation, conference.

consultar, to consult.

consultório, m. (dr's) office.

contar, to tell (story), to count.

contente, adj. pleased, happy.

contrato, m. contract.

conversa, /é/ f. chat, conversation.

conversar, to chat, to talk.

convidar (para), to invite (to).

copo /ó/, m. glass.

cor /ô/, f. color.

coração, m. heart.

correio, m. mail, post office.

correr, to run, to hurry.

    correr perigo, to run risk.

cortar, to cut.

costa /ó/, f. coast.
couve, f. kale.
cozido, adj. boiled, stewed.
cozinha, f. kitchen, cuisine.
cozinhar, to cook.
crer (em), to believe (in).
crescer, to grow.
criança, f. child.
criar, to raise (animals)
cruzeiro, m. Braz. monetary unit.
cultivado, adj. cultivated.
curso, m. course.
curto, adj. short.
custar, to cost, to be difficult.
custa-me crer, it's hard for me to
    believe.

da, das, contraction, of the
daí, contr. from there, from then on
    thence.
dança, f. dance.
dançar, to dance.
daquele, /ê/, contr. of that.
daqui, contr. from here.
dar, to give, to strike.
    dar a aula, to recite.
    dar bom dia, to say good morning.
    dar cartas, to deal cards.
    dar com, to run into.
    dar duas horas, to strike two.
    dar em, to hit, hit upon.
    dar para a rua, to face the street
    dar para a música, to be good at
    music.
    dar um grito, to yell.
    dar uma olhada, to take a look.
    dar um passeio, to take a stroll.
    dar uma volta, tõ take a stroll.
    dar-se bem com, to get along with.
    dar-se conta de, to realize.
data, f. date (on calendar)
de, prep. of, from.
décimo, adj. tenth.
dedo /ê/, m. finger, toe.
    dedo da mão, finger.
    dedo do pé, toe.
deitar, to lay, to lie down.
    deitar-se, to lie down, go to bed.
deixar, to let, allow, permit.
    to leave. abandon.
    deixar de fazer, to stop doing.

dela, dele, contr. of her, her, of him, his.
demorar, to delay, to be long in.
dente, m. tooth.
dentro, adv. inside, within.
    dentro de, inside of.
depois, adv. afterwards, later.
    depois que, conj. after.
depressa, /é/ adv. quick, fast.
descer, to go down, come down.
desejar, to desire.
desejável, adj. desirable.
desfilar, to parade.
desfile, m. parade.
despedir, to discharge, fire
    (a person)
    despedir-se, to take leave.
despir, to undress, to take off.
desse, /ê/ contr. of that.
deste, /ê/ contr. of this.
Deus, m. God.
devagar, adv. slow (ly).
dever, to owe, ought, should.
dezembro, m. December.
dia, m. day.
    o dia 2 de março, March 2.
    de dia, in the daytime.
diante adv. in front, out ahead.
    diante de, prep. in front of.
diferença. f. difference.
difícil, adj. difficult, hard.
dinheiro, m. money.
dirigir, to direct, to drive
    (a car).
    dirigir-se a, to go to.
distrito, m. district:
    Distrito Federal, Federal District.
dito, p. p. of dizer.
divertir, to amuse.
    divertir-se, to have a good time.
dividido, p. p. divided.
dizer, to say, to tell.
do, dos, contr. of the.
dobrar, to fold, to turn (corner).
doce /ô/, adj. sweet.
doente, adj. sick, ill.
doentio, adj. sickly.
dois, num. two.
doméstico, adj. domestic.
domingo, m. Sunday.
    aos domingos, on Sunday.
do que, conj. than.

dor /ô/, f. pain, grief.
dormir, to sleep, to go to sleep.
duas, f. of dois.
dum, duma, contr. of a.
durante, prep. during.
dúvida, f. doubt.
    sem dúvida, no doubt.
duvidar, to doubt.
duzentos, two hundred.

e, conj. and.
edifício, m. building.
ela, /é/ pron. she.
elas, /é/ pron. they (f).
ele, /ê/ pron. he.
eles, /ê/ pron. they.
em, prep. in, on, at (place)
    em cima, adv. above, up there.
    em cima de, prep. above, over.
    em frente, adv. in front.
    em frente de, prep. in front of.
    em vez de, prep. instead of.
embora, /ó/, adv. away
    conj. although, even if.
embrulho, m. package.
empregada, f. maid. employee,,
emprestar, to lend.
encher (de), to fill with.
encontrar, to meet, to find.
    encontrar com, to run into.
    encontrar-se com, to meet (accidental)
encrenca, f. difficulty, mess.
enfim, adv. in short.
engolir, to swallow.
enquanto, conj. while.
    enquanto . . . não, until.
    por enquanto, for the time being.
ensinar (a), to teach (how to).
então, adv. then.
entrar (em), to enter
entre, prep. between, among.
entregar, p. p. entregue. to deliver
enxergar, to catch sight of, manage to
    see.
errado, adj. incorrect, wrong.
escada, f. stair, ladder.
escândalo, m. loud talk, quarrel.
escola, /ó/ f. school.
escolher, to choose, select, pick.
escrever, to write
    p.p. escrito.

escuro, dark (without light).
escutar, to listen to.
espalhar, to spread, scatter.
espanhol, /ó/ Spanish, Spaniard.
espécie, f. kind.
esperar, to hope, to wait, to expect.
esporte, /ô/, m. sport.
esquecer, to forget.
    esquecer-se de, to forget (to)
esquina, f. corner.
esse /ê/, f. essa /é/, adj. & pron. that.
estação f., station; season.
estado, m. state.
    Estados Unidos, m. pl. United
    States.
estar, to be.
    estar com, to have.
estar com sono, to be sleepy.
estar em falta, to be out of stock.
    estar sem, not to have.
    estar sem sono, not to be sleepy.
este /ê/, f. esta /é/, adj. & pron. this.
estender-se, to extend.
estrada, f. road.
estreito, adj. narrow.
estudante, m. or f., student.
estudar, to study.
existir, to exist.
explicar, to explain.
expor, to expose

faca, f. knife.
fácil, adj. easy; likely.
faculdade, f. college; school (of a univer-
    sity)
falar, to speak, to talk.
    falar com, to speak to.
falta, f. lack, need, shortage.
    estar em falta, to be out of stock.
    fazer falta, to be needed, to be
    missed.
faltar, to be lacking.
    faltar à aula, to miss class.
família, f. family.
famoso, adj. famous.
fantasia, f. (Carnival) costume.
fato, m. fact.
fazenda, f. farm; ranch.
fazendeiro, m. farmer; rancher.

fazer, to do; to make.
    fazer anos, to have a birthday.
    fazer a barba, to shave.
    fazer calor, to be hot (weather).
    fazer falta, to be needed.
    fazer favor de, please.
    fazer frio, to be cold (weather)
    fazer um piquenique, to have a picnic.
    fazer uma pergunta, to ask a question.
    fazer uma viagem, to take a trip.
fechar, to shut, close.
federal, adj. federal.
feijão, m. beans.
feio, adj. ugly.
feito, p.p. of fazer, made, done.
    prep. like.
feliz, adj. happy.
feriado, m. holiday.
férias, f. pl. vacation.
    tirar férias, to take a vacation.
festa, /é/ f. party.
fevereiro, m. February.
ficar, to stay, remain; to be (permanently
    located); to become.
ficar noivo (noiva), to get engaged.
fiel, /é/ adj. faithful.
filha, f. daughter.
filho, m. son.
firme, adj. firm, steady.
flor /ô/, f. flower, blossom.
fogo /ô/, pl. fogos /ó/, fire.
fome, f. hunger.
    ter fome, to be hungry.
    com fome, hungry.
fora /ó/, adv. outside, away.
    lá fora, out there.
    cá fora, out here.
    fora de, prep. outside (of).
formar, to form; to graduate.
    formar-se, to be graduated.
forte, /ó/, adj. strong.
foto (grafia), f. photo (graph).
fraco, adj. weak.
francês, adj. & n. French (man).
frente, f. front.
    em frente de, prep. in front of.
freqüência, f. frequency.
freqüentar, to attend (regularly)
freqüente, adj. frequent.
fresco /ê/, adj. cool.

frio, m. cold.
    adj. cold.
    ter frio, to be cold.
    fazer frio, to be cold (weather).
fritar, to fry.
    p. p. fritado, frito.
frito, adj. fried.
fruta, f. fruit.
futebol, /ó/ m. soccer.

galinha, f. hen.
    as galinhas, the chickens.
ganhar, to earn (money), to get (a present),
    to win (a game).
    p. p. ganho.
garçom, m. waiter.
garçonete, /é/ f. waitress.
garfo, m. fork.
garoto, /ô/ m. boy.
gastar, to spend (money).
    p. p. gasto.
gelo, /ê/ m. ice.
gente, f. people.
    a gente, one, they, people.
geografia, f. geography.
geral, adj. general.
geralmente, adv. generally.
giz, m. chalk.
gostar (de), to like, to love.
gosto /ô/, pl. gostos /ó/, m. taste, pleasure.
grande, adj. big, large, great.
grosso /ô/, pl. & f. /ó/, adj. thick.
grupo, m. group.
guardar, to guard, to keep, put away.
guerra /é/, f. war.

há, there is (are); ago.
habitante, m. or f. inhabitant.
haja, subj. of haver.
haver, auxiliary of fut.
hein? adv. Eh?
história, f. story, history.
hoje, /ô/ adv. today.
    hoje à noite, tonight.
homem, m. man.
hora, /ó/ f. hour; o'clock.
horta, /ó/ f. (vegetable) garden.

igreja, /ê/ f. church.
importante, adj. important.
impor, to impose.

impossível, adj. impossible.
improvável, adj. improbable.
incrível, adj. incredible.
indesejável, adj. undesirable.
induzir, to induce.
inevitável, adj. inevitable.
inglês, adj. & n. English (man).
injusto, adj. unjust.
inteiro, adj. entire.
interior, m. interior.
introduzir (em) introduce into, to lead
    into.
inverno, /é/ m. winter.
ir, to go
    como vai? How are you?
    vou bem. I am well.
irmã, f. sister.
irmão, m. brother.
isso, neuter pron. that.
isto, neuter pron. this.

já, adv. already; immediately.
jaca, f. jack fruit.
janeiro, m. January.
janela, /é/ f. window.
jantar, m. dinner.
    v. to have dinner.
japonês, adj. & n. Japanese.
jaqueira, f. jack fruit tree.
jardim, m. garden, lawn, yard.
jeito, m. way, manner.
    de jeito que, so, so that.
João, m. John.
jogar, to play, to throw, to gamble.
    jogar fora, to throw out.
    jogar a bola, to pitch the ball.
jogo /ô/, pl. /ó/, m. game.
jornal, m. newspaper.
José, m. Joseph.
julho, m. July.
junho, m. June.
juntos, pl. adj., together.
justo, adj. just.

lá, adv. there.
    para lá, there (to that place)
    lá atrás, back there.
lado, m. side.
    do lado de lá, on the other side.
lago, m. lake.
lamentável, adj. lamentable, unfortunate.

lançar, to launch, to throw.
lápis, m. pencil.
laranja, f. orange.
laranjeira, f. orange tree.
largo, m. (city) square. adj. wide.
lateral, lateral.
lavar (-se), to wash.
legume, m. vegetable.
leite, m. milk.
leiteiro, m. milkman.
leitura, f. reading.
lembrar (a), to remind.
    lembrar (-se) (de) to remember.
ler, to read.
leste /é/, m. east.
    a leste de, east of.
levantar, to raise.
    levantar (-se) to rise, get up.
levar, to take, carry.
    levar tempo, to take time.
leve /é/, adj. light (in weight).
    de leve, adv. lightly.
lhe, lhes, indirect obj. prons.
    to him, them, you, etc.
lição, f. lesson.
ligar, to connect.
    ligar a luz, to turn on the light.
    ligar o rádio, to turn on the radio.
limpo, adj. clean.
lindo, adj. beautiful.
língua, f. tongue; language.
livraria, f. bookstore.
livreiro, m. bookseller.
livro, m. book.
lixo, m. trash.
logo /ó/, adv. soon, immediately.
    logo que, conj. as soon as.
    até logo, see you soon.
    mais logo, later.
loja /ó/, f. shop, store.
    Lojas Brasileiras, variety stores
longe, adv. far away.
    longe de, prep. far from.
longo, adj. long (in time)
    ao longo de, prep. along.
louro, adj. blond.
lua, f. moon.
lugar, m. place.
luz, f. light.

má, f. of mau, bad.
maçã, f. apple.
mãe, f. mother.
maio, m. May.
maiô, m. (woman's) bathing suit,
maior /ó/, adj. larger, greater.
mais, adv. more, most.
mal, adv. badly, poorly
    mal passado, rare (meat).
mala, f. suitcase, trunk.
Mamãe, Mommy.
mamão, m. papaya.
mandão, f. mandona adj. bossy.
mandar, to order, to have (something done),
    to send.
maneira, f. way, manner.
    de maneira que, conj. so, so that.
manga, f. mango (fruit).
mangueira, f. mango tree.
manhã, f. morning.
    de manhã, in the morning.
    da manhã, a.m.
manteiga, f. butter.
mão, f. hand. pl. mãos.
    à mão, by hand.
máquina, f. machine.
mar, m. sea.
marcha. f march (music).
março, m. March.
Maria, f. Mary.
marrom, adj. maroon, brown,
mas, conj. but.
mata, f. forest.
mato, m. bush, low woody growth.
mau, adj. f. má, bad.
médico, m. doctor (physician).
medo /ê/, m. fear.
    com medo, afraid.
    ter medo, be afraid.
meio, adj. half.
meia-noite, f. midnight.
meio-dia, m. noon, midday.
melhor /ó/, adj. better, best
menina, f. girl.
menino, m. boy.
menor /ó/, adj. smaller, littler.
menos, adv. less, fewer, minus.
me, pron. me.
mês, pl. meses, m. month.
mesa /ê/, f. table.

mesmo /ê/, adj. & pron. same, self.
    adv. really, even.
meu, f. minha, poss. pron. my
mexer, to stir, to mix, scramble.
mexido, adj, scrambled.
mil, num. one thousand.
milhão, m. million.
milhar, m. (group of) one thousand.
milho, m. corn.
mim, pron., obj. of prep. me.
minuto, m. minute.
missa, f. mass (at church).
moça /ô/, f. girl, young woman, "lady"
modo /ó/, m. way, manner.
    de modo que, conj. so, so that.
montanha, f. mountain.
montar, to ride (a horse).
morango, m. strawberry.
morar, to live, dwell.
moreno, dark (complexion).
morro /ô/, m. hill.
motel /é/, m. motel.
mudar, to move, to change.
    mudar a roupa, to change clothes.
    mudar de casa, move away.
    mudar-se, to move, change.
muito, adj, much, lots of
    adv. very, too (too much).
    nem muito, not much.
mulher /é/, f. woman.
mundo, m. world.
música, f. music.

na, nas, contr. in the.
nada, pron. nothing.
nadar, to swim.
nalguma parte, somewhere.
namorada, f. girl-friend.
namorado, m. boy-friend.
namorar, to "date," "go with."
não, adv. no, not.
naquele, /ê/, contr. in that.
nascer, to be born.
    (plant, sun, etc.) come up.
natural, adj. natural.
necessário, adj. necessary.
nem, conj. nor.
    nem . . . nem, neither nor.
    nem muito, not much.
    nem sempre, not always.

nenhum, f. nenhuma, adj., pron.
    no, none.
nesse, nessa, contr. in that.
neste, nesta, contr., in this.
nevar, to snow.
neve /é/, f. snow.
ninguém, pron. no one.
no, nos, contr. in the.
noite, f. night.
    boa noite, good night.
    hoje à noite, tonight.
    ontem à noite, last night.
    de noite, at night.
noiva, f. fiancée, bride.
noivo, m. fiancé, groom.
nome, m. name.
nono, adj. ninth.
norte /ó/, m. north.
    ao norte de, north of.
nos, pron. us.
nós, pron. we; us (obj. of prep.)
nosso /ó/, poss, pron. our.
noutra parte, elsewhere.
nove, /ó/ num. nine
novecentos, num. nine hundred.
novembro, m. November.
noventa, num. ninety.
novo /ô/, pl. /ó/, adj. new; young.
nublado, adj. cloudy
num, numa, contr. in a.
número, m. number.
nunca, adv. never.

o, os, def. art. the.
obrigado, adj. thanks, thank you.
odiar, to hate,
oeste, /é/, m. west.
    a oeste de, west of.
oitavo, adj. eighth.
oitenta, num. eighty.
oito, num. eight.
oitocentos, num. eight hundred.
olhada, f. look.
olhar (para), to look (at).
olho /ô/, pl. /ó/, m. eye.
onde, adv. where.
ônibus, m. bus.
ontem, adv. yesterday.
    ontem à noite, last night.
opor-se a, to oppose.
o qual, rel pron. which.

o que, interrog. pron. what.
    rel. pron. what.
ordem, f. order.
    dar ordem de, to order to.
    pôr em ordem, put in order
órfã, f. orphan.
órfão, m. orphan.
organização, f. organization.
ou, conj. or.
    ou . . . ou, either . . or.
outono, m. autumn, fall.
outro, adj., pron. other, another.
outra parte, elsewhere.
outubro, m. October.
ouvir, to hear.
    ouvir dizer, to hear (that).
ovo /ô/, pl. /ó/, m. egg.

pá, f. spade.
padeiro, m. baker.
pagar, to pay.
    p.p. pago.
pai, m. father.
    os pais, the parents.
país, m. country, nation.
palavra, f. word.
paletó, m. (suit) coat.
pão, pl. pães, m. bread.
Papai, Daddy.
papel, /é/, m. paper.
par, m. (dancing) partner; pair.
para, prep. for. to, toward, in order to
    para que, conj. so that, in order that
parar, to stop.
parecer, to seem, to look like.
    parecer (-se) com, to look like.
parente, m. or f. relative.
parque, m. park.
parte, f. part.
    alguma parte, somewhere.
    outra parte, elsewhere.
    nenhuma parte, nowhere.
    toda parte, everywhere.
partir, to depart, go away
    partir para, to leave for.
Páscoa, f. Easter.
passado, n. & adj. past, last.
passagem, f. passage, ticket.
passar, to pass.
    passar tempo, to spend time.
pássaro, m. bird.

passear, to walk, ride, drive, etc.
for pleasure.
passeio, m. walk, ride, drive, etc.
for pleasure.
passo, m. step.
dar um passo, take a step.
pato, m. duck.
patrão, m. boss, employer.
patroa, /ô/, f. boss, employer.
pé, foot.
pedaço, m. piece.
pedir, to ask for, to beg.
pedir para, to ask to.
pedra /é/, f. stone, rock.
pegar, to catch.
pegar uma doença, to catch a disease.
pegar a bola, to catch the ball.
pelo, pela, /ê/, contr. by the.
pena, f. trouble, pity.
sentir pena de, to feel sorry for.
pena, f. penpoint.
escrever com pena, to write with pen.
pensar (em), to think (of).
Que pensa dele? What do you think
of him?
pentear (-se), to comb.
pequeno, adj. little (size)., small.
perder, to lose,
perder o trem, to miss the train.
pergunta, f. question.
fazer uma pergunta, to ask a question.
perguntar, to ask (question).
permitir, to permit, allow.
perna /é/, f. leg.
pertencer (a), to belong (to).
perto /é/, adv. near., nearby.
perto de, prep. near.
pesado, adj. heavy
pêssego, m. peach.
pessoa, /ô/, f. person.
peteca /é/, f. Braz. game, with racket or
hand.
pior /ó/, adj. adv. worse.
piquenique, m. picnic.
piscina, f. swimming pool.
planejar, to plan.
planície, f. plain.
planta, f. plant.
plantar, to plant, raise (crops).
pobre /ó/, adj. poor.
poder, can, to be able, may.

pomar, m. archard.
popular, adj. popular, of the people.
pôr, to put; to put on (clothes);
to lay (eggs); to set (table);
to pour (water).
pôr-se, to set (sun).
por, prep. for, by, through, along, per.
por que, adv. why.
porque, conj. because.
porta, /ó/, f. door.
português, n., adj. Portuguese.
possível, adj. possible.
posto /ô/, f. /ó/, p.p. of pôr.
posto que, conj. although, even if.
pouco, adj. little (quantity)
um pouco, a little (bit).
poucos, few
adv. little; somewhat.
povo /ô/, pl. /ó/, m. people (nation)
praça, f. (city) square.
praia, f. beach.
prato, m. plate, dish.
prazer /ê/ m. pleasure
muito prazer em conhecê-lo,
very glad to meet you.
preceder, to precede.
precisar de, to need.
preciso, adj. necessary.
preço /ê/, m. price.
preferir, to prefer, like better.
prêmio, m. prize, premium.
preparar, to prepare, get ready.
presente, m. gift, present.
adj. present.
pressa, /é/, f. haste, hurry.
com pressa, in a hurry, hastily.
prestar atenção, to pay attention.
presunto, m. ham.
preto /ê/, adj. black.
prima, f. cousin.
primavera, f. spring (season).
primeiro, adj., adv. first.
primo, m. cousin.
procurar, to look for; to try to.
produzir, to produce.
professor, /ô/, m. teacher, professor.
professora /ô/, f. teacher, professor.
profissão, f. profession.
profissional, adj. professional.
proibir, to prohibit, forbid.
promover, to promote.

propor, to propose, suggest.
prova, /ó/, f. test; proof.
próximo (x=/s/), adj. next, nearest.
    próximo de, prep. near.

quadro, m. picture, painting.
quadro-negro, /ê/, m. blackboard.
qual, interrog. pron. which, what.
    o qual, rel. pron. which.
quando, adv., conj. when.
quanto, adj., pron. how much.
quarenta, num. forty.
Quaresma, /é/, f. Lent.
quarta-feira, f. Wednesday.
quarto, m. quarter; bedroom.
    adj. fourth.
quase, adv. almost.
quatro, num. four.
quatrocentos, num. four hundred.
que, conj. that.
    interrog. pron. & adj., what.
    rel. pron. who, which, that.
    conj. than.
quebrar, to break.
queimar, to burn.
quem, rel. pron. he who, the one who.
    interrog. pron. who.
quente, adj. warm, hot.
querer, to wish, want.
    quer? querem? will you?
    querer dizer, to mean.
    eu queria saber, I wonder
quiabo, m. okra.
quiçá, adv. perhaps.
quinhentos, num. five hundred.
quinta-feira, f. Thursday.
quinto, adj. fifth.

rádio, m. radio.
raiva, f. anger, rage.
    ter raiva de, to be angry at.
rapaz, m. (older) boy, young man, fellow.
rasgado, adj. torn, ripped.
razão, f. reason.
    ter razão, to be right.
receber, to receive, get.
recompor, to recompose.
rede /ê/, f. net, network; hammock.
reduzir, to reduce.
refeição, f. meal (e.g., dinner).
rei, m. king.

relógio, m. watch. clock.
repor, to put back.
reproduzir, to reproduce.
responder (a), to answer.
restaurante /tô/, m. restaurant.
reunião, f. meeting, reunion.
reunir-se, to meet, gather.
rico, adj. rich.
rio, m. river.
rir, to laugh.
    rir-se de, to laugh at.
roça, /ó/, f., (cultivated) field; the
    country.
roda, /ó/, f., wheel; group of friends.
roupa, f. clothes
    roupa de banho, swimming clothes.
rua, f. street.
ruim, adj. bad, "terrible,"
    poor (quality).

sábado, m. Saturday.
saber, to know (fact), to know how;
    to find out.
    eu sei lá. I don't know.
saco, m. sack.
sair, to go out, come out.
    sair de, to leave.
sal, m. salt.
sala, f. room.
    sala de aula, classroom.
saltar, to jump, jump down, get off.
samba, m. samba (Braz. music)
sanduíche, m. sandwich.
sapateiro, m. shoemaker, shoe seller.
sapato, m. shoe.
saudade, f. longing.
    ter saudade de, to miss (person).
saúde, f. health.
se, reflex. pron. yourself, himself,
    yourselves, themselves, etc.
se, conj. if
    se . . . não, unless.
sede /ê/, f. thirst.
    ter sede, to be thirsty.
sede /é/, f. seat, base.
seguinte, adj. following.
seguir, to follow, to go on.
segunda-feira, f. Monday.
segundo, adj. second.
    prep. according to.
seguro, adj. sure, certain.

seis, num. six.
seiscentos, num. six hundred.
selva, /é/, f. jungle.
sem, prep. without.
    sem que, conj. without.
semana, f. week.
sempre, adv. always.
seja, /ê/, pres. subj. of ser.
senhor, /ô/, m. Mr., sir.
    o senhor, you.
senhora /ó/, f. Mrs., ma'am.
    a senhora, you.
senhorita, f. Miss, ma'am.
sentar (-se), to sit down.
sentir, to feel; to be sorry;
    to hear (noise); to smell (odor).
    sentir-se bem, to feel well.
ser, to be.
serra, /é/, f. mountain range.
sessenta, num. sixty.
sete, /é/, num. seven.
setecentos, num. seven hundred.
setembro, m. September.
setenta, num. seventy.
sétimo, adj. seventh.
seu, f. sua, adj. your.
sexta-feira, /ê/, f. Friday.
sexto, /ê/, adj. sixth.
si, pron. obj. of prep., himself, etc.
sim, adv. yes (used mostly for emphasis.)
simpático, adj. nice, agreeable.
simples, adj. simple.
situação, f. situation.
só, adj. alone.
    adv. only; just.
sobre /ô/, prep. on (top of);
    concerning.
sócio, m. member.
sol /ó/, m. sun.
    dia de sol, sunny day.
soldado, m. soldier.
sonhar (com), to dream (about)
sonho, m. dream.
sono, m. sleep; sleepiness.
    ter sono, to be sleepy.
    pegar no sono, go to sleep.
sorrir, to smile.
sorte /ó/, m., (good) luck.
    ter sorte, to be lucky.
sorvete /ê/, m. ice cream.
sotaque, m. (foreign) accent.

sozinho /só/, adj. alone.
sua, f. of seu, your (s).
subir, to go up, come up.
    o preço subiu, the price has risen.
sujo, adj. dirty.
sul, m. south.
    ao sul de, south of.
sumir, to disappear.
    ele sumiu, he's gone.
surpreender, to surprise.

tal, adj. such a.
talvez, /ê/, adv. perhaps, maybe.
também, adv. also, too.
    também não, not either, neither.
tanto, adj., adv. so much, as much.
tão, adv. so.
tarde, f. afternoon.
    boa tarde, good afternoon.
    de tarde, in the afternoon.
    adv. late.
táxi, m. taxi.
teatro, m. theater.
telefone, m. telephone.
televisão, f. television.
temer, to fear.
tempo, m. time; weather.
tentar, to try (to).
ter, to have.
    tem, there is (are).
    ter azar, to be unlucky.
    ter calor, to be warm (person).
    ter fome, to be hungry.
    ter frio, to be cold.
    ter medo (de), to be afraid (of).
    ter raiva (de), to be mad (at).
    ter razão, to be right.
    ter sede, to be thirsty.
    ter sono, to be sleepy.
    ter sorte, to be lucky.
    ter vergonha, to be ashamed.
    ter vontade (de), to feel like.
    ter que (de), to have to.
    ter trabalho para fazer, to have work
    to do.
terça-feira, /ê/, f. Tuesday.
terceiro, adj. third.
terra, /é/, f. land; earth.
território, m. territory.
tia, f. aunt.
time, m. team.

tio, m. uncle.

tirar, to take off, take out.

    tirar uma foto, to take a picture.

    tirar a mesa, to clear off the table.

Titia, f. Aunty.

Titio, m. Uncle.

toalha, f. towel.

    toalha de mesa, f. tablecloth.

tocar, to touch, to ring (bell),
    to play (music).

    tocar piano, to play the piano.

tomar, to take (possession);
    to accept; to drink.

    tomar banho, to take a bath.

tomara, I wish; would (that).

trabalhador, m. & adj. worker.

trabalhar, to work.

tratar, to treat.

trazer, to bring.

trem, m. train.

três, num. three.

treze, /ê/, num. thirteen.

trezentos, num. three hundred.

trinta, num. thirty.

tudo, pron. all, everything.

turma, f. class (people); the "gang".

ultimamente, adv. lately.

último, adj. last (in a series).

um, uma, indef. art. & num. one.

universidade, f. university.

urgente, adj. urgent.

usar, to use, to wear (clothes, hair, etc.)

útil, adj. useful

vaca, f. cow.

valer, to be worth.

    valer a pena, to be worth while.

vamos, form of ir, let's.

    vamos? shall we?

variar, to vary,

vários, adj. several.

vazio, adj. empty.

velho, /é/, adj. old.

vender, to sell.

ventar, to blow.

vento, m. wind.

ver, to see.

    ver televisão, to look at TV.

verão, m. summer.

verdade, f. truth.

verde, adj. green.

vergonha, f. shame; bashfulness.

    ter vergonha, to be ashamed (bashful).

vestido, m. dress.

vestir-se, to dress, to put on.

vez, /ê/, f. time (occasion).

    em vez de, prep. instead of.

    de uma vez, once and for all.

    desta vez, this time.

viagem, f. trip, voyage.

viajar, to travel.

vindo, p.p. of vir, come.

vinte, num. twenty.

vir, to come.

vírgula, f. comma.

visita, f. visit; visitor.

    de visita, on a visit.

visto, p.p. of ver, to see.

vitela, /é/, f. veal.

viver, to live, to be alive.

você, vocês, pron. you.

volta, /ó/, f. turn; return; stroll.

    dar uma volta, to take a stroll.

    está de volta, he's back.

voltar, to return, come back.

vontade, f. wish, desire, will.

    ter vontade de, to want to.

voz, /ó/, f. voice.

xícara, f. cup.

xicrinha, f. demi-tasse.

zero /é/, num. zero.

Index

Numbers refer to pages.